The Complete Keto Diet Cookbook for Beginners

800

Effortless Low Carbs Ketogenic Recipes with
21-Day Meal Plan to Keep Fit and Increase Energy Level

By Oster Davis

Table of Content

Part I

Part II

Chapter 12 Fish and Seafood 71

Chapter 13 Meats 88

Chapter 14 Poultry 110

Chapter 15 Appetizers and Snacks 130

Chapter 16 Desserts 145

Chapter 17 Side Dishes 163

INTRODUCTION

The Keto diet is just like every other dietary plan. You may have read about other diet plans out there, and you want to know the buzz about the keto diet. You will know what the keto diet is and more. Ketosis involves reducing and converting body fats into ketones while making your body attain a metabolic state. When your body is in a metabolic state, it takes only nutrients and components that are beneficial to the body and uses ketones rather than carbohydrates to fuel the body. To attain ketosis, you need to follow a Keto diet. A Keto diet is a dietary plan that you follow so that you can become healthier. It involves cutting on carbohydrates, eating more fats and proteins.

People adopt a ketogenic diet for different reasons, whether personally or it was recommended by their doctor. Some of the reasons people adopt the keto diet are they can lose weight and belly fat or so as to reduce their risk of having certain illnesses like diabetes, etc. Keto is beneficial in many ways to your body, and when followed well, will yield optimum results.

In this book, you will be educated about what the keto diet is, the stages, why you need to have a keto dietary plan, meals that fall under the keto diet. If you are looking into starting a keto diet plan or you need a reason to, this book will help you all through the way. Read and enjoy!

PART I

Chapter 1 Unveiling Keto Diet

Trying to lose weight, maintain low blood pressure, cure diabetes, and maintain overall body wellness can be quite challenging, especially if you have tried different means without getting the desired result. There are tons of procedures, diet, and ways to lose weight, but only a few of them work. If you ask me, I would tell you how many different methods I've tried to lose weight and maintain overall wellness, and how many of them failed to deliver results but instead led to more complications due to their adverse side effects. However, the Keto diet was a ball game for me. Over time, I was able to lose weight and achieve overall well-being without complications.

If you are trying to lose weight and achieve a healthy overall-being without experiencing complications, I would recommend you try the keto diet. It is about the safest, natural, and most effective way to lose weight and achieve the best results in your journey to overall wellness.

What Is Keto Diet?

A keto diet is an eating plan focused on foods that offer a high amount of healthful fat, moderate level of protein, and very low carbohydrates. People who say they are on a 'keto diet' are people who ensure that their regular food intake contains a lot of healthful fat, an adequate amount of protein, and very low carbohydrates. This means their dietary macronutrients are divided into about 55% to 60% fat, 30% to 35% protein, and 5% to 10% carbohydrate. In the end, the goal of the keto diet is to get more energy from healthful fats than from carbohydrates.

How Does It Work?

Your body makes use of any energy source it finds readily available, which is often glucose converted from carbohydrates. By increasing the level of healthful fat you take and reducing your carbohydrate intake, your glycogen level depletes, which forces your body to go through metabolic changes. Two metabolic processes occur when your body stores low-level carbohydrates. They are called gluconeogenesis and ketogenesis.

Glycogenesis is the production of glucose in your body, and when the glucose production level stops due to low carbohydrate level, the production of glucose becomes too low to keep up with the needs of your body, which forces your body to adapt to ketogenesis as an alternative. Ketogenesis begins to produce the energy for your body, and ketone bodies become your body's primary source of energy, which is known as the 'ketosis state' that continues to be as long as your body is deprived of carbohydrates. Because your body is deprived of carbohydrates, which is primarily the cause of weight gain, your body is able to burn fat faster and convert the available fat into energy.

The ketone bodies are integrated into your body system and are used to produce energy through the heart, muscle tissue, and kidneys and also cross the blood-brain barrier to be an alternative source of energy to the brain.

History and Origin of Keto Diet

The Keto diet was first used to treat epilepsy in 1921 by Russel Wilder, after which it became a widely acceptable dietary therapy to treat epilepsy. However, its popularity ceased after the 1930s due to the introduction of antiepileptic drugs.

The keto diet recently became a widely accepted procedure for weight loss, treatment for diabetes, cancer, and other illnesses and has proven, based on experience and scientific studies, to be safe and highly effective.

How Does Keto Diet Compare to other Diet?

The Keto diet has proven to be a much more effective procedure to achieve weight loss, cure diabetes, control blood sugar levels and maintain an overall healthy body system than a low-fat diet.

Here is what research says:

Weight Loss

A review of 13 studies showed that a consistent intake of very low carbohydrate was more effective than undergoing a low-fat diet. Participants who followed the keto diet lost an average of 2 pounds (0.9kg) more than the participants that followed a low-fat diet.

A study carried on 34 older adults found out that the participants who underwent the keto diet for eight weeks lost about five times as much total body fat as those who followed a low-fat diet.

Diabetes

Research conducted by NCBI in 349 participants with type 2 diabetes discovered that those who practiced the keto diet lost an average of 26.2 pounds (11.9kg) in 2 years. The research also noted that those participants also experienced a significant decrease in their blood sugar level.

Another study conducted by PubMed in 2019 on women with type 2 diabetes discovered that women who practiced the keto diet for 90 days greatly reduced the level of hemoglobin AIC which shows a high level of long-term blood sugar management.

There are tons of studies that have proven the keto diet to be a much more effective way for weight loss, diabetes treatment, control of blood sugar level, and general well-being. But I've only selected a few of them in order not to bore you with too many statistics. If you want to find out more, I encourage you to do further research to make a personal conclusion.

That being said, let's dive into the numerous reasons to adopt the keto diet in the next chapter.

Chapter 2 Why You Need Keto Diet

The Keto diet has many health benefits to offer. This probably suggests why it has a large fan-base and why it is recommended by top medical experts as the key to successful weight loss and effective treatment for a wide range of health complications. In this chapter, I'm going to take you through a detailed analysis of the different health benefits of the ketosis diet.

Let's dive right in.

Epilepsy

Ketosis diet has been used to treat epileptic seizures in children and adults since the early 1920s. A ketosis diet is often recommended by medical experts for people with Lennox –Gastaut syndrome or Rett syndrome and don't respond to antiepileptic medications.

During a seizure, the neurons tend to fire when they are not required to, basically because the brain cells are overly excited and are releasing excitatory neurotransmitters such as glutamate, or perhaps, it is neighboring brain cells that have lost their ability to control the level of their excitability as they should through inhibitory neurotransmitters like GABA.

Either way, a ketosis diet helps reduce the amount of glutamate present in the brain, which promotes the amalgamation of GABA, which reduces the possibility of a seizure occurring.

A ketosis diet is a safer way to stop epilepsy. There are tons of cases where patients have been able to control epilepsy through drugs but whose quality of life has been greatly affected by several side effects, one of which is sedation. A ketosis diet, however, helps cure epilepsy in patients without affecting the quality of their lives through sedation or any other side effects. In fact, I think it empowers them and gives them a greater ability to take control of their lives.

Weight Loss

Although epilepsy is the foremost ailment that was ever cured with a ketosis diet, a recent and most common reason people partake in a ketosis diet is to lose weight.

You lose weight because your body does not have enough carbohydrates to burn for energy. Instead, it burns fat and produces ketones, which your body uses as fuel for energy. Once your body is used to the ketosis diet, you begin to feel less weak and hungry because your body has a steady supply of energy. So, you won't have to wake at 3 am in the morning to 'snack' because you've been working for long hours and you are weak, which ultimately cuts down on the way you eat and aids your weight loss journey.

Type 2 Diabetes

Many people think preventing and controlling diabetes is how much you eat. However, when it comes to type 2 diabetes, reducing your food intake doesn't completely cut it as it isn't just about how much you eat but what you eat.

The Keto diet is a proven regimen in the treatment of type 2 diabetes as it helps you lose weight and reduce your sugar level; here is how it works:

Reducing carbohydrate intake is important for people with diabetes because carbohydrates convert to sugar and too much sugar increases the blood sugar level. By switching the focus to healthy fat instead of carbohydrates, you will start to experience a low blood sugar level.

Cancer

The Keto diet is an additional means to fight cancer. This is because reducing the glucose level helps take away the energy source of many cancer cells because cancer cells have difficulty adapting to areas with low glucose levels, which destroys their ability to survive. Keto diet also reduces the tumor's power to produce cancer's growth signal known as IGF-1, a protein growth signal, and VEGF that cut off the blood supply for tumors, which inhibits the growth of cancer cells.

Alzheimer Disease

Alzheimer's disease is associated with impaired glucose metabolism and amyloid plaques. However, ketones serve as an alternative source of metabolic precursors to glucose in the brain, which helps reduce amyloid plaques and reverse their neurotoxicity. The ketogenic diet also helps reduce carbohydrate intake, which helps manage Alzheimer's.

Apart from the benefits I listed above, the keto diet also helps reduce high sugar levels, which causes inflammation—more on that in the next chapter.

Chapter 3 How Sugar Causes Chronic Inflammation

Inflammation plays a significant role in healing in protecting your immune system and keeping you safe and healthy, but it leads to a whole lot of health complications like heart disease, arthritis, and Alzheimer's if left to run wild. There are majorly two types of inflammation: acute and chronic inflammation.

Acute inflammation is the good guy that sends an army of white blood cells to fight invaders that may harm yourv immune system and also contributes significantly to your healing. Chronic inflammation, on the other hand, is excessive inflammation that attacks healthy tissue and organs.

How Does Sugar Cause Chronic Inflammation?

Sugar causes inflammation in the body system in so many ways. For instance, sugar stimulates the production of free fatty acids in the liver. When the body digests these free fatty acids, the resulting compounds are trigger inflammatory processes.

Also, when fat and protein join with sugar in the blood, it results in the production of harmful substances named Advanced Glycation End Products, commonly known as (AGEs) which can lead to inflammation when produced in excess quantities.

Sugar and other inflammatory food lead to the rise in LDL cholesterol, which results in more C-reactive protein that causes inflammation. More so, sugar makes you gain weight, which results in inflammation.

Symptoms of Inflammation

Acute inflammation usually shows up with very noticeable symptoms such as redness, swelling, and pain. However, symptoms of chronic information include tiredness, fever, rashes, mouth sores, abdominal pain, and chest pain. The tricky thing about these symptoms is that they are very subtle and generic, so it's easier to overlook them or mistake them for other illnesses that come with similar symptoms.

How Does Chronic Inflammation Affect the Body?

Chronic inflammation leads to a wide range of health complications. During chronic inflammation, the body's inflammatory response starts to damage healthy cells, tissues, and organs, which finally results in the DNA damage, internal scarring, and the death of tissue cells and can lead to the development of chronic diseases such as cancer, heart diseases, type 2 diabetes, obesity, rheumatoid arthritis, asthma, and Alzheimer disease.

How Does Ketosis Help Reduce Inflammation?

Three ketone bodies are released at the stage of ketosis, but the most important of these keto bodies is the beta-hydroxybutyrate. The hydroxybutyrate helps obstruct the NLRP3 inflammasome, an immune system receptor that is connected to inflammation. Although the NLRP3 inflammasome responds quickly to the threats to the body system, it gets highly activated when the body is exposed to inflammation. Beta-hydroxybutyrate helps reduce the production of the NLRP3 inflammasome in the body, thereby preventing chronic inflammation.

Chapter 4 The Ketosis Stages

Before starting out on your keto diet, you need to know the process and phases involved in ketosis. The Keto diet isn't about eating bacon and eating sugar-free peanut butter-like most people think. Keto is different from your usual chocolate, sweets, and carbohydrate filled meals. If you are going to give all of that up to live a very healthy life, you should know what you are getting yourself into. It is an eating lifestyle that you have to stick to if you want to see optimum results. Whether you are getting into ketosis so that you can lose weight, or because you are diabetic, whatever reason that it is, have it in mind that you are doing this to become better. So, you need to know what you are getting into and prepare yourself for the things you will experience.

Keto diet is in stages just like everything that has stages, like beginning, middle, and end, but keto is a continuous lifestyle rather than it is for a while. What are the stages you should prepare for as you are about to adopt the keto diet?

The Three Ketosis Stages

There are three stages between ketosis and ketosis adaptation, that is, starting the keto diet and maintaining the diet for a healthy life, and there is more to the three stages. They are packed with information that will tell you what to expect. The three stages of the keto diet you should go through are:

Induction stage

This is your introduction stage into the keto diet. At this stage, you are just getting into the diet. This stage is the first few weeks of your diet, and you are going to experience rapid weight loss. During the first few weeks, you may not like the experience because it's a new chance for you, but it's what you signed up for. What should you expect at this stage?

You need to get your body to produce ketones, which are by-products of the liver when the body breaks down fat. How will your liver start to produce ketones? What you need to do is deplete the liver's glycogen. This may be hard for you, and you may get a keto flu-like headache, fatigue, irritation, sugar craving, etc., which will probably last only a few days. The objective of this stage is to cut on your carbohydrate and increase your fat consumption. You should eat 60% to 80% fat, 15% to 30% proteins, and carbohydrate as small as 5% to 10%. The fat you should consume should be healthy fats like grass-fed butter, healthy oils, dairy, fatty fish, etc.

You will also need to fast as you start. You can adopt intermittent daily fasting for three days because committing to a full 72 hours of fasting may be too much for you to handle. You can eat for 8 to 10 hours and fast for 14 to 16 hours daily. That way, you can get into ketosis as easily as possible. Ensure you don't last any longer than 16 hours because that may make it difficult for you to get into ketosis. Fasting will cause your glycogens to expend and make it use its fat reserves as energy for your body, thereby making you lose weight. You may lose muscle during this induction stage.

Keto Adaptation

At this stage, your body is already getting used to ketosis; that is, you are already into it. Therefore, you need to teach your body to adapt to it. You have probably achieved your weight loss aim, but there's more to it than cutting on your carb and losing weight. For you to adapt, you should incorporate exercise into your diet. Rather than going to the gym to sweat and stress your body, you can try yoga, aerobics class, or high interval intensive training. Going intense in the gym isn't that beneficial for you and will only stress your body.

You also need to be strategic with your carbohydrate intake. You can start eating your carbohydrate in a strategic way, such that it won't affect everything you have been working for. A little intake of carbohydrates wouldn't hurt. You can do this by carb cycling, which is rotating your carb and adding quality carb into your diet. Eating sweet potatoes or whole-grain once a week will help your body's metabolism. On the day you decide to eat a carb, you can feed yourself with 60% to 70% carbohydrate, 15% to 25% protein, and 15% fat for a healthy balance. The rest of the week will be your regular keto diet. Carb cycling isn't an excuse for you to slack on your diet and eat all the chocolate and ice cream in your fridge or at the store.

You can also be strategic with your carbohydrate intake through a targeted ketogenic diet, which means that on your exercise days, you can eat as much carbohydrate as you want. However, on this day, you have to lower your fat intake to the barest minimum, so you don't pile up calories in your body. Before exercising, you can eat 25 to 30-gram carbohydrates.

Including carbohydrates, as you use either of the methods in your diet, is good for you in many ways. It will help boost your energy, help you sleep better, balance any hormonal fluctuation, and offer variety in your diet.

Metabolic Flexibility

This is the final stage and the stage you should aim to attain because, at this stage, you have control over your metabolism. At this stage, you can be flexible with your diet, and you don't have to stick rigidly to a keto diet, and accidentally eating sugar or a high carb-filled food won't harm you in any way.

When you have gotten to this stage, your metabolism won't be as fragile as it was before you started, and would be able to adapt and handle any food you eat without it harming your body. So, you can eat whichever way you want while still sticking to the keto diet, and your body will be able to handle it and only pick on things that are only beneficial to your body, whether fat, glucose, or ketones. To get to this stage, you need to have stuck with a full keto diet from the beginning.

After you have achieved metabolic flexibility and the reason why you started this diet, you need to keep tweaking and modifying your keto diet so as to maintain your healthy state permanently. You can become more creative with your diet at this stage. You can include fiber, starch, supplements, fermented food, etc. You don't necessarily have to stick to ketosis every day of the week, and you can chip in a little variety here and there and remain healthy.

Whichever stage you are on; you shouldn't give up. If you are at the induction or keto-adaptation stage, picture the metabolism flexibility in your mind and your goal in mind. That should keep you going. You are not giving up your chocolate or pizza for life. You only need to be ready to do this and keep going. Once your body adapts, and your metabolism is flexible, you are good to go, and you can enjoy varieties once in a while.

Chapter 5 Choosing Keto Foods

Adopting the Keto diet means you would have to do away with some of the foods you love and inculcate healthier foods into your diet. I know how that sounds, and trust me, it would be worth it in the long run.

Like I explained earlier at the beginning of this book, the Keto diet means healthier fat, an adequate amount of protein, and a really low level of carbohydrates. In other words, non-starchy vegetables are in, sugary foods are out, and bread is completely off the menu.

In this chapter, I compiled what you can eat on a keto diet and what you can't eat on a keto diet because, let's be real: there are tons of supposed keto foods out there, and it can be hard to make the right choice.

Let's get right into it.

Fish and Seafood

Fish and seafood are ideal for the keto diet because they are high in protein and very low in carbohydrates. They also contain Omega 3 and Omega 3 fatty acids. Trying out different varieties of fish and seafood will help you explore and pick favorites. With that in mind, I compiled a list of the best seafood to try out on a keto diet below.

Salmon

Salmon has an enriching flavor and is particularly rich in omega- 3 fatty acids with other nutrients such as Vitamin B, D, and selenium, which jointly contribute to the health of your body and brain. You can grill or broil and dust with olive oil to bring about its best taste.

Mackerel

Just like Salmon, Mackerel is packed with omega 3s and many other nutrients. You can broil, pan-fry, or grilled to achieve the desired taste.

Oysters

Oysters are highly nutritious and can supply your body with zinc, copper, and vitamin B12. You can either cook or enjoy them raw for best results.

Eggs

Eggs are one of the healthiest food options out there, keto diet or not. There are about 6 grams of protein and as low as 1 gram of carbohydrate in one egg, which makes it a suitable recommendation for the keto diet.

More so, eggs make you feel satiated and full, which makes you eat less and prevent gaining weight. Eggs do not increase blood cholesterol levels, although they are known to be high in cholesterol. Instead, they help to fix the size of LDL particles thereby, reducing the chances the heart failure.

Leafy and Green Vegetables

Non-starchy vegetables provide a good amount of fiber and are very low on carbohydrates. They help aid digestion and help play a huge role in lowering the cholesterol level and are enriched in abundant vitamins and minerals such as vitamin A, K, and C. Examples of non-starchy vegetables are eggplant, cucumber, Turnip, and many more.

Cheese

Cheese is very low in carbohydrates and very high in fat, which makes them ideal for the keto diet. Cheese aid weight loss as it is enriched with conjugated linoleic acid, which helps you lose weight and improve your body composition. One Ounce of cheddar cheese offers 1 gram of carbs, 6.5 grams of protein, and a high level of calcium, which contributes to your overall well-being.

There is a wide range of cheese you can choose from; some of them are blue cheese chevre, cheddar, camembert, and a whole lot of others.

Avocados

Avocados are highly enriched in vitamins, minerals, and potassium, which make them fit into the Keto diet. They help to reduce the cholesterol level, which helps prevent diabetes.

Meat

Meats are a great source of protein and are very low on carbohydrates, so you can inculcate them into your keto diet. However, you should note that the keto diet is based on accumulating a higher amount of fat, not protein, and meat contain a high level of protein and not fat. This means you should avoid taking them in large quantities, as an excess amount of protein can be converted to glucose, which might make it harder for you to reach the state of ketosis.

Food to Avoid on Keto Diet

There are certain foods you must avoid if you want to actually make your keto diet work and produce the right results. Below are some of them:

Food Grains

Food grains are wheat flour, oatmeal, whole wheat flour that is enriched with a high amount of carbohydrates and has the ability to alter your ketosis state if you are on the keto diet. Avoid grains such as rice, rye, barley, corn, oatmeal, whole wheat flour, and their products if you are on the keto diet.

Certain Vegetables

You must avoid certain vegetables as they are not keto-friendly and could alter your progress with your keto diet. These vegetables include potatoes (sweet and baked), corn, peas, carrots, and yam.

Beverages

Many drinks we consume have a high level of sugar and carbohydrate, which may hinder the production of ketones in the body system. If you are on the keto diet, you should absolutely avoid taking beverages. Examples of beverages you should avoid include cola, soda, fruit bear, vitamin water, lemonade, margarita, protein shake fruit bear, Iced tea, energy drinks, and Frappuccino.

Legumes and Beans

Although legumes and beans are highly nutritional, they are high in carbohydrates, which makes them unfit for your keto diet. Examples of legumes and peas include baked beans, lima beans, kidney beans, green peas, lentils, labia, baked beans, and black beans.

Artificial Sweetener

Artificial sweeteners contain aspartame, acesulfame, sucralose, and saccharin, which can lead to so many health complications like increased blood sugar level and cholesterol level. You must therefore avoid them whether you are on a keto diet or not.

The Keto diet is all about living strictly on a low carb, moderate protein, and high-fat diet plan. It will definitely require a lot of discipline and commitment, but over time, it gets easier. Follow these food suggestions in this chapter and avoid the foods that need to be avoided, then see yourself achieving your weight goals and overall wellness.

Chapter 6 Keto Diet and Intermittent Fasting

Intermittent fasting, or what some call "IF," is quite a relatively new trend, and you have surely read about it briefly in the previous chapters. Intermittent fasting is different from regular fasting, and some people get it confused or are not so informed about it. When you eat, the interval at which you eat is very important for IF, or that would defeat the purpose of even trying it in the first place. It involves routine fasting, and there are different routines to intermittent fasting. You can stick to whichever routine works for you. There is the 5:2 methods, the warrior diet, alternate-day fasting, and the most popular one, which was mentioned in the last two chapters, which is the 16/8 intermittent fasting, which involves eating during an eight-hour time frame and fasting for the remaining 16 hours in the day.

People do intermittent fasting so as to lose weight, and some people combine it with the keto diet; if that doesn't make you happy or feel good, you don't need to. However, if you want to see rapid results, it's a good combination.

In intermittent fasting, timing and discipline are important if you want to see a satisfying result. You have to stick to the plan you draw down for you to follow. During the timeframe you are fasting, you shouldn't be tempted to reach into your fridge and eat something. You shouldn't also miss the timeframe you set aside for eating. If you are inconsistent, you may not achieve the goal you want to. It would be a bonus for you to achieve your aim if you already have a keto diet plan in place to go with it. Through intermittent fasting, you reduce your insulin production, increase ketone productions, and induce autography, which is necessary for you to lose fat and improve your health during the process and after.

Benefits of Intermittent Fasting

Lose weight and belly fat

One of the main goals or intentions behind intermittent fasting is so as to lose weight. One effective way to lose weight is through IF, and you will see evident results if you stick to it diligently. It helps you to accumulate fewer calories, except if during your window timeframe, you fill up your stomach with a lot of calories. It increases your metabolism rate as well and is a good effective way to lose weight.

Lower your risk of type 2 diabetes

Intermittent fasting reduces insulin resistance in your body, and lower blood sugar level, thereby protecting you from being at risk of being diabetic. It can also protect the kidney from damage, which is a serious diabetes complication.

Beneficial to the heart

Intermittent fasting helps to reduce calories, fat, and cholesterol level, which are risk factors for heart disease. Therefore, intermittent fasting is good for your heart in a way that helps decrease your risk of developing heart disease.

Beneficial to the brain

IF is beneficial to the brain and can help protect the brain from damage. It also reduces oxidative stress, inflammation, blood sugar, insulin resistance, which is beneficial to brain health. It also multiplies a brain hormone brain-derived neurotrophic factor that may cause depression or other brain problems when it is deficient.

Changes functions of cell, hormones, and genes

Intermittent fasting reduces insulin level, increases hormonal growth, repairs the cells and genes, and enable them to function better, and help you live a longer life.

Other benefits of intermittent fasting are:

- It makes you fit.

- It makes your mind clearer and makes you focus more.

- It helps reduce oxidative stress and inflammation in the body.

- It may help prevent Alzheimer's disease.

- It may help prevent cancer and make chemotherapy less painful.

Keto Diet and Intermittent Fasting

Starting a keto diet so that you can lose weight is good, and combining both will take you closer to your goal within a short period of time. Combining the two isn't dangerous for your health, and if you are up for it, you can combine both together. Not combining them doesn't mean you won't achieve the result you have in mind, but doing them both makes it easier.

Combining the two will:

- Make adapting to ketosis easier for you.

- Help you lose weight and belly fat faster.

You don't have to adopt intermittent fasting all through your ketosis. You may stop when you get the result you want. You may combine both for six months and stick to your keto diet alone.

You may be excited to combine the two together because you want fast results, but you should consult your doctor first before you go ahead with it, even though combining them may not be harmful to your health. You also need to be careful when combining both. Plan out your keto diet carefully and ensure that it is not poorly planned, which may lead to a nutritional deficiency in your body. That coupled with fasting may be bad for your health and cause you to lose weight drastically and muscle.

Chapter 7 21-day Meal Plan

Ready to get started on your keto diet plan? In this chapter, I compiled a twenty-one-day meal plan to help you get started on your keto diet journey. Remember, this is not a hard and fast rule diet plan. Feel free to be flexible; just ensure you stick to a low carbohydrate, moderate protein, and high level of healthy fat meals. Enjoy!

[Handwritten note in left margin:] I Lunch/Dinner: 74-Salmon w/ Garlic Yogurt + Steam Broccoli + one plum

DAYS	BREAKFAST	SNACKS	LUNCH	DESSERT	DINNER
Day 1	Cheddar Spinach Omelet (22) *2g* + KIWI	~~One Orange~~ *1g*	Almond-Coated Catfish (74)	~~One plum~~	Broccoli with Garlic Mayo Sauce (60) *6g*
Day 2	Mozzarella Bacon Pizza (23) *5g*	One raspberry	Parmesan Filet Mignon (94) *3g*	Slow cooker vegetable soup	Mozzarella Beef Casserole (101) *2.2g*
Day 3	Pork Sausage and Egg Cup (24) *1g*	One cup of raspberry	Zucchini and Spinach Croquettes (59) *14.3g*	One medium pear	Balsamic Tilapia Fillet (71) *0g*
Day 4	Lemon Cake with Poppy Seeds (31) *15g*	One medium apple	Parmesan Pork Cutlets in Red Wine (107) *1g*	Half cup of raspberry	Cauliflower Masala Curry (59) *7.7g*
Day 5	Mushroom and Egg Cups (24) *4.7g*	Half cup of raspberry and one almond	Pork Meatballs with Parmesan Cheese (99) *2g*	Pecan Pie with Strawberry Cream	Pork and Pepper Casserole (100) *8g*
Day 6	Spaghetti Squash Patties (32) *5g*	A quarter cup of raspberry	Asparagus with Lemony Vinaigrette (58) *13.4g*	Chocolate Fat Bombs with Nuts	Vinegary Skirt Steak with Dill (91) *1g*
Day 7	Egg and Cheese Stuffed Mushrooms (26) *7g*	One medium plum	Sweet and Sour Tilapia Fillets (16) *0g*	Two plums and six almonds	Rosemary Chicken Thighs in Wine (110) *16g*
Day 8	Cheese Cauliflower with Avocado (30) *8g*	One medium orange	Pork and Lettuce Salad (109) *5.2g*	One cup of raspberry	Peppery Eggplant with Cheese (57) *7g*
Day 9	Breakfast Chicken and Tomato Pizza (21) *6.3g*	Half cup of blueberry	Cauliflower Rice with Cilantro (61) *4.0g*	Cheddar cheese	Chive Chicken with Cauliflower (110) *7g*

Day 10	Pancake Bites 2.2g (27)	Half cup of raspberry	Basil Chicken Fillets with Cheese Sauce (124)	One medium-sized orange	Mediterranean Zoodles (64) 10.7g
Day 11	Cheddar Eggs with Tomatoes 2.4 (29)	One medium-sized pear	Curried Chicken Fillets with Bacon (111)	Pumpkin Cheese Cookie	Smoky Beef Steak with Brussels Sprouts (92)
Day 12	Almond and Coconut Porridge 2.6g (37)	One medium-sized orange	Creamy Broccoli with Turmeric 3.3g (66)	Vanilla Butter Cake	Cheese Almond Spinach (131)
Day 13	Egg and Chorizo Lettuce Wraps 4.1g (34)	One medium-sized pear	Cumin Short Ribs in Red Wine (88)	15 almonds	Lemon Salmon and Avocado Salad 3.1g (72)
Day 14	Sausage-Stuffed Mushrooms (169)	Half cup of raspberry	Cinnamon Celery with Coriander (?)	One medium-sized orange	Turkey and Cucumber Salad (127)
Day 15	Vanilla-Cinnamon Cake 11g (34)	Two boiled eggs	Cheese Shrimp 6g (80)	One cup of raspberry	Paprika Turkey Breasts with Basil (126)
Day 16	Mediterranean Eggs with Cheddar 3.5g (35)	One medium-sized pear	Chicken and Celery Salad (142)	Vanilla Monkey Bread	Parsley Scallops in White Wine 5.4g (74)
Day 17	Bacon and Kale Quiche with Basil 2.7g (28)	One cup of raspberry	Chuck Kebab with Tahini Sauce 4g (88)	One plum	Chicken Thighs in Vinegar Sauce (128)
Day 18	Fried Eggs with Cheddar Cheese 1g (30)	One medium-sized orange	Cilantro Chicken Legs with Mayo Sauce (116)	One medium-sized pear	Shrimp and Veggie Salad with Mustard 3.4g (86)
Day 19	Pumpkin Walnuts Cake with Coconut 3.0g (30)	Half cup of raspberry	Shrimp and Cucumber Salad (?)	Almond Vanilla Crème	Cayenne Cabbage with Bacon (143)
Day 20	Cheese Cauliflower Mash 2.9g (36)	Two boiled eggs	Paprika Egg Salad with Green Onions (143)	One medium-sized orange	Sesame Chicken Thighs with Lime (125)
Day 21	Spinach and Mushroom Frittata 2.0g (31)	One Plum	Chicken, Egg and Spinach Salad (142)	One cup of raspberry	Halibut, Clam and Bacon Chowder 7.6 (85)

Chapter 8 Maintaining Ketosis

At this stage of this book, you already know what the keto diet is, what it entails, the stages, and you are armed with a meal plan as well. So, how do you maintain it? Whether you have started or you are about to start, you need to be consistent so that you can get a satisfactory result. You need to be able to control yourself, so you don't go sneaking to the kitchen at night to eat a chocolate bar. It may not be easy at first to maintain a keto diet, but once you start and your body adapts to it, you will enjoy both the diet and the results you get in return.

Maintaining ketosis isn't hard because you don't have to say goodbye to your regular meal forever. It's just for a while, and you can throw carbohydrates into the diet once in a while for a balance. Once you attain metabolism flexibility, you can go right ahead and eat what you want. Reaching the third stage doesn't also equal tucking your keto diet under the pillow or shoving it under your bed. You have to stick to eat in a more flexible way so that you can live healthily for as long as you want to. How do you maintain ketosis?

Staying in Ketosis

Staying in ketosis isn't rigorous work, and you can maintain your keto diet by:

Eating and Exercising

That means you eat the right food, shun carbohydrates, and have an exercise routine. Lower your carb intake and avoid high carb vegetables, bread, starchy foods, whole-grain meals, and any other high carb meals. Instead, eat healthier fats like meat (beef, chicken, seafood, bacon), eggs, high-fat vegetables, dairy products like cheese, milk, butter, and heavy cream, nut, legumes, eggs, etc.

At the same time, create your exercise routine and stick to eat. Avoid rigorous exercises because they only stress you. Exercise on days you eat carbohydrates.

Fasting

Fasting is another way to maintain your keto diet. Start your diet by fasting. Fasting coupled with a keto diet will give you a more rapid result than ketosis alone. Not just any fasting, combine intermittent fasting with ketosis. However, you shouldn't get fast when you have a metabolic disorder, which is why you should consult your doctor before you embark on it. You don't have to fast for long hours. Figure out which routine you are comfortable with, and stick with it. You should also try fat fasting. Cut on high-fat foods and eat only a small amount of high-fat meals daily.

Afterward, track your calory level to know how far you have come, and much further you have to go. Tracking your progress will help you stay focused and motivated.

Consult professionals

Before beginning your keto diet, consult your doctor so that you can know your health status, to know if you are fit for the keto diet, and he/she may recommend a keto diet that he/she may think will work for you. Your doctor will also warn you about keto flu and how you can handle it. A while after you have started your keto diet, test your blood for ketone levels, blood sugar, protein level so you can know how far you have gone in your keto diet. You can also purchase a ketone meter so that you can measure your ketone level every day or at intervals so as to keep you on track and keep you going till you achieve your aim.

For your exercise routine, talk to a fitness trainer who will recommend a routine that will fit into your keto diet plan and help you achieve your goals faster. Also, talk to a nutritionist or dietician who will help you draft a diet plan that will work for you after considering different factors like your age, gender, size, health conditions, etc.

You also need to find out why you started a keto diet. This will help you make a decision to carry on with your keto diet. Whether you want to lose weight, or you just want to live a healthy life, it will motivate you to continue even after you have achieved your aim.

Should you continue with a keto diet? Keto diet could just be a one-time plan for you to achieve your aim. It is not unhealthy to maintain keto as a lifetime diet plan. Many people usually start keto to lose weight, and maybe the longest they can go is six months or 12 months, and they are done. It is fine if you want to stick to the diet because you are now used to it. Ketosis is a good way to maintain a healthy lifestyle through dieting.

PART II

Chapter 9 Breakfasts

Bacon and Broccoli Frittata with Feta

Prep time: 5 minutes | Cook time: 19 minutes | Serves 2

2 teaspoons avocado oil
4 slices bacon
2 cups chopped broccoli
½ teaspoon sea salt
¼ teaspoon ground black pepper
4 large eggs
¼ cup heavy whipping cream
¼ teaspoon ground cumin
¾ cup crumbled Feta cheese
1 cup water

1. Use the avocado oil to grease a baking dish that fits inside your Instant Pot.
2. Set the Instant Pot to Sauté mode. When hot, add the bacon and cook, flipping occasionally, until the bacon is crispy. Remove to a plate.
3. Add the broccoli to the pot and season with ¼ teaspoon of the salt and ⅛ teaspoon of the pepper. Sauté for 3 minutes, then transfer the broccoli to a small bowl.
4. In a medium bowl, lightly beat together the eggs, cream, cumin, and the remaining ¼ teaspoon salt and ⅛ teaspoon pepper. Crumble the bacon and stir it into the eggs, along with half the feta cheese. Pour the egg mixture into the prepared baking dish. Quickly stir in the broccoli. Sprinkle with the remaining feta cheese. Cover with a metal or silicone lid, or use foil.
5. Wipe out the Instant Pot if desired. Pour in the water and place the trivet inside. Arrange the sling over it so the two ends stick up like handles, then lower the baking dish onto the sling and the trivet.
6. Lock the lid. Select the Manual mode and set the cooking time for 16 minutes on High Pressure. Once the timer goes off, perform a natural pressure release for 5 minutes, then release any remaining pressure. Carefully open the lid.
7. Use the sling to carefully remove the hot baking dish. Serve hot or at room temperature.

Per Serving
calories: 605 | fat: 52.2g | protein: 28.7g
carbs: 5.4g | net carbs: 4.2g | fiber: 1.2g

German Pancake

Prep time: 5 minutes | Cook time: 1 hour 30 minutes | Serves 6

4 large eggs
½ cup unsweetened almond milk
½ teaspoon lemon juice
1 teaspoon vanilla extract
1 cup almond flour
¼ cup erythritol and oligosaccharide-blend
granular sweetener
½ teaspoon baking powder
¼ teaspoon ground sea salt
3 tablespoons melted butter, divided
2 tablespoons no-sugar-added berry jam

1. In a large bowl, combine the eggs, almond milk, lemon juice, and vanilla extract. Whisk to combine. Set aside.
2. In a medium bowl, combine the almond flour, sweetener, baking powder, and sea salt. Mix well.
3. Add the wet ingredients to the dry ingredients and mix until the batter is well combined and no lumps remain.
4. Coat the bottom of the inner pot with 1 tablespoon of the melted butter and then add the batter.
5. Set the lid in place. Select the Slow Cook mode and set the cooking time for 1 hour 30 minutes on High Pressure.
6. When the cook time is complete, open the lid and insert a toothpick into the center of the pancake to check for doneness. (The toothpick should come out clean.)
7. Remove the inner pot from the base. Using a spatula, carefully loosen the edges of the pancake from the sides of the pot and transfer the pancake to a large plate. Use the spatula to flip the pancake over so the browned side is facing up.
8. Slice into 6 equal-sized wedges. Drizzle 1 teaspoon of the melted butter over each wedge and then top each serving with 1 teaspoon of the berry jam. Serve warm.

Per Serving (1 slice)
calories: 137 | fat: 10.6g | protein: 5.0g
carbs: 4.8g | net carbs: 2.9g | fiber: 1.9g

Cheddar Spinach Omelet {*very good; light*}

Prep time: 5 minutes | Cook time: 12 minutes | Serves 2

4 large eggs
1½ cups chopped fresh spinach leaves
2 tablespoons peeled and chopped ~~yellow onion~~ *Shallots*

2 tablespoons salted butter, melted
½ cup shredded mild Cheddar cheese
¼ teaspoon salt

Whisk eggs. Add other ingredients. Use a

1. In an ungreased 6-inch round ~~baking dish, whisk eggs. Stir in spinach,~~ (nonstick) *pan, (Med. temp)* ~~onion, butter, Cheddar, and salt.~~ *(4)*
2. ~~Place dish into~~ air fryer ~~basket. Adjust the temperature to 320°F (160ºC) and set the timer for 12 minutes. Omelet will be done when browned on the top and firm in the middle.~~
3. Slice in half and serve warm on two medium plates. *Slice 1 kiwi for each person. Carbs for kiwi = _____*

Per Serving
calories: 368 | fat: 28g | protein: 20g
carbs: 3g | net carbs:2g | fiber: 1g

Cheese Soufflés

Prep time: 15 minutes | Cook time: 12 minutes | Serves 4

3 large eggs, whites and yolks separated
¼ teaspoon cream of tartar

½ cup shredded sharp Cheddar cheese
3 ounces (85 g) cream cheese, softened

1. In a large bowl, beat egg whites together with cream of tartar until soft peaks form, about 2 minutes.
2. In a separate medium bowl, beat egg yolks, Cheddar, and cream cheese together until frothy, about 1 minute. Add egg yolk mixture to whites, gently folding until combined.
3. Pour mixture evenly into four 4-inch ramekins greased with cooking spray. Place ramekins into air fryer basket. Adjust the temperature to 350°F (180ºC) and set the timer for 12 minutes. Eggs will be browned on the top and firm in the center when done. Serve warm.

Per Serving
calories: 183 | fat: 14g | protein: 9g
carbs: 1g | net carbs: 1g | fiber: 0g

Pork Sausage and Cheese Meatball

Prep time: 10 minutes | Cook time: 15 minutes | Serves 18 meatballs

1 pound (454 g) ground pork breakfast sausage
½ teaspoon salt
¼ teaspoon ground black pepper

½ cup shredded sharp Cheddar cheese
1 ounce (28 g) cream cheese, softened
1 large egg, whisked

1. Combine all ingredients in a large bowl. Form mixture into eighteen 1-inch meatballs.
2. Place meatballs into ungreased air fryer basket. Adjust the temperature to 400°F and set the timer for 15 minutes, shaking basket three times during cooking. Meatballs will be browned on the outside and have an internal temperature of at least 145°F (63ºC) when completely cooked. Serve warm.

Per Serving
calories: 288 | fat: 24g | protein: 11g
carbs: 1g | net carbs: 1g | fiber: 0g

Turkey Sausage Burger with Mayo

Prep time: 5 minutes | Cook time: 15 minutes | Serves 4

1 pound (454 g) ground turkey breakfast sausage
½ teaspoon salt
¼ teaspoon ground black pepper
¼ cup seeded and

chopped green bell pepper
2 tablespoons mayonnaise
1 medium avocado, peeled, pitted, and sliced

1. In a large bowl, mix sausage with salt, black pepper, bell pepper, and mayonnaise. Form meat into four patties.
2. Place patties into ungreased air fryer basket. Adjust the temperature to 370°F and set the timer for 15 minutes, turning patties halfway through cooking. Burgers will be done when dark brown and they have an internal temperature of at least 165°F (74ºC).
3. Serve burgers topped with avocado slices on four medium plates.

Per Serving
calories: 276 | fat: 17g | protein: 22g
carbs: 4g | net carbs: 1g | fiber: 3g

Mozzarella Bacon Pizza

Prep time: 5 minutes | Cook time: 10 minutes | Serves 2

1 cup shredded Mozzarella cheese
1 ounce (28 g) cream cheese, broken into small pieces
4 slices cooked sugar-free bacon, chopped
¼ cup chopped pickled jalapeños
1 large egg, whisked
¼ teaspoon salt

1. Place Mozzarella in a single layer on the bottom of an ungreased 6-inch round nonstick baking dish. Scatter cream cheese pieces, bacon, and jalapeños over Mozzarella, then pour egg evenly around baking dish.
2. Sprinkle with salt and place into air fryer basket. Adjust the temperature to 330°F (166ºC) and set the timer for 10 minutes. When cheese is brown and egg is set, pizza will be done.
3. Let cool on a large plate 5 minutes before serving.

Per Serving
calories: 361 | fat: 24g | protein: 26g
carbs: 5g | net carbs: 5g | fiber: 0g

Pepperoni Egg with Mozzarella

Prep time: 5 minutes | Cook time: 10 minutes | Serves 2

1 cup shredded Mozzarella cheese
7 slices pepperoni, chopped
1 large egg, whisked
¼ teaspoon dried oregano
¼ teaspoon dried parsley
¼ teaspoon garlic powder
¼ teaspoon salt

1. Place Mozzarella in a single layer on the bottom of an ungreased 6-inch round nonstick baking dish. Scatter pepperoni over cheese, then pour egg evenly around baking dish.
2. Sprinkle with remaining ingredients and place into air fryer basket. Adjust the temperature to 330°F (166ºC) and set the timer for 10 minutes. When cheese is brown and egg is set, dish will be done.
3. Let cool in dish 5 minutes before serving.

Per Serving
calories: 241 | fat: 15g | protein: 19g
carbs: 4g | net carbs: 4g | fiber: 0g

Parmesan Turkey Rolls

Prep time: 5 minutes | Cook time: 5 minutes | Serves 3

½ teaspoon olive oil
3 turkey lunch meat slices
3 ounces (85 g) grated Parmesan cheese
1 tablespoon cream cheese
½ teaspoon minced garlic

1. Press the Sauté button on the Instant Pot and heat the olive oil. Add the turkey slices to the pot and cook for 2 minutes on each side.
2. Meanwhile, in a bowl, stir together the remaining ingredients.
3. Transfer the cooked turkey slices to a plate and spread the cheese mixture over the turkey slices.
4. Roll up the turkey slices and secure them with the toothpicks.
5. Serve immediately.

Per Serving
calories: 159 | fat: 7.9g | protein: 21.5g
carbs: 1.2g | net carbs: 1.2g | fiber: 0g

Breakfast Beef and Jalapeños

Prep time: 10 minutes | Cook time: 16 minutes | Serves 6

1 teaspoon coconut oil
2 cups ground beef
1 teaspoon chili flakes
3 jalapeño peppers, chopped
2 eggs, beaten
½ avocado, chopped
¾ cup black olives, sliced
⅓ cup coconut milk

1. Press the Sauté button on the Instant Pot and melt the coconut oil for 2 minutes. Add the ground beef and chili flakes to the pot and sauté for 4 minutes, or until lightly browned, stirring constantly. Stir in the remaining ingredients.
2. Set the lid in place. Select the Manual mode and set the cooking time for 10 minutes on High Pressure. When the timer goes off, do a quick pressure release. Carefully open the lid.
3. Serve immediately.

Per Serving
calories: 200 | fat: 15.8g | protein: 11.5g
carbs: 3.8g | net carbs: 1.5g | fiber: 2.3g

Broccoli Frittata with Bell Pepper

Prep time: 15 minutes | Cook time: 12 minutes | Serves 4

6 large eggs
¼ cup heavy whipping cream
½ cup chopped broccoli
¼ cup chopped yellow onion
¼ cup chopped green bell pepper

1. In a large bowl, whisk eggs and heavy whipping cream. Mix in broccoli, onion, and bell pepper.
2. Pour into a 6-inch round oven-safe baking dish. Place baking dish into the air fryer basket.
3. Adjust the temperature to 350°F (180°C) and set the timer for 12 minutes.
4. Eggs should be firm and cooked fully when the frittata is done. Serve warm.

Per Serving
calories: 168 | fat: 11g | protein: 10g
carbs: 3g | net carbs: 2g | fiber: 1g

Pork Sausage and Egg Cup

Prep time: 10 minutes | Cook time: 15 minutes | Serves 6

12 ounces (340 g) ground pork breakfast sausage
6 large eggs
½ teaspoon salt
¼ teaspoon ground black pepper
½ teaspoon crushed red pepper flakes

1. Place sausage in six 4-inch ramekins (about 2 ounces (57 g) per ramekin) greased with cooking oil. Press sausage down to cover bottom and about ½-inch up the sides of ramekins. Crack one egg into each ramekin and sprinkle evenly with salt, black pepper, and red pepper flakes.
2. Place ramekins into air fryer basket. Adjust the temperature to 350°F (180°C) and set the timer for 15 minutes. Egg cups will be done when sausage is fully cooked to at least 145°F (63°C) and the egg is firm. Serve warm.

Per Serving
calories: 267 | fat: 21g | protein: 14g
carbs: 1g | net carbs: 1g | fiber: 0g

Bacon Quiche with Cheddar Cheese

Prep time: 5 minutes | Cook time: 12 minutes | Serves 2

3 large eggs
2 tablespoons heavy whipping cream
¼ teaspoon salt
4 slices cooked sugar-free bacon, crumbled
½ cup shredded mild Cheddar cheese

1. In a large bowl, whisk eggs, cream, and salt together until combined. Mix in bacon and Cheddar.
2. Pour mixture evenly into two ungreased 4-inch ramekins. Place into air fryer basket. Adjust the temperature to 320°F (160°C) and set the timer for 12 minutes. Quiche will be fluffy and set in the middle when done.
3. Let quiche cool in ramekins 5 minutes. Serve warm.

Per Serving
calories: 380 | fat: 28g | protein: 24g
carbs: 2g | net carbs: 2g | fiber: 0g

Mushroom and Egg Cups

Prep time: 10 minutes | Cook time: 7 to 8 minutes | Serves 4

4 eggs, beaten
1 cup diced mushrooms
½ cup grated sharp Cheddar cheese
¼ cup heavy cream
1 teaspoon salt
1 teaspoon freshly ground black pepper
2 tablespoons chopped fresh cilantro

1. In a medium bowl, stir together all the ingredients. Divide the mixture among four glass jars. Place the lids on top of the jars, but do not tighten.
2. Pour 2 cups water and insert the trivet in the Instant Pot. Place the egg jars on the trivet.
3. Set the lid in place. Select the Manual mode and set the cooking time for 5 minutes on High Pressure. When the timer goes off, do a quick pressure release. Carefully open the lid.
4. Remove the jars from the pot and remove the lids from the jars. Serve warm.

Per Serving
calories: 238 | fat: 16.8g | protein: 15.1g
carbs: 6.7g | net carbs: 4.7g | fiber: 2.0g

Cheddar Ham Egg

Prep time: 10 minutes | Cook time: 15 minutes | Serves 4

4 medium green bell peppers, tops removed, seeded	sugar-added ham
	¼ cup peeled and chopped white onion
1 tablespoon coconut oil	4 large eggs
	½ teaspoon salt
3 ounces (85 g) chopped cooked no-	1 cup shredded mild Cheddar cheese

1. Place peppers upright into ungreased air fryer basket. Drizzle each pepper with coconut oil. Divide ham and onion evenly among peppers.
2. In a medium bowl, whisk eggs, then sprinkle with salt. Pour mixture evenly into each pepper. Top each with ¼ cup Cheddar.
3. Adjust the temperature to 320°F (160°C) and set the timer for 15 minutes. Peppers will be tender and eggs will be firm when done.
4. Serve warm on four medium plates.

Per Serving
calories: 281 | fat: 18g | protein: 18g
carbs: 8g | net carbs: 6g | fiber: 2g

Cinnamon Cheese Roll

Prep time: 10 minutes | Cook time: 20 minutes | Makes 12 rolls

2½ cups shredded Mozzarella cheese	½ teaspoon vanilla extract
2 ounces (57 g) cream cheese, softened	½ cup erythritol
1 cup blanched finely ground almond flour	1 tablespoon ground cinnamon

1. In a large microwave-safe bowl, combine Mozzarella cheese, cream cheese, and flour. Microwave the mixture on high 90 seconds until cheese is melted.
2. Add vanilla extract and erythritol, and mix 2 minutes until a dough forms.
3. Once the dough is cool enough to work with your hands, about 2 minutes, spread it out into a 12-inch × 4-inch rectangle on ungreased parchment paper. Evenly sprinkle dough with cinnamon.
4. Starting at the long side of the dough, roll lengthwise to form a log. Slice the log into twelve even pieces.
5. Divide rolls between two ungreased 6-inch round nonstick baking dishes. Place one dish into air fryer basket. Adjust the temperature to 375°F (190°C) and set the timer for 10 minutes.
6. Cinnamon rolls will be done when golden around the edges and mostly firm. Repeat with second dish. Allow rolls to cool in dishes 10 minutes before serving.

Per Serving
calories: 145 | fat: 10g | protein: 8g
carbs: 10g | net carbs: 9g | fiber: 1g

Kale and Bacon Frittatas with Dried Herbs

Prep time: 10 minutes | Cook time: 20 minutes | Serves 4

6 eggs, beaten	½ teaspoon dried cilantro
4 slices bacon, finely cut, cooked	½ teaspoon dried basil
1 cup chopped kale	½ teaspoon chili powder
2 tablespoons coconut oil	½ teaspoon kosher salt
½ teaspoon full-fat coconut milk	½ teaspoon freshly ground black pepper
½ teaspoon dried parsley	1 cup water

1. Pour the water and insert the trivet in the Instant Pot.
2. In a large bowl, stir together the remaining ingredients.
3. Divide the mixture evenly among four well-greased ramekins. Make sure to leave room on top of each for possible expansion during cooking. Place all the ramekins on the trivet.
4. Lock the lid. Select the Manual mode and set the cooking time for 20 minutes on High Pressure. Once the timer goes off, perform a natural pressure release for 10 minutes, then release any remaining pressure. Carefully open the lid.
5. Remove the ramekins from the pot and let cool for 5 to 10 minutes. Serve warm.

Per Serving
calories: 275 | fat: 21.4g | protein: 16.5g
carbs: 4.6g | net carbs: 3.8g | fiber: 0.8g

Cauliflower Hash Browns with Cheddar

Prep time: 20 minutes | Cook time: 12 minutes | Serves 4

1 (12-ounce / 340-g) steamer bag cauliflower

1 large egg
1 cup shredded sharp Cheddar cheese

1. Place bag in microwave and cook according to package instructions. Allow to cool completely and put cauliflower into a cheesecloth or kitchen towel and squeeze to remove excess moisture.
2. Mash cauliflower with a fork and add egg and cheese.
3. Cut a piece of parchment to fit your air fryer basket. Take ¼ of the mixture and form it into a hash brown patty shape. Place it onto the parchment and into the air fryer basket, working in batches if necessary.
4. Adjust the temperature to 400°F (205ºC) and set the timer for 12 minutes.
5. Flip the hash browns halfway through the cooking time. When completely cooked, they will be golden brown. Serve immediately.

Per Serving
calories: 153 | fat: 9g | protein: 10g
carbs: 5g | net carbs: 3g | fiber: 2g

Egg and Cheese Stuffed Mushrooms

Prep time: 15 minutes | Cook time: 14 minutes | Serves 2

1 tablespoon olive oil
2 cloves garlic, minced
¼ teaspoon dried thyme
2 portobello mushrooms, stems removed and gills scraped out
2 Roma tomatoes, halved lengthwise

Salt and freshly ground black pepper
2 large eggs
2 tablespoons grated Pecorino Romano cheese
1 tablespoon chopped fresh parsley, for garnish

1. Preheat the air fryer to 400°F (205ºC).
2. In a small bowl, combine the olive oil, garlic, and thyme. Brush the mixture over the mushrooms and tomatoes until thoroughly coated. Season to taste with salt and freshly ground black pepper.

3. Arrange the vegetables, cut side up, in the air fryer basket. Crack an egg into the center of each mushroom and sprinkle with cheese. Air fry for 10 to 14 minutes until the vegetables are tender and the whites are firm. When cool enough to handle, coarsely chop the tomatoes and place on top of the eggs. Scatter parsley on top just before serving.

Per Serving
calories: 255 | fat: 20g | protein: 11g
carbs: 10g | net carbs: 7g | fiber: 3g

Pork Sausage Stuffed Peppers

Prep time: 15 minutes | Cook time: 15 minutes | Serves 4

½ pound (227 g) spicy ground pork breakfast sausage
4 large eggs
4 ounces (113 g) full-fat cream cheese, softened
¼ cup canned diced tomatoes and green

chiles, drained
4 large poblano peppers
8 tablespoons shredded pepper jack cheese
½ cup full-fat sour cream

1. In a medium skillet over medium heat, crumble and brown the ground sausage until no pink remains. Remove sausage and drain the fat from the pan. Crack eggs into the pan, scramble, and cook until no longer runny.
2. Place cooked sausage in a large bowl and fold in cream cheese. Mix in diced tomatoes and chiles. Gently fold in eggs.
3. Cut a 4-inch–5-inch slit in the top of each poblano, removing the seeds and white membrane with a small knife. Separate the filling into four servings and spoon carefully into each pepper. Top each with 2 tablespoons pepper jack cheese.
4. Place each pepper into the air fryer basket.
5. Adjust the temperature to 350°F (180ºC) and set the timer for 15 minutes.
6. Peppers will be soft and cheese will be browned when ready. Serve immediately with sour cream on top.

Per Serving
calories: 489 | fat: 35g | protein: 23g
carbs: 13g | net carbs: 9g | fiber: 4g

Breakfast Chicken and Tomato Pizza

Prep time: 15 minutes | Cook time: 20 minutes | Serves 4 to 5

2 tablespoons avocado oil
1 pound (454 g) ground chicken
¼ cup water
½ teaspoon crushed red pepper
½ teaspoon freshly ground black pepper
½ teaspoon dried parsley
½ teaspoon kosher salt
½ teaspoon dried basil
1 (14-ounce / 397-g) can unsweetened crushed tomatoes, drained
1 cup shredded Cheddar cheese
2 to 4 slices bacon, cooked and finely cut

1. Press the Sauté button on the Instant Pot and melt the avocado oil. Add the ground chicken to the pot and sauté for 5 minutes, or until browned. Pour in the water. Push the chicken down with a spatula to form a flat, even layer, covering the bottom of the pot.
2. In a small bowl, stir together the red pepper, black pepper, parsley, salt and basil.
3. Spread the tomatoes over the chicken. Add a layer of cheese and then the bacon. Top with the spice and herb mixture.
4. Lock the lid. Select the Manual mode and set the cooking time for 15 minutes on High Pressure. Once the timer goes off, perform a natural pressure release for 10 minutes, then release any remaining pressure. Carefully open the lid.
5. Remove the pizza with a spatula. Serve hot.

Per Serving
calories: 173 | fat: 11.6g | protein: 10.2g
carbs: 8.7g | net carbs: 6.3g | fiber: 2.4g

Pancake Bites

Prep time: 5 minutes | Cook time: 20 minutes | Serves 7

2 eggs
1 cup almond flour
⅔ cup Swerve
¼ cup full-fat coconut milk
1 tablespoon butter, softened
½ teaspoon kosher salt
¼ teaspoon baking soda
1 cup water

1. Pour the water and insert the trivet in the Instant Pot.

2. In a large bowl, stir together the remaining ingredients. Transfer the mixture into two well-greased egg bites molds.
3. Using a sling, place the molds onto the trivet. Stack two egg bites molds on top of each other. Cover loosely with aluminum foil.
4. Lock the lid. Select the Manual mode and set the cooking time for 20 minutes on High Pressure. Once the timer goes off, perform a natural pressure release for 10 minutes, then release any remaining pressure. Carefully open the lid.
5. Remove the molds from the pot. Let cool for 5 minutes before serving.

Per Serving
calories: 186 | fat: 17.3g | protein: 4.9g
carbs: 4.2g | net carbs: 2.2g | fiber: 2.0g

Egg and Bacon Bake with Broccoli

Prep time: 10 minutes | Cook time: 19 minutes | Serves 2 to 3

5 eggs
3 slices bacon, cooked and finely chopped
½ cup chopped broccoli
½ cup chopped kale
½ cup heavy whipping cream
2 tablespoons avocado oil
½ teaspoon dried basil
½ teaspoon ground cayenne pepper
½ teaspoon kosher salt
½ teaspoon freshly ground black pepper
1 cup water

1. Pour the water and insert the trivet in the Instant Pot.
2. In a large bowl, stir together the remaining ingredients.
3. Transfer the mixture into a well-greased baking pan and cover loosely with aluminum foil.
4. Lock the lid. Select the Manual mode and set the cooking time for 19 minutes on High Pressure. Once the timer goes off, perform a natural pressure release for 10 minutes, then release any remaining pressure. Carefully open the lid.
5. Transfer the dish to a plate and serve.

Per Serving
calories: 301 | fat: 23.8g | protein: 17.7g
carbs: 4.4g | net carbs: 3.2g | fiber: 1.2g

Bacon and Kale Quiche with Basil

Prep time: 10 minutes | Cook time: 20 minutes | Serves 4 to 5

6 eggs
6 slices bacon, cooked and finely chopped
¼ small onion, thinly sliced
½ cup shredded full-fat Cheddar cheese
½ cup Ricotta cheese
½ cup chopped kale
¼ cup full-fat coconut

milk
2 tablespoons coconut oil
½ teaspoon dried basil
½ teaspoon dried parsley
½ teaspoon kosher salt
½ teaspoon freshly ground black pepper

1. Add all the ingredients to a baking pan and stir to combine.
2. Pour 1 cup water and insert the trivet in the Instant Pot. Put the pan on the trivet. Cover with aluminium foil.
3. Lock the lid. Select the Manual mode and set the cooking time for 20 minutes on High Pressure. Once the timer goes off, perform a natural pressure release for 10 minutes, then release any remaining pressure. Carefully open the lid.
4. Serve immediately.

Per Serving
calories: 339 | fat: 22.6g | protein: 13.2g
carbs: 3.3g | net carbs: 2.7g | fiber: 0.6g

Pork Sausage Eggs

Prep time: 20 minutes | Cook time: 12 minutes | Serves 8

1 pound (454 g) pork sausage
8 soft-boiled or hard-boiled eggs, peeled
Smoky Mustard Sauce:
¼ cup mayonnaise
2 tablespoons sour cream
1 tablespoon Dijon

1 large egg
2 tablespoons milk
1 cup crushed pork rinds

mustard
1 teaspoon chipotle hot sauce

1. Preheat the air fryer to 390°F (199°C).
2. Divide the sausage into 8 portions. Take each portion of sausage, pat it down into a patty, and place 1 egg in the middle, gently wrapping the sausage around the egg until the egg is completely covered. (Wet your hands slightly if you find the sausage to be too sticky.) Repeat with the remaining eggs and sausage.

3. In a small shallow bowl, whisk the egg and milk until frothy. In another shallow bowl, place the crushed pork rinds. Working one at a time, dip a sausage-wrapped egg into the beaten egg and then into the pork rinds, gently rolling to coat evenly. Repeat with the remaining sausage-wrapped eggs.
4. Arrange the eggs in a single layer in the air fryer basket, and lightly spray with olive oil. Air fry for 10 to 12 minutes, pausing halfway through the baking time to turn the eggs, until the eggs are hot and the sausage is cooked through.
5. To make the sauce: In a small bowl, combine the mayonnaise, sour cream, Dijon, and hot sauce. Whisk until thoroughly combined. Serve with the Scotch eggs.

Per Serving
calories: 340 | fat: 28g | protein: 22g
carbs: 1g | net carbs: 1g | fiber: 0g

Spicy Turkey Sausage

Prep time: 15 minutes | Cook time: 20 minutes | Serves 8

1½ pounds (680g) 85% lean ground turkey
3 cloves garlic, finely chopped
¼ onion, grated
1 teaspoon Tabasco

sauce
1 teaspoon Creole seasoning
1 teaspoon dried thyme
½ teaspoon paprika
½ teaspoon cayenne

1. Preheat the air fryer to 370°F (188°C).
2. In a large bowl, combine the turkey, garlic, onion, Tabasco, Creole seasoning, thyme, paprika, and cayenne. Mix with clean hands until thoroughly combined. Shape into 16 patties, about ½ -inch thick. (Wet your hands slightly if you find the sausage too sticky to handle.)
3. Working in batches if necessary, arrange the patties in a single layer in the air fryer basket. Pausing halfway through the cooking time to flip the patties, air fry for 15 to 20 minutes until a thermometer inserted into the thickest portion registers 165°F (74°C).

Per Serving
calories: 170 | fat: 11g | protein: 16g
carbs: 1g | net carbs: 1g | fiber: 0g

Cheddar Eggs with Tomatoes

Prep time: 5 minutes | Cook time: 20 minutes | Serves 4

2 tablespoons coconut oil
6 eggs
1 (14-ounce / 397-g) can sugar-free crushed tomatoes
1 cup shredded full-fat Cheddar cheese
½ teaspoon dried cilantro
½ teaspoon chili powder
½ jalapeño, finely chopped
½ teaspoon kosher salt
½ teaspoon freshly ground black pepper
½ cup water

1. Pour the water and insert the trivet in the Instant Pot.
2. In a large bowl, stir together the remaining ingredients.
3. Transfer the mixture into a well-greased baking pan and cover loosely with aluminum foil.
4. Using a sling, place the pan on top of the trivet.
5. Lock the lid. Select the Manual mode and set the cooking time for 20 minutes on High Pressure. Once the timer goes off, perform a natural pressure release for 10 minutes, then release any remaining pressure. Carefully open the lid.
6. Transfer the dish to a plate and serve.

Per Serving
calories: 276 | fat: 22.7g | protein: 15.5g
carbs: 3.1g | net carbs: 2.4g | fiber: 0.7g

Vanilla Mug Cakes with Strawberries

Prep time: 5 minutes | Cook time: 20 minutes | Serves 3 to 4

2 eggs
⅔ cup almond flour
½ cup Swerve
1 tablespoon butter, softened
1 teaspoon vanilla
extract
1 teaspoon smooth almond butter
4 strawberries, hulled and chopped

1. In a large bowl, stir together all the ingredients.
2. Pour the mixture evenly into mugs, filling each about halfway. Cover each loosely with aluminum foil.
3. Pour 1 cup water and insert the trivet in the Instant Pot. Put the mugs on the trivet.

4. Lock the lid. Select the Manual mode and set the cooking time for 20 minutes on High Pressure. Once the timer goes off, perform a natural pressure release for 10 minutes, then release any remaining pressure. Carefully open the lid.
5. Transfer the mugs to a cooling rack. Let cool completely before serving.

Per Serving
calories: 93 | fat: 7.6g | protein: 3.7g
carbs: 2.6g | net carbs: 1.5g | fiber: 1.1g

Bell Pepper Egg Cups with Arugula

Prep time: 5 minutes | Cook time: 3 minutes | Serves 8

4 large eggs
4 medium bell peppers, tops and
Sauce:
¼ cup mayonnaise
1 teaspoon Dijon mustard
½ teaspoon lemon juice
½ teaspoon white vinegar
seeds removed
6 baby arugula leaves

¼ teaspoon fine grind sea salt
⅛ teaspoon ground black pepper
¼ teaspoon ground turmeric

Instant Pot?

1. Place the trivet in the inner pot and add 1 cup water to the bottom of the pot.
2. Make the sauce by combining the mayonnaise, Dijon mustard, lemon juice, vinegar, sea salt, black pepper, and turmeric in a small bowl. Whisk until blended. Cover and refrigerate.
3. Carefully crack 1 egg into each bell pepper cup, making sure to keep the yolk intact, and cover the top of each pepper with a small square of aluminum foil. Place the covered peppers on the trivet.
4. Lock the lid. Select the Manual mode and set the cooking time for 3 minutes on High Pressure. Once the timer goes off, perform a natural pressure release for 2 minutes, then release any remaining pressure. Carefully open the lid.
5. Transfer the peppers to a serving platter.
6. Remove the foil and top each pepper with 1 tablespoon of the sauce, and then garnish with the arugula leaves. Serve hot.

Per Serving
calories: 199 | fat: 14.8g | protein: 8.2g
carbs: 8.3g | net carbs: 8.0g | fiber: 0.3g

Fried Eggs with Cheddar Cheese

Prep time: 5 minutes | Cook time: 15 minutes | Serves 2

4 large eggs
2 tablespoons unsalted butter, melted

½ cup shredded sharp Cheddar cheese

1. Crack eggs into 2-cup round baking dish and whisk. Place dish into the air fryer basket.
2. Adjust the temperature to 400°F (205ºC) and set the timer for 10 minutes.
3. After 5 minutes, stir the eggs and add the butter and cheese. Let cook 3 more minutes and stir again.
4. Allow eggs to finish cooking an additional 2 minutes or remove if they are to your desired liking.
5. Use a fork to fluff. Serve warm.

Per Serving
calories: 359 | fat: 27g | protein: 20g
carbs: 1g | net carbs: 1g | fiber: 0g

Pumpkin Walnuts Cake with Coconut

Prep time: 5 minutes | Cook time: 40 minutes | Serves 5 to 6

Base:
3 eggs
1 cup almond flour
¾ cup chopped walnuts
½ cup organic pumpkin purée
¼ cup heavy whipping cream
2 tablespoons butter,

softened
½ teaspoon ground cinnamon
½ teaspoon ground nutmeg
½ teaspoon baking powder
½ teaspoon salt

Topping:
¼ cup heavy whipping cream
½ cup Swerve

½ cup unsweetened coconut flakes

1. Pour 1 cup water and insert the trivet in the Instant Pot.
2. Using an electric mixer, combine all the ingredients for the cake. Mix thoroughly. Transfer the mixture into a well-greased baking pan.
3. Place the pan onto the trivet and cover loosely with aluminum foil.
4. Lock the lid. Select the Manual mode and set the cooking time for 40 minutes on High Pressure.

5. Meanwhile, in a large bowl, whisk together all the ingredients for the topping.
6. Once the timer goes off, perform a natural pressure release for 10 minutes, then release any remaining pressure. Carefully open the lid.
7. Remove the pan from the pot. Sprinkle the topping mixture evenly over the cake. Let cool for 5 minutes before serving.

Per Serving
calories: 333 | fat: 30.5g | protein: 7.9g
carbs: 7.8g | net carbs: 3.0g | fiber: 4.8g

Cheese Cauliflower with Avocado

Prep time: 15 minutes | Cook time: 8 minutes | Serves 2

1 (12-ounce / 340-g) steamer bag cauliflower
1 large egg
½ cup shredded Mozzarella cheese

1 ripe medium avocado
½ teaspoon garlic powder
¼ teaspoon ground black pepper

1. Cook cauliflower according to package instructions. Remove from bag and place into cheesecloth or clean towel to remove excess moisture.
2. Place cauliflower into a large bowl and mix in egg and Mozzarella. Cut a piece of parchment to fit your air fryer basket. Separate the cauliflower mixture into two, and place it on the parchment in two mounds. Press out the cauliflower mounds into a ¼-inch-thick rectangle. Place the parchment into the air fryer basket.
3. Adjust the temperature to 400°F (205ºC) and set the timer for 8 minutes.
4. Flip the cauliflower halfway through the cooking time.
5. When the timer beeps, remove the parchment and allow the cauliflower to cool 5 minutes.
6. Cut open the avocado and remove the pit. Scoop out the inside, place it in a medium bowl, and mash it with garlic powder and pepper. Spread onto the cauliflower. Serve immediately.

Per Serving
calories: 278 | fat: 15g | protein: 14g
carbs: 16g | net carbs: 8g | fiber: 8g

Lemon Cake with Poppy Seeds

Prep time: 10 minutes | Cook time: 14 minutes | Serves 6

1 cup blanched finely ground almond flour
½ cup powdered erythritol
½ teaspoon baking powder
¼ cup unsalted butter, melted
¼ cup unsweetened almond milk
2 large eggs
1 teaspoon vanilla extract
1 medium lemon
1 teaspoon poppy seeds

1. In a large bowl, mix almond flour, erythritol, baking powder, butter, almond milk, eggs, and vanilla.
2. Slice the lemon in half and squeeze the juice into a small bowl, then add to the batter.
3. Using a fine grater, zest the lemon and add 1 tablespoon zest to the batter and stir. Add poppy seeds to batter.
4. Pour batter into nonstick 6-inch round cake pan. Place pan into the ==air fryer basket==.
5. Adjust the temperature to 300°F (150ºC) and set the timer for 14 minutes.
6. When fully cooked, a toothpick inserted in center will come out mostly clean. The cake will finish cooking and firm up as it cools. Serve at room temperature.

Per Serving
calories: 204 | fat: 18g | protein: 6g
carbs: 17g | net carbs: 15g | fiber: 2g

Cheddr Bacon Eggs with Avocado

Prep time: 15 minutes | Cook time: 20 minutes | Serves 4

6 large eggs
¼ cup heavy whipping cream
1½ cups chopped cauliflower
1 cup shredded medium Cheddar cheese
1 medium avocado,
peeled and pitted
8 tablespoons full-fat sour cream
2 scallions, sliced on the bias
12 slices sugar-free bacon, cooked and crumbled

1. In a medium bowl, whisk eggs and cream together. Pour into a 4-cup round baking dish.
2. Add cauliflower and mix, then top with Cheddar. Place dish into the ==air fryer== basket.

3. Adjust the temperature to 320°F (160ºC) and set the timer for 20 minutes.
4. When completely cooked, eggs will be firm and cheese will be browned. Slice into four pieces.
5. Slice avocado and divide evenly among pieces. Top each piece with 2 tablespoons sour cream, sliced scallions, and crumbled bacon.

Per Serving
calories: 512 | fat: 38g | protein: 27g
carbs: 8g | net carbs: 5g | fiber: 3g

Spinach and Mushroom Frittata

Prep time: 5 minutes | Cook time: 30 minutes | Serves 6

1 cup sliced fresh mushrooms
1 cup fresh baby spinach leaves
6 large eggs
¼ cup heavy cream
1 teaspoon sea salt
½ teaspoon ground black pepper
½ cup shredded Monterey Jack cheese
½ avocado, sliced
Cooking spray

1. Spray a soufflé dish with cooking spray.
2. Arrange the mushrooms and spinach leaves in the bottom of the dish. Set aside.
3. In a large bowl, combine the eggs, heavy cream, sea salt, and black pepper. Mix well to combine. Gently pour the egg mixture over the mushrooms and spinach.
4. Add 1½ cups water to the bottom of the ==inner pot==. Place the soufflé dish on the *Instant Pot* trivet and grasp the ==trivet== handles to lower the trivet and dish into the pot.
5. Lock the lid. Select the Manual mode and set the cooking time for 30 minutes on High Pressure. Once the timer goes off, perform a natural pressure release for 10 minutes, then release any remaining pressure. Carefully open the lid.
6. Sprinkle the Jack cheese over top of the frittata. Replace the lid and allow the residual heat to melt the cheese for 5 minutes.
7. Open the lid and carefully grasp the trivet handles to lift the trivet and dish out of the pot. Transfer the frittata to a serving platter, cut into 6 equal-sized wedges, and top with the sliced avocado. Serve warm.

Per Serving
calories: 169 | fat: 12.6g | protein: 10.2g
carbs: 3.3g | net carbs: 2.0g | fiber: 1.3g

Spaghetti Squash Patties

Prep time: 15 minutes | Cook time: 8 minutes | Serves 4

2 cups cooked spaghetti squash
2 tablespoons unsalted butter, softened
1 large egg
¼ cup blanched finely ground almond flour

2 stalks green onion, sliced
½ teaspoon garlic powder
1 teaspoon dried parsley

1. Remove excess moisture from the squash using a cheesecloth or kitchen towel.
2. Mix all ingredients in a large bowl. Form into four patties.
3. Cut a piece of parchment to fit your air fryer basket. Place each patty on the parchment and place into the air fryer basket.
4. Adjust the temperature to 400°F (205°C) and set the timer for 8 minutes.
5. Flip the patties halfway through the cooking time. Serve warm.

Per Serving
calories: 131 | fat: 10g | protein: 4g
carbs: 7g | net carbs: 5g | fiber: 2g

Chicken Sausage Egg Muffins

Prep time: 5 minutes | Cook time: 9 to 10 minutes | Serves 2

3 teaspoons avocado oil, divided
4 ounces (113 g) fully cooked chicken sausage, diced
4 small kale leaves, finely chopped
½ teaspoon kosher

salt, divided
½ teaspoon ground black pepper, divided
4 large eggs
¼ cup heavy whipping cream
1 cup water

1. Grease the bottom and insides of four silicone muffin cups with 1 teaspoon of the avocado oil.
2. Press the Sauté button on the Instant Pot and heat the remaining 2 teaspoons of the avocado oil. Add the sausage to the pot and sauté for 2 minutes. Add the chopped kale and ¼ teaspoon of the salt and black pepper. Sauté for 2 to 3 minutes, or until the kale is wilted.
3. Meanwhile, in a medium bowl, lightly whisk together the eggs, cream and the remaining ¼ teaspoon of the salt and pepper.
4. Divide the kale and sausage mixture among the four muffin cups. Pour the egg mixture evenly over the kale and sausage and stir lightly with a fork. Loosely cover the cups with foil.
5. Pour the water and insert the trivet in the Instant Pot. Put the muffin cups on the trivet.
6. Lock the lid. Select the Manual mode and set the cooking time for 5 minutes on High Pressure. Once the timer goes off, perform a natural pressure release for 10 minutes, then release any remaining pressure. Carefully open the lid.
7. Remove the muffins from the Instant Pot. Serve hot.

Per Serving
calories: 389 | fat: 32.9g | protein: 19.1g
carbs: 3.4g | net carbs: 3.1g | fiber: 0.3g

Bacon, Tomato and Lettuce Wrap

Prep time: 20 minutes | Cook time: 13 minutes | Serves 4

8 ounces (227 g) (about 12 slices) reduced-sodium bacon
8 tablespoons mayonnaise
8 large romaine

lettuce leaves
4 Roma tomatoes, sliced
Salt and freshly ground black pepper

1. Arrange the bacon in a single layer in the air fryer basket. (It's OK if the bacon sits a bit on the sides.) Set the air fryer to 350°F (180°C) and cook for 10 minutes. Check for crispiness and cook for 2 to 3 minutes longer if needed. Cook in batches, if necessary, and drain the grease in between batches.
2. Spread 1 tablespoon of mayonnaise on each of the lettuce leaves and top with the tomatoes and cooked bacon. Season to taste with salt and freshly ground black pepper. Roll the lettuce leaves as you would a burrito, securing with a toothpick if desired.

Per Serving
calories: 370 | fat: 34g | protein: 11g
carbs: 7g | net carbs: 4g | fiber: 3g

Pecan Granola with Coconut

Prep time: 10 minutes | Cook time: 5 minutes | Serves 6

2 cups pecans, chopped
1 cup unsweetened coconut flakes
1 cup almond slivers
1/3 cup sunflower seeds
1/4 cup golden flaxseed
1/4 cup low-carb,
sugar-free chocolate chips
1/4 cup granular erythritol
2 tablespoons unsalted butter
1 teaspoon ground cinnamon

1. In a large bowl, mix all ingredients.
2. Place the mixture into a 4-cup round baking dish. Place dish into the air fryer basket.
3. Adjust the temperature to 320°F (160°C) and set the timer for 5 minutes.
4. Allow to cool completely before serving.

Per Serving
calories: 617 | fat: 55g | protein: 11g
carbs: 32g | net carbs: 21g | fiber: 11g

Coconut Porridge with Hemp Hearts

Prep time: 5 minutes | Cook time: minutes | Serves 3

1/4 cup unsweetened shredded coconut
1/2 cup hemp hearts
3 large eggs
1/3 cup water
1 (13.5-ounce / 383-g) can full-fat coconut
milk
1/2 teaspoon vanilla extract
1 1/2 teaspoons pumpkin pie spice
1/4 teaspoon sea salt

1. Set the Instant Pot to Sauté mode. Add the coconut and hemp to the dry pot insert and cook, stirring frequently, until lightly browned and the hemp starts to smell nutty, 3 minutes.
2. Meanwhile, in a blender, combine the eggs, water, coconut milk, vanilla, pumpkin pie spice, and salt.
3. Pour the egg mixture into the pot and stir.
4. Lock the lid. Select the Manual mode and set the cooking time for 1 minute on High Pressure.
5. Once the timer goes off, perform a natural pressure release for 5 minutes, then release any remaining pressure. Carefully open the lid.

6. Give the porridge a good stir. Spoon the porridge into individual serving bowls.

Per Serving
calories: 547 | fat: 51.3g | protein: 14.5g
carbs: 14.2g | net carbs: 8.5g | fiber: 5.7g

Ham Frittata with Bell Peppers

Prep time: 10 minutes | Cook time: 40 minutes | Serves 2

2 tablespoons avocado oil, divided
1/4 cup chopped onion
1/4 cup chopped green bell pepper
1/4 cup chopped red bell pepper
1/2 pound (227 g) cooked ham, cubed
6 large eggs
1/2 cup heavy whipping
cream
1/2 teaspoon sea salt
1/4 teaspoon ground black pepper
1/4 teaspoon dried basil
1/4 teaspoon dried parsley
1/4 teaspoon red pepper flakes
1 cup water

1. Grease a baking pan with 2 teaspoons of the avocado oil.
2. Press the Sauté button on the Instant Pot and heat the remaining 1 1/3 tablespoons of the avocado oil. Add the onion and bell peppers to the pot and sauté for 3 minutes, or until tender. Add the ham and continue to sauté for 2 minutes. Transfer the ham and onion mixture to a bowl. Clean the pot.
3. In a medium bowl, whisk together the eggs, cream, salt, black pepper, basil, parsley and pepper flakes. Pour the mixture into the prepared baking pan. Stir in the ham and onion mixture. Cover the pan with foil.
4. Pour the water and insert the trivet in the Instant Pot. Put the pan on the trivet.
5. Lock the lid. Select the Manual mode and set the cooking time for 35 minutes on High Pressure. Once the timer goes off, perform a natural pressure release for 10 minutes, then release any remaining pressure. Carefully open the lid.
6. Remove the baking pan from the pot. Serve hot.

Per Serving
calories: 571 | fat: 43.4g | protein: 39.1g
carbs: 6.0g | net carbs: 5.1g | fiber: 0.9g

Egg and Chorizo Lettuce Wraps

Prep time: 5 minutes | Cook time: 12 minutes | Serves 6

2 tablespoons avocado oil
1½ pounds (680 g) fresh chorizo
¾ cup sour cream
½ cup chicken broth
6 large eggs, washed
6 large lettuce leaves

1. Press the Sauté button on the Instant Pot and heat the oil. Crumble in the chorizo. Sauté for 2 minutes, breaking up the meat with a wooden spoon or meat chopper.
2. Stir in the sour cream and broth.
3. Place a long-legged metal trivet directly on top of the sausage mixture. Place the eggs on the trivet.
4. Set the lid in place. Select the Manual mode and set the cooking time for 10 minutes on High Pressure.
5. Meanwhile, fill a medium bowl with ice water for the eggs.
6. When the timer goes off, do a quick pressure release. Carefully open the lid.
7. Use tongs or a large spoon to transfer the eggs immediately to the ice bath. Stir the chorizo mixture and allow it to rest in the Instant Pot on Keep Warm.
8. When the eggs are cool enough to handle, peel and slice them.
9. To serve, use a slotted spoon to spoon the chorizo into lettuce leaves.

Per Serving
calories: 671 | fat: 55.9g | protein: 35.0g
carbs: 4.9g | net carbs: 4.7g | fiber: 0.2g

Vanilla-Cinnamon Cake

Prep time: 10 minutes | Cook time: 7 minutes | Serves 4

½ cup blanched finely ground almond flour
¼ cup powdered erythritol
½ teaspoon baking powder
2 tablespoons unsalted butter, softened
1 large egg
½ teaspoon unflavored gelatin
½ teaspoon vanilla extract
½ teaspoon ground cinnamon

1. In a large bowl, mix almond flour, erythritol, and baking powder. Add butter, egg, gelatin, vanilla, and cinnamon. Pour into 6-inch round baking pan.
2. Place pan into the air fryer basket.
3. Adjust the temperature to 300°F (150ºC) and set the timer for 7 minutes.
4. When the cake is completely cooked, a toothpick will come out clean. Cut cake into four and serve.

Per Serving
calories: 153 | fat: 13g | protein: 5g
carbs: 13g | net carbs: 11g | fiber: 2g

Beef and Cabbage Bowl

Prep time: 10 minutes | Cook time: 7 minutes | Serves 4

1 tablespoon avocado oil
1 pound (454 g) ground beef
1 clove garlic, minced
½ teaspoon sea salt
½ teaspoon ground black pepper
½ teaspoon ground turmeric
¼ teaspoon ground cinnamon
¼ teaspoon ground coriander
¼ cup almond butter
½ cup full-fat coconut milk
1 small head green cabbage, shredded

1. Press the Sauté button on the Instant Pot and heat the oil. Crumble in the ground beef and cook for 3 minutes, breaking up the meat with a wooden spoon or meat chopper.
2. Stir in the garlic, salt, black pepper, turmeric, cinnamon, and coriander.
3. Add the almond butter and coconut milk. Stir constantly until the almond butter melts and mixes with the coconut milk. Layer the cabbage on top of the meat mixture but do not stir.
4. Set the lid in place. Select the Manual mode and set the cooking time for 4 minutes on High Pressure. When the timer goes off, do a quick pressure release. Carefully open the lid.
5. Stir the meat mixture. Taste and adjust the salt and black pepper, and add more red pepper flakes if desired. Use a slotted spoon to transfer the mixture to a serving bowl. Serve hot.

Per Serving
calories: 534 | fat: 43.2g | protein: 26.4g
carbs: 15.0g | net carbs: 9.2g | fiber: 5.8g

Broccoli and Mushroom Frittata

Prep time: 15 minutes | Cook time: 20 minutes | Serves 2

1 tablespoon olive oil
1½ cups broccoli florets, finely chopped
½ cup sliced brown mushrooms
¼ cup finely chopped onion
½ teaspoon salt
¼ teaspoon freshly ground black pepper
6 eggs
¼ cup Parmesan cheese

1. In an 8-inch nonstick cake pan, combine the olive oil, broccoli, mushrooms, onion, salt, and pepper. Stir until the vegetables are thoroughly coated with oil. Place the cake pan in the air fryer basket and set the air fryer to 400°F (205°C). Air fry for 5 minutes until the vegetables soften.
2. Meanwhile, in a medium bowl, whisk the eggs and Parmesan until thoroughly combined. Pour the egg mixture into the pan and shake gently to distribute the vegetables. Air fry for another 15 minutes until the eggs are set.
3. Remove from the air fryer and let sit for 5 minutes to cool slightly. Use a silicone spatula to gently lift the frittata onto a plate before serving.

Per Serving
calories: 360 | fat: 25g | protein: 25g
carbs: 10g | net carbs: 8g | fiber: 2g

Almond Porridge with Berries

Prep time: 5 minutes | Cook time: 2 minutes | Serves 4

8 tablespoons unsalted and shelled raw sunflower seeds
10 tablespoons almond flour
4 tablespoons golden flaxseed meal
2½ tablespoons butter, melted
2⅓ cups water
1 cup unsweetened
almond milk
½ teaspoon vanilla extract
½ teaspoon ground cinnamon
4 teaspoons erythritol-oligosaccharide granular sweetener blend
2 cups mixed berries

1. Add the sunflower seeds to a small food processor or blender. Pulse until a flour-like texture is achieved.
2. In a medium bowl, combine the sunflower meal, almond flour, and flaxseed meal. Mix until well combined.
3. Add the melted butter to the pot and then add the almond-flaxseed mixture and water. Stir until well combined.

Instant Pot

4. Set the lid in place. Select the Manual mode and set the cooking time for 2 minutes on High Pressure. When the timer goes off, do a quick pressure release. Carefully open the lid.
5. Stir in the almond milk and vanilla extract.
6. Spoon the porridge into serving bowls. Top each serving with ⅛ teaspoon cinnamon, 1 teaspoon sweetener, and ½ cup of the berries. Serve warm.

Per Serving (½ cup porridge with ½ cup berries)
calories: 309 | fat: 26.8g | protein: 10.1g
carbs: 6.8g | net carbs: 5.9g | fiber: 0.9g

Mediterranean Eggs with Cheddar

Prep time: 5 minutes | Cook time: 1 minute | Serves 2 to 4

2 tablespoons coconut oil
1 (14-ounce / 397-g) can roasted sugar-free tomatoes
1 garlic clove, minced
2 cups shredded full-fat Cheddar cheese
½ teaspoon ground cayenne pepper
½ teaspoon ground
cumin
½ teaspoon dried oregano
½ teaspoon dried cilantro
½ teaspoon kosher salt
½ teaspoon freshly ground black pepper
6 eggs

1. Press the Sauté button on the Instant Pot and melt the coconut oil. Stir in the remaining ingredients, except for the eggs, to the pot.
2. Carefully crack the eggs into the mixture, maintaining the yolks. Make sure they are spaced evenly apart.
3. Set the lid in place. Select the Manual mode and set the cooking time for 1 minute on High Pressure. When the timer goes off, do a quick pressure release. Carefully open the lid.
4. Serve warm.

Per Serving
calories: 396 | fat: 32.1g | protein: 22.7g
carbs: 4.4g | net carbs: 3.5g | fiber: 0.9g

Ham and Broccoli Frittata with Peppers

Prep time: 10 minutes | Cook time: 20 minutes | Serves 4

1 cup sliced bell peppers
8 ounces (227 g) ham, cubed
2 cups frozen broccoli florets
4 eggs
1 cup heavy cream
1 cup grated Cheddar cheese
1 teaspoon salt
2 teaspoons freshly ground black pepper

1. Arrange the pepper slices in a greased pan. Place the cubed ham on top. Cover with the frozen broccoli.
2. In a bowl, whisk together the remaining ingredients. Pour the egg mixture over the vegetables and ham. Cover the pan with aluminum foil.
3. Pour 2 cups water and insert the trivet in the Instant Pot. Put the pan on the trivet.
4. Lock the lid. Select the Manual mode and set the cooking time for 20 minutes on High Pressure. Once the timer goes off, perform a natural pressure release for 10 minutes, then release any remaining pressure. Carefully open the lid.
5. Carefully remove the pan from the pot and remove the foil. Let the frittata sit for 5 to 10 minutes before transferring the frittata onto the plate.
6. Serve warm.

Per Serving
calories: 395 | fat: 26.8g | protein: 30.1g
carbs: 8.8g | net carbs: 5.7g | fiber: 3.1g

Cauliflower Bake with Chicken

Prep time: 10 minutes | Cook time: 15 minutes | Serves 4

4 eggs, beaten
1 cup shredded cauliflower
1 tablespoon Italian seasonings
½ teaspoon salt
½ cup ground chicken
¼ cup shredded Cheddar cheese
1 cup water

1. In a bowl, stir together the beaten eggs, shredded cauliflower, Italian seasonings and salt. Pour the mixture into four ramekins.
2. Add the ground chicken to the ramekins and top with the Cheddar cheese.

3. Pour the water and insert the trivet in the Instant Pot. Put the ramekins on the trivet.
4. Set the lid in place. Select the Manual mode and set the cooking time for 15 minutes on High Pressure. When the timer goes off, do a quick pressure release. Carefully open the lid.
5. Serve immediately.

Per Serving
calories: 141 | fat: 9.0g | protein: 13.0g
carbs: 2.0g | net carbs: 1.3g | fiber: 0.7g

Cheese Cauliflower Mash

Prep time: 5 minutes | Cook time: 8 to 10 minutes | Serves 4

2 cups cauliflower, cut into florets
2 tablespoons cream cheese, at room temperature
½ cup heavy cream
½ cup grated sharp Cheddar cheese
1 teaspoon salt
1 teaspoon freshly ground black pepper

1. In a blender, place the cauliflower florets and pulse until puréed.
2. In a heatproof bowl, mix the cauliflower along with the remaining ingredients. Cover the bowl with aluminum foil.
3. Pour 2 cups water and insert the trivet in the Instant Pot. Put the bowl on the trivet.
4. Lock the lid. Select the Manual mode and set the cooking time for 5 minutes on High Pressure. Once the timer goes off, perform a natural pressure release for 10 minutes, then release any remaining pressure. Carefully open the lid.
5. Place the cooked cauliflower in a broiler and broil for 3 to 5 minutes, or until the cheese is browned and bubbling.
6. Serve immediately.

Per Serving
calories: 133 | fat: 10.7g | protein: 6.1g
carbs: 3.9g | net carbs: 2.9g | fiber: 1.0g

Almond and Coconut Porridge

Prep time: 5 minutes | Cook time: 5 minutes | Serves 4

½ cup chopped almonds
4 tablespoons shredded unsweetened coconut
2 tablespoons flaxseed
2 tablespoons pumpkin seeds
1 teaspoon ground cinnamon
½ teaspoon grated nutmeg
¼ teaspoon ground cloves
Himalayan salt, to taste
1 cup boiling water

1. Add all the ingredients to the Instant Pot and stir to combine.
2. Set the lid in place. Select the Manual mode and set the cooking time for 5 minutes on High Pressure. When the timer goes off, do a quick pressure release. Carefully open the lid.
3. Serve immediately.

Per Serving
calories: 172 | fat: 14.9g | protein: 5.0g
carbs: 7.5g | net carbs: 2.6g | fiber: 4.9g

Cauliflower Rice Pudding with Blueberries

Prep time: 5 minutes | Cook time: 3 minutes | Serves 4

2 tablespoons coconut oil
4 cups raw cauliflower rice
1 cup unsweetened almond milk
2 scoops vanilla-flavored protein powder
¼ teaspoon sea salt
½ cup blueberries

1. Press the Sauté button on the Instant Pot and heat the oil. Add the cauliflower rice and stir to coat it with the cacao butter. Add the almond milk, protein powder, salt and blueberries and stir very well to combine.
2. Lock the lid. Select the Manual mode and set the cooking time for 3 minutes on High Pressure. Once the timer goes off, perform a natural pressure release for 5 minutes, then release any remaining pressure. Carefully open the lid.

3. Stir the pudding. Spoon the pudding into individual bowls and allow it to cool for a few minutes. Serve warm or at room temperature.

Per Serving
calories: 221 | fat: 10.4g | protein: 16.6g
carbs: 17.6g | net carbs: 13.5g | fiber: 4.1g

Breakfast Turkey Casserole

Prep time: 10 minutes | Cook time: 10 minutes | Serves 4 to 5

2 tablespoons coconut oil
1 pound (454 g) ground turkey
3 slices bacon, cooked and crumbled
1 cup chopped bell peppers
½ cup chopped spinach
½ cup heavy cream
¼ cup shredded full-fat Cheddar cheese
1 teaspoon dried oregano
½ teaspoon crushed red pepper
½ teaspoon kosher salt
½ teaspoon freshly ground black pepper

1. Press the Sauté button on the Instant Pot and melt the coconut oil.
2. Add the turkey to the pot and sauté for 5 minutes. Stir in the remaining ingredients and continue to cook for 5 minutes, or until the turkey is browned and cooked all the way through.
3. Transfer the dish to plates and serve immediately.

Per Serving
calories: 373 | fat: 25.0g | protein: 33.2g
carbs: 3.1g | net carbs: 2.4g | fiber: 0.7g

Breakfast Green Salad with Sardines

Prep time: 10 minutes | Cook time: 14 to 15 minutes | Serves 2

2 large eggs
1 cup water
1 tablespoon avocado oil
4 slices bacon, cut into small pieces
2 tablespoons minced shallots
1 tablespoon apple cider vinegar
1 (4.4-ounce / 125-g) can oil-packed sardines
¼ cup fresh parsley leaves
4 cups chopped romaine lettuce
2 cups baby spinach, torn into smaller pieces
¼ teaspoon ground black pepper
1 medium avocado, sliced

1. Pour the water into the Instant Pot. Place the trivet inside and place the eggs on top.
2. Set the lid in place. Select the Manual mode and set the cooking time for 10 minutes on High Pressure.
3. Meanwhile, prepare a bowl with ice water to cool the eggs.
4. When the timer goes off, do a quick pressure release. Carefully open the lid. Use tongs to transfer the eggs to the ice bath. When cool, peel and slice the eggs.
5. Carefully pour the water out of the Instant Pot and wipe it dry. Set the Instant Pot to Sauté mode and heat the avocado oil. Add the bacon and cook for 3 minutes. Add the shallots and cook until the bacon is crispy, another 1 to 2 minutes. Press Cancel.
6. Deglaze the pot with the vinegar, scraping the bottom with a wooden spoon to loosen any browned bits. Use a fork to break up the sardines and add them, along with their oil, to the pot. Stir in the parsley.
7. Place the lettuce, spinach, and pepper in the pot and mix well to coat the greens with the oil. Divide the mixture between two large serving bowls, scraping any remaining dressing from the pot.
8. Top each salad with half the sliced avocado and 1 sliced egg. Crack some black pepper over the top and serve immediately.

Per Serving
calories: 679 | fat: 55.1g | protein: 33.4g
carbs: 16.0g | net carbs: 6.0g | fiber: 10.0g

Sausage-Stuffed Mushrooms

Prep time: 10 minutes | Cook time: 15 to 16 minutes | Serves 2

12 large white mushrooms, washed, stems removed and reserved
1 tablespoon avocado oil
¼ teaspoon kosher salt
¼ teaspoon ground black pepper
1 tablespoon butter
6 ounces (170 g) sugar-free bulk pork breakfast sausage
1 clove garlic, minced
¼ cup full-fat coconut milk
1 cup finely chopped Swiss chard
1 cup water

1. Finely chop the mushroom stems and set aside. Place the mushroom caps stemmed side down in a medium bowl and pour the avocado oil over them. Season with the salt and pepper. Toss gently to coat the mushrooms with oil without breaking them.
2. Set the Instant Pot to Sauté mode and melt the butter. When it is melted, crumble in the sausage and add the chopped mushroom stems. Sauté, stirring occasionally, until only a little pink remains in the pork, 3 to 4 minutes. Add the garlic and sauté until the pork is cooked through.
3. Deglaze the pot with the coconut milk, scraping the bottom with a wooden spoon to loosen any browned bits. Stir in the chopped chard and cook just until they are wilted.
4. Transfer the pork to a bowl. Taste and adjust the salt and pepper. Wipe or wash out the pot insert.
5. Stuff the pork mixture into the mushrooms. Place the mushrooms stem side up in two stackable stainless steel insert pans, 6 mushrooms per pan. Stack and secure the lid on the pans.
6. Pour the water into the Instant Pot and lower the stacked pans into the pot.
7. Set the lid in place. Select the Steam mode and set the cooking time for 12 minutes on High Pressure. When the timer goes off, do a quick pressure release. Carefully open the lid.
8. Transfer the pan from the pot. Open the insert pans and transfer the mushrooms to serving plates. Serve warm.

Per Serving
calories: 453 | fat: 40.8g | protein: 16.1g
carbs: 8.1g | net carbs: 6.3g | fiber: 1.8g

Chapter 10 Soups and Stews

Cheddar Bacon Soup

Prep time: 10 minutes | Cook time: 20 minutes | Serves 4

3 ounces (85 g) bacon, chopped
1 tablespoon chopped scallions
1 teaspoon curry powder
1 cup coconut milk
3 cups beef broth
1 cup Cheddar cheese, shredded

1. Heat the the Instant Pot on Sauté mode for 3 minutes and add bacon. Cook for 5 minutes. Flip constantly.
2. Add the scallions and curry powder. Sauté for 5 minutes more.
3. Pour in the coconut milk and beef broth. Add the Cheddar cheese and stir to mix well.
4. Select Manual mode and set cooking time for 10 minutes on High Pressure.
5. When timer beeps, use a quick pressure release. Open the lid.
6. Blend the soup with an immersion blender until smooth. Serve warm.

Per Serving
calories: 398 | fat: 33.6g | protein: 20.0g
carbs: 5.1g | net carbs: 3.6g | fiber: 1.5g

Cauliflower and Bacon Soup with Leek

Prep time: 15 minutes | Cook time: 15 minutes | Serves 6

6 slices bacon
1 leek, remove the dark green end and roots, sliced in half lengthwise, rinsed, cut into ½-inch-thick slices crosswise
½ medium yellow onion, sliced
4 cloves garlic, minced
3 cups chicken broth
1 large head
cauliflower, roughly chopped into florets
1 cup water
1 teaspoon kosher salt
1 teaspoon ground black pepper
²⁄₃ cup shredded sharp Cheddar cheese, divided
½ cup heavy whipping cream

1. Set the Instant Pot to Sauté mode. When heated, place the bacon on the bottom of the pot and cook for 5 minutes or until crispy.

2. Transfer the bacon slices to a plate. Let stand until cool enough to handle, crumble it with forks.
3. Add the leek and onion to the bacon fat remaining in the pot. Sauté for 5 minutes or until fragrant and the onion begins to caramelize. Add the garlic and sauté for 30 seconds more or until fragrant.
4. Stir in the chicken broth, cauliflower florets, water, salt, pepper, and three-quarters of the crumbled bacon.
5. Secure the lid. Press the Manual button and set cooking time for 3 minutes on High Pressure.
6. When timer beeps, perform a quick pressure release. Open the lid.
7. Stir in ½ cup of the Cheddar and the cream. Use an immersion blender to purée the soup until smooth.
8. Ladle into bowls and garnish with the remaining Cheddar and crumbled bacon. Serve immediately.

Per Serving
calories: 251 | fat: 18.9g | protein: 10.5g
carbs: 12.0g | net carbs: 8.6g | fiber: 3.4g

Beef Broth with Bay Leaf

Prep time: 20 minutes | Cook time: 50 minutes | Serves 4

1 pound (454 g) T-bone beef steak, chopped
1 bay leaf
1 teaspoon peppercorns
1 teaspoon salt
3 cups water

1. Put all ingredients in the Instant Pot. Stir to mix well. Close the lid.
2. Set Manual mode and set cooking time for 50 minutes on High Pressure.
3. When timer beeps, use a natural pressure release for 15 minutes, then release the remaining pressure and open the lid.
4. Strain the cooked mixture and shred the meat. Serve the beef broth with the shredded beef.

Per Serving
calories: 303 | fat: 23.1g | protein: 22.1g
carbs: 0.5g | net carbs: 0.3g | fiber: 0.2g

Beef and Cauliflower Soup with Oregano

Prep time: 10 minutes | Cook time: 14 minutes | Serves 4

1 cup ground beef
½ cup cauliflower, shredded
1 teaspoon unsweetened tomato purée
¼ cup coconut milk
1 teaspoon minced garlic
1 teaspoon dried oregano
½ teaspoon salt
4 cups water

1. Put all ingredients in the Instant Pot and stir well.
2. Close the lid. Select Manual mode and set cooking time for 14 minutes on High Pressure.
3. When timer beeps, make a quick pressure release and open the lid.
4. Blend with an immersion blender until smooth.
5. Serve warm.

Per Serving
calories: 106 | fat: 7.7g | protein: 7.3g
carbs: 2.2g | net carbs: 1.3g | fiber: 0.9g

White Mushroom Soup with Scallions

Prep time: 15 minutes | Cook time: 20 minutes | Serves 4

2 cups chopped white mushrooms
3 tablespoons cream cheese
4 ounces (113 g) scallions, diced
4 cups chicken broth
1 teaspoon olive oil
½ teaspoon ground cumin
1 teaspoon salt
2 ounces (57 g) blue cheese, crumbled

1. Combine the mushrooms, cream cheese, scallions, chicken broth, olive oil, and ground cumin in the Instant Pot.
2. Seal the lid. Select Manual mode and set cooking time for 20 minutes on High Pressure.
3. When timer beeps, use a quick pressure release and open the lid.
4. Add the salt and blend the soup with an immersion blender.
5. Ladle the soup in the bowls and top with blue cheese. Serve warm.

Per Serving
calories: 142 | fat: 9.4g | protein: 10.1g
carbs: 4.8g | net carbs: 3.7g | fiber: 1.1g

Beef and Eggplant Tagine with Scallions

Prep time: 15 minutes | Cook time: 25 minutes | Serves 6

1 pound (454 g) beef fillet, chopped
1 eggplant, chopped
6 ounces (170 g) scallions, chopped
4 cups beef broth
1 teaspoon ground allspices
1 teaspoon erythritol
1 teaspoon coconut oil

1. Put all ingredients in the Instant Pot. Stir to mix well.
2. Close the lid. Select Manual mode and set cooking time for 25 minutes on High Pressure.
3. When timer beeps, use a natural pressure release for 15 minutes, then release any remaining pressure. Open the lid.
4. Serve warm.

Per Serving
calories: 158 | fat: 5.3g | protein: 21.1g
carbs: 8.2g | net carbs: 4.7g | fiber: 3.5g

Beef and Okra Stew with Basil

Prep time: 15 minutes | Cook time: 25 minutes | Serves 3

8 ounces (227 g) beef sirloin, chopped
¼ teaspoon cumin seeds
1 teaspoon dried basil
1 tablespoon avocado
oil
¼ cup coconut cream
1 cup water
6 ounces (170 g) okra, chopped

1. Sprinkle the beef sirloin with cumin seeds and dried basil and put in the Instant Pot.
2. Add avocado oil and roast the meat on Sauté mode for 5 minutes. Flip occasionally.
3. Add coconut cream, water, and okra.
4. Close the lid and select Manual mode. Set cooking time for 25 minutes on High Pressure.
5. When timer beeps, use a natural pressure release for 10 minutes, the release any remaining pressure. Open the lid.
6. Serve warm.

Per Serving
calories: 216 | fat: 10.2g | protein: 24.6g
carbs: 5.7g | net carbs: 3.2g | fiber: 2.5g

Broccoli Soup with Feta Cheese

Prep time: 10 minutes | Cook time: 25 minutes | Serves 4

1 cup broccoli, chopped
½ cup coconut cream
1 teaspoon unsweetened tomato
purée
4 cups beef broth
1 teaspoon chili flakes
6 ounces (170 g) feta, crumbled

1. Put broccoli, coconut cream, tomato purée, and beef broth in the Instant Pot. Sprinkle with chili flakes and stir to mix well.
2. Close the lid and select Manual mode. Set cooking time for 8 minutes on High Pressure.
3. When timer beeps, make a quick pressure release and open the lid.
4. Add the feta cheese and stir the soup on Sauté mode for 5 minutes or until the cheese melt.
5. Serve immediately.

Per Serving
calories: 229 | fat: 17.7g | protein: 12.3g
carbs: 6.1g | net carbs: 4.8g | fiber: 1.3g

Avocado and Tomatillo Soup

Prep time: 10 minutes | Cook time: 7 minutes | Serves 4

2 avocados
1 small fresh tomatillo, quartered
2 cups chicken broth
2 tablespoons avocado oil
1 tablespoon butter
2 tablespoons finely minced onion
1 clove garlic, minced
½ Serrano chile,
deseeded and ribs removed, minced, plus thin slices for garnish
¼ teaspoon sea salt
Pinch of ground white pepper
½ cup full-fat coconut milk
Fresh cilantro sprigs, for garnish

1. Scoop the avocado flesh into a food processor. Add the tomatillo and chicken broth and purée until smooth. Set aside.
2. Set the Instant Pot to Sauté mode and add the avocado oil and butter. When the butter melts, add the onion and garlic and sauté for a minute or until softened. Add the Serrano chile and sauté for 1 minute more.
3. Pour the puréed avocado mixture into the pot, add the salt and pepper, and stir to combine.

4. Secure the lid. Press the Manual button and set cooking time for 5 minutes on High Pressure.
5. When timer beeps, use a quick pressure release. Open the lid and stir in the coconut milk.
6. Serve hot topped with thin slices of Serrano chile, and cilantro sprigs.

Per Serving
calories: 333 | fat: 32.1g | protein: 3.8g
carbs: 14.5g | net carbs: 6.6g | fiber: 7.9g

Chicken and Avocado Soup with Jalapeños

Prep time: 15 minutes | Cook time: 25 minutes | Serves 5

2 tablespoons olive oil
1 pound (454 g) boneless, skinless chicken thighs, cut into bite-sized pieces
4 garlic cloves, minced
½ medium yellow onion, diced
2 jalapeño, stems and seeds removed, chopped
½ cup diced fresh tomato
5 cups chicken broth
Juice of 2 limes
2 teaspoons sea salt
1 teaspoon chili powder
½ teaspoon garlic powder
¼ teaspoon ground black pepper
1 medium avocado, chopped
⅓ cup shredded pepper Jack cheese

1. Select the Instant Pot on Sauté mode and add the olive oil. Once the oil is hot, add the chicken and sauté for 3 minutes per side or until browned.
2. Add the garlic, onions, and jalapeños to the pot. Continue sautéing or until the vegetables are softened.
3. Add the diced tomatoes, chicken broth, lime juice, sea salt, chili powder, garlic powder, and black pepper. Stir to combine.
4. Lock the lid. Select Manual mode and set cooking time for 20 minutes on High Pressure.
5. When cooking is complete, allow the pressure to release naturally for 15 minutes and then release the remaining pressure.
6. Open the lid and ladle the soup into serving bowls. Top each serving with equal amounts of the avocado and pepper Jack cheese. Serve hot.

Per Serving
calories: 337 | fat: 16.8g | protein: 13.6g
carbs: 28.5g | net carbs: 23.5g | fiber: 5.0g

Buffalo Chicken Soup with Celery

Prep time: 7 minutes | Cook time: 10 minutes | Serves 2

1 ounce (28 g) celery stalk, chopped
4 tablespoons coconut milk
¾ teaspoon salt
¼ teaspoon white pepper
1 cup water

2 ounces (57 g) Mozzarella, shredded
6 ounces (170 g) cooked chicken, shredded
2 tablespoons keto-friendly Buffalo sauce

1. Place the chopped celery stalk, coconut milk, salt, white pepper, water, and Mozzarella in the Instant Pot. Stir to mix well.
2. Set the Manual mode and set timer for 7 minutes on High Pressure.
3. When timer beeps, use a quick pressure release and open the lid.
4. Transfer the soup on the bowls. Stir in the chicken and Buffalo sauce. Serve warm.

Per Serving
calories: 287 | fat: 14.8g | protein: 33.5g
carbs: 4.3g | net carbs: 2.8g | fiber: 1.5g

Chicken and Cauliflower Soup

Prep time: 15 minutes | Cook time: 13 minutes | Serves 5

2 cups cauliflower florets
1 pound (454 g) boneless, skinless chicken thighs
4½ cups chicken broth
½ yellow onion, chopped
2 garlic cloves, minced
1 tablespoon unflavored gelatin powder
2 teaspoons sea salt
½ teaspoon ground black pepper

½ cup sliced zucchini
1/3 cup sliced turnips
1 teaspoon dried parsley
3 celery stalks, chopped
1 teaspoon ground turmeric
½ teaspoon dried marjoram
1 teaspoon dried thyme
½ teaspoon dried oregano

1. Add the cauliflower florets to a food processor and pulse until a ricelike consistency is achieved. Set aside.
2. Add the chicken thighs, chicken broth, onions, garlic, gelatin powder, sea salt, and black pepper to the pot. Gently stir to combine.

3. Lock the lid. Select Manual mode and set cooking time for 10 minutes on High Pressure.
4. When cooking is complete, quick release the pressure and open the lid.
5. Transfer the chicken thighs to a cutting board. Chop the chicken into bite-sized pieces and then return the chopped chicken to the pot.
6. Add the cauliflower rice, zucchini, turnips, parsley, celery, turmeric, marjoram, thyme, and oregano to the pot. Stir to combine.
7. Lock the lid. Select Manual mode and set cooking time for 3 minutes on High Pressure.
8. When cooking is complete, quick release the pressure.
9. Open the lid. Ladle the soup into serving bowls. Serve hot.

Per Serving
calories: 247 | fat: 10.4g | protein: 30.2g
carbs: 8.3g | net carbs: 6.1g | fiber: 2.2g

Cod and Tomato Stew

Prep time: 10 minutes | Cook time: 20 minutes | Serves 4

8 ounces (227 g) cod, chopped
½ teaspoon ground turmeric
½ teaspoon ground cumin
½ teaspoon ground

paprika
½ teaspoon sesame seeds
1 teaspoon coconut oil
½ cup crushed tomatoes

1. Sprinkle the chopped cod with turmeric, cumin, paprika, and sesame seeds on a clean work surface.
2. Melt the coconut oil in the Instant Pot on Sauté mode.
3. Add the seasoned cod and cook for 2 minutes for each side.
4. Pour in the crushed tomatoes and close the lid.
5. Select Manual mode and set cooking time for 15 minutes on Low Pressure.
6. When timer beeps, perform a quick pressure release. Open the lid.
7. Serve warm.

Per Serving
calories: 87 | fat: 1.9g | protein: 13.9g
carbs: 3.0g | net carbs: 1.8g | fiber: 1.2g

Chicken Zoodles Soup

Prep time: 25 minutes | Cook time: 15 minutes | Serves 2

2 cups water
6 ounces (170 g) chicken fillet, chopped
1 teaspoon salt
2 ounces (57 g) zucchini, spiralized
1 tablespoon coconut aminos

1. Pour water in the Instant Pot. Add chopped chicken fillet and salt. Close the lid.
2. Select Manual mode and set cooking time for 15 minutes on High Pressure.
3. When cooking is complete, perform a natural pressure release for 10 minutes, then release any remaining pressure. Open the lid.
4. Fold in the zoodles and coconut aminos.
5. Leave the soup for 10 minutes to rest. Serve warm.

Per Serving

calories: 175 | fat: 6.3g | protein: 24.8g
carbs: 4.5g | net carbs: 1.5g | fiber: 3.0g

Cajun Chicken and Shrimp Stock

Prep time: 10 minutes | Cook time: 15 minutes | Serves 4

2 chicken thighs, boneless, chopped
4 ounces (113 g) shrimps, peeled
3 ounces (85 g) sausages, chopped
½ bell pepper, chopped
1 cup beef broth
1 teaspoon unsweetened tomato purée
1 celery stalk, chopped
½ teaspoon Cajun seasonings

1. Heat the the Instant Pot on Sauté mode for 3 minutes.
2. Add the chicken thighs, shrimps, sausages, bell pepper, beef broth, unsweetened tomato purée, celery stalk, and Cajun seasonings.
3. Gently mix the the ingredients and close the lid.
4. Select Manual mode and set time to 15 minutes on High Pressure.
5. When cooking is complete, use a quick pressure release and open the lid.
6. Serve immediately.

Per Serving

calories: 261 | fat: 12.3g | protein: 33.2g
carbs: 2.2g | net carbs: 1.9g | fiber: 0.3g

Cheese Chicken Soup

Prep time: 10 minutes | Cook time: 25 minutes | Serves 4

1 pound (454 g) chicken breast, skinless, boneless
5 cups chicken broth
½ cup Cheddar
cheese, shredded
2 ounces (57 g) chili Verde sauce
1 tablespoon dried cilantro

1. Put chicken breast and chicken broth in the Instant Pot.
2. Add the cilantro, Close the lid. Select Manual mode and set cooking time for 15 minutes on High Pressure.
3. When timer beeps, make a quick pressure release and open the lid.
4. Shred the chicken breast with a fork.
5. Add the Cheddar and chili Verde sauce in the soup and cook on Sauté mode for 10 minutes.
6. Mix in the dried cilantro. Serve immediately.

Per Serving

calories: 257 | fat: 10.2g | protein: 34.5g
carbs: 4.0g | net carbs: 3.8g | fiber: 0.2g

Coconut Beef and Spinach Stew

Prep time: 20 minutes | Cook time: 30 minutes | Serves 4

1 pound (454 g) beef sirloin, chopped
2 cups spinach, chopped
3 cups chicken broth
1 cup coconut milk
1 teaspoon allspices
1 teaspoon coconut aminos

1. Put all ingredients in the Instant Pot. Stir to mix well.
2. Close the lid. Set the Manual mode and set cooking time for 30 minutes on High Pressure.
3. When timer beeps, use a natural pressure release for 10 minutes, then release any remaining pressure. Open the lid.
4. Blend with an immersion blender until smooth.
5. Serve warm.

Per Serving

calories: 383 | fat: 22.2g | protein: 39.9g
carbs: 5.1g | net carbs: 3.3g | fiber: 1.8g

Chicken Stew with Cilantro

Prep time: 15 minutes | Cook time: 10 minutes | Serves 3

9 ounces (255 g) chicken fillet, chopped
2 chipotle chili in adobo sauce, chopped
2 tablespoons sesame seeds
1 ounce (28 g) fresh cilantro, chopped
1 teaspoon ground paprika
¼ teaspoon salt
1 cup chicken broth

1. In a mixing bowl, combine the chicken fillet, chipotle chili, sesame seeds, cilantro, ground paprika, and salt.
2. Transfer the mixture in the Instant Pot and pour in the chicken broth.
3. Select Manual mode and set cooking time for 10 minutes on High Pressure.
4. When timer beeps, use a natural pressure release for 10 minutes, then release any remaining pressure. Open the lid.
5. Serve warm.

Per Serving
calories: 230 | fat: 10.6g | protein: 27.6g
carbs: 4.5g | net carbs: 1.9g | fiber: 2.6g

Curried Chicken Stew

Prep time: 10 minutes | Cook time: 12 minutes | Serves 4

1 teaspoon lemon zest
1 tablespoon coconut cream
1 teaspoon curry paste
4 ounces (113 g) leek, chopped
2 cups water
4 chicken thighs, skinless, boneless, chopped

1. In a mixing bowl, mix the lemon zest, coconut cream, and curry paste.
2. Combine the chopped chicken thighs, leek, and curry paste mixture in the Instant Pot. Pour in the the water
3. Close the lid and select Manual mode. Set cooking time for 12 minutes on High Pressure.
4. When timer beeps, use a quick pressure release and open the lid.
5. Transfer the stew in bowls and serve.

Per Serving
calories: 145 | fat: 4.6g | protein: 20.4g
carbs: 4.7g | net carbs: 4.1g | fiber: 0.6g

Cabbage and Pork Soup with Chili

Prep time: 10 minutes | Cook time: 12 minutes | Serves 3

1 teaspoon butter
½ cup shredded white cabbage
½ teaspoon ground coriander
½ teaspoon salt
½ teaspoon chili flakes
2 cups chicken broth
½ cup ground pork

1. Melt the butter in the Instant Pot on Sauté mode.
2. Add cabbage and sprinkle with ground coriander, salt, and chili flakes.
3. Fold in the chicken broth and ground pork.
4. Close the lid and select Manual mode. Set cooking time for 12 minutes on High Pressure.
5. When timer beeps, use a quick pressure release. Open the lid.
6. Ladle the soup and serve warm.

Per Serving
calories: 350 | fat: 23.9g | protein: 30.2g
carbs: 1.3g | net carbs: 1.0g | fiber: 0.3g

Cheese Ham Soup

Prep time: 15 minutes | Cook time: 6 minutes | Serves 4

7 ounces (198 g) ham, chopped
3 ounces (85 g) Mozzarella cheese, shredded
2 tablespoons ricotta cheese
4 cups chicken broth
2 ounces (57 g) scallions, chopped
½ teaspoon salt
1 teaspoon ground black pepper

1. Put all ingredients in the Instant Pot and stir to mix well.
2. Close the lid and select Manual mode. Set cooking time for 6 minutes at High Pressure.
3. When timer beeps, use a natural pressure release for 10 minutes, then release any remaining pressure. Open the lid.
4. Ladle the soup into the bowls. Serve warm.

Per Serving
calories: 196 | fat: 10.1g | protein: 20.3g
carbs: 5.3g | net carbs: 4.1g | fiber: 1.2g

Egg Drop Soup with Dill

Prep time: 5 minutes | Cook time: 10 minutes | Serves 4

4 cups chicken broth
1 teaspoon salt
2 eggs, beaten

2 tablespoons fresh dill, chopped

1. Pour chicken broth in the Instant Pot. Add the salt and bring to a boil on Sauté mode.
2. Add beaten eggs and stir the mix well. Add dill and Sauté for 5 minutes.
3. Serve immediately.

Per Serving
calories: 74 | fat: 3.6g | protein: 7.9g
carbs: 2.0g | net carbs: 1.8g | fiber: 0.2g

Beef Meatball and Veggie Minestrone

Prep time: 5 minutes | Cook time: 35 minutes | Serves 6

1 pound (454 g) ground beef
1 large egg
1½ tablespoons golden flaxseed meal
⅓ cup shredded Mozzarella cheese
¼ cup unsweetened tomato purée
1½ tablespoons Italian seasoning, divided
1½ teaspoons garlic powder, divided
1½ teaspoons sea salt, divided
1 tablespoon olive oil

2 garlic cloves, minced
½ medium yellow onion, minced
¼ cup pancetta, diced
1 cup sliced yellow squash
1 cup sliced zucchini
½ cup sliced turnips
4 cups beef broth
14 ounces (397 g) can diced tomatoes
½ teaspoon ground black pepper
3 tablespoons shredded Parmesan cheese

1. Preheat the oven to 400°F (205°C) and line a large baking sheet with aluminum foil.
2. In a large bowl, combine the ground beef, egg, flaxseed meal, Mozzarella, unsweetened tomato purée, ½ tablespoon of Italian seasoning, ½ teaspoon of garlic powder, and ½ teaspoon of sea salt. Mix the ingredients until well combined.
3. Make the meatballs by shaping 1 heaping tablespoon of the ground beef mixture into a meatball. Repeat with the remaining mixture and then transfer the meatballs to the prepared baking sheet.
4. Place the meatballs in the oven and bake for 15 minutes. When the baking time is complete, remove from the oven and set aside.
5. Select Sauté mode of the Instant Pot. Once the pot is hot, add the olive oil, garlic, onion, and pancetta. Sauté for 2 minutes or until the garlic becomes fragrant and the onions begin to soften.
6. Add the yellow squash, zucchini, and turnips to the pot. Sauté for 3 more minutes.
7. Add the beef broth, diced tomatoes, black pepper, and remaining garlic powder, sea salt, and Italian seasoning to the pot. Stir to combine and then add the meatballs.
8. Lock the lid. Select Manual mode and set cooking time for 15 minutes on High Pressure.
9. When cooking is complete, allow the pressure to release naturally for 10 minutes and then release the remaining pressure.
10. Open the lid and gently stir the soup. Ladle into serving bowls and top with Parmesan. Serve hot.

Per Serving
calories: 373 | fat: 18.8g | protein: 34.7g
carbs: 15.0g | net carbs: 11.3g | fiber: 3.7g

Cauliflower Soup with Cilantro

Prep time: 10 minutes | Cook time: 6 minutes | Serves 4

2 cups chopped cauliflower
2 tablespoons fresh cilantro
1 cup coconut cream

2 cups beef broth
3 ounces (85 g) Provolone cheese, chopped

1. Put cauliflower, cilantro, coconut cream, beef broth, and cheese in the Instant Pot. Stir to mix well.
2. Select Manual mode and set cooking time for 6 minutes on High Pressure.
3. When timer beeps, allow a natural pressure release for 4 minutes, then release any remaining pressure. Open the lid.
4. Blend the soup and ladle in bowls to serve.

Per Serving
calories: 244 | fat: 20.7g | protein: 10.2g
carbs: 6.9g | net carbs: 4.3g | fiber: 2.6g

Coconut Asparagus Soup

Prep time: 10 minutes | Cook time: 17 minutes | Serves 4

1 cup asparagus, chopped
3 ounces (85 g) scallions, diced
1 teaspoon olive oil
½ teaspoon cayenne pepper
1 teaspoon salt
2 cups coconut milk

1. Sauté the chopped asparagus, scallions, and olive oil in the Instant Pot on Sauté mode for 7 minutes.
2. Add cayenne pepper, salt, and coconut milk.
3. Select Manual mode and set cooking time for 10 minutes on High Pressure.
4. When timer beeps, make a quick pressure release and open the lid.
5. Blend the soup until creamy. Serve warm.

Per Serving
calories: 300 | fat: 29.9g | protein: 3.9g
carbs: 9.6g | net carbs: 5.6g | fiber: 4.0g

Cauliflower and Bacon Chowder

Prep time: 10 minutes | Cook time: 25 minutes | Serves 6

2 cups chicken broth
8 ounces (227 g) diced bacon, uncooked
5 ounces (142 g) diced onion (about 1 small onion)
1 teaspoon salt
½ teaspoon black pepper
1 (2-pound / 907-g)
large head cauliflower, stem and core removed, cut into florets
8 ounces (227 g) cream cheese, softened and cut into small cubes
½ cup heavy cream, at room temperature

1. Pour the chicken broth into the pot. Add the bacon, onion, salt, and pepper. Stir to combine. Place the large florets in the pot.
2. Close the lid. Select Manual mode and set cooking time for 25 minutes on High Pressure.
3. When timer beeps, perform a quick pressure release. Open the lid.
4. Use a potato masher to break the cauliflower apart into little pieces.
5. Stir in the cream cheese and heavy cream. Serve warm.

Per Serving
calories: 328 | fat: 24.6g | protein: 16.3g
carbs: 9.1g | net carbs: 6.4g | fiber: 2.7g

Beef and Tomato Soup

Prep time: 15 minutes | Cook time: 20 minutes | Serves 6

1 tablespoon coconut oil
1 cup ground beef
1 teaspoon taco seasonings
½ cup crushed
tomatoes
2 tablespoons cream cheese
1 bell pepper, chopped
1 garlic clove, diced
4 cups beef broth

1. Heat the the coconut oil in the Instant Pot on Sauté mode.
2. Add the ground beef and sprinkle with taco seasonings. Stir well and cook the meat on Sauté mode for 5 minutes.
3. Add crushed tomatoes, cream cheese, bell pepper, garlic clove, and beef broth.
4. Close the lid and select Manual mode. Set cooking time for 15 minutes on High Pressure.
5. When cooking is complete, perform a natural pressure release for 10 minutes and open the lid.
6. Ladle the soup and serve.

Per Serving
calories: 117 | fat: 7.1g | protein: 8.6g
carbs: 4.4g | net carbs: 3.4g | fiber: 1.0g

Pancetta Chowder with Celery

Prep time: 5 minutes | Cook time: 8 minutes | Serves 3

1 cup coconut milk
1 ounce (28 g) celery stalk, chopped
1 teaspoon ground paprika
¼ teaspoon salt
4 ounces (113 g) pancetta, chopped, fried

1. Pour the coconut milk in the Instant Pot, then add celery stalk in the Instant Pot. Sprinkle with paprika and salt.
2. Lock the lid. Press the Manual button and set the timer for 3 minutes on High Pressure.
3. When timer beeps, use a naturally pressure release for 5 minutes, then release any remaining pressure. Open the lid.
4. Top the chowder with fried pancetta. Serve warm.

Per Serving
calories: 392 | fat: 35.0g | protein: 16.0g
carbs: 5.6g | net carbs: 3.4g | fiber: 2.2g

Lamb and Turnip Stew

Prep time: 10 minutes | Cook time: 52 minutes | Serves 4

1 teaspoon olive oil
1 pound (454 g) lamb shank, chopped
1 turnip, chopped
1 teaspoon dried rosemary
½ teaspoon salt
1 teaspoon unsweetened tomato purée
2 cups water

Instant Pot

1. Heat the olive oil on Sauté mode for 2 minutes or until shimmering.
2. Add the chopped lamb shank, turnip, and dried rosemary. Sprinkle with salt. Sauté the ingredients for 5 minutes.
3. Pour in the unsweetened tomato purée and water. Close the lid and set to Manual mode. Set cooking time for 15 minutes on High Pressure.
4. When timer beeps, use a natural pressure release for 5 minutes, then release any remaining pressure. Open the lid.
5. Serve warm.

Per Serving
calories: 185 | fat: 7.7g | protein: 25.8g
carbs: 1.9g | net carbs: 1.3g | fiber: 0.6g

Chicken Soup with Dill

Prep time: 10 minutes | Cook time: 20 minutes | Serves 2

2 cups water
8 ounces (227 g) chicken breast, skinless, boneless
1 tablespoon scallions,
diced
1 teaspoon salt
1 tablespoon fresh dill, chopped

1. Pour water in the ==Instant Pot.==
2. Chop the chicken breast and add it in the water.
3. Add scallions and salt. Close the lid.
4. Select Manual mode. Set cooking time for 20 minutes at High Pressure.
5. When timer beeps, make a quick pressure release and carefully open the lid.
6. Ladle the soup in the bowls. Top the soup with fresh dill. Serve immediately.

Per Serving
calories: 134 | fat: 2.9g | protein: 24.4g
carbs: 1.1g | net carbs: 0.8g | fiber: 0.3g

Chorizo and Scallion Soup

Prep time: 10 minutes | Cook time: 17 minutes | Serves 3

1 teaspoon avocado oil
8 ounces (227 g) chorizo, chopped
1 teaspoon unsweetened tomato purée
1 tablespoon dried cilantro
4 ounces (113 g) scallions, diced
½ teaspoon chili powder
2 cups beef broth

Instant Pot

1. Heat the avocado oil on Sauté mode for 1 minute.
2. Add the chorizo and cook for 6 minutes, stirring frequently.
3. Add the tomato purée, cilantro, scallions, and chili powder. Stir well.
4. Pour in the beef broth. Close the lid. Select Manual mode and set cooking time for 10 minutes on High Pressure.
5. When timer beeps, make a quick pressure release. Open the lid.
6. Serve warm.

Per Serving
calories: 387 | fat: 30.2g | protein: 22.3g
carbs: 5.5g | net carbs: 4.2g | fiber: 1.3g

Cheddar Spinach and Mushroom Soup

Prep time: 10 minutes | Cook time: 15 minutes | Serves 4

1 cup spinach, chopped
1 cup mushrooms, chopped
2 ounces (57 g) Cheddar cheese, shredded
3 ounces (85 g)
scallions, diced
1 cup unsweetened almond milk
2 cups chicken broth
1 teaspoon cayenne pepper
½ teaspoon salt

1. Put all ingredients in the ==Instant Pot== and close the lid. Stir to mix well.
2. Set the Manual mode and set cooking time for 15 minutes on High Pressure.
3. When timer beeps, make a quick pressure release. Open the lid.
4. Blend the soup with an immersion blender until smooth.
5. Serve warm.

Per Serving
calories: 228 | fat: 19.9g | protein: 8.5g
carbs: 6.6g | net carbs: 4.3g | fiber: 2.3g

Pork and Daikon Stew with Green Onions

Prep time: 15 minutes | Cook time: 3 minutes | Serves 6

1 pound (454 g) pork tenderloin, chopped
1 ounce (28 g) green onions, chopped
½ cup daikon, chopped
1 lemon slice
1 tablespoon heavy cream
1 tablespoon butter
1 teaspoon ground black pepper
3 cups water

1. Put all ingredients in the Instant Pot and stir to mix with a spatula.
2. Seal the lid. Set Manual mode and set cooking time for 20 minutes on High Pressure.
3. When cooking is complete, use a natural pressure release for 15 minutes, then release any remaining pressure. Open the lid.
4. Serve warm.

Per Serving
calories: 137 | fat: 5.5g | protein: 20.1g
carbs: 0.9g | net carbs: 0.6g | fiber: 0.3g

Creamy Chicken Salsa Soup

Prep time: 15 minutes | Cook time: 35 minutes | Serves 6

1⅓ cups chunky salsa
½ teaspoon ground chipotle powder
3 cups chicken broth
½ teaspoon ground coriander
½ teaspoon ground cumin
1 teaspoon garlic powder
1 teaspoon sea salt
½ teaspoon ground black pepper
½ dried parsley
1 pound (454 g) boneless, skinless chicken thighs
8 ounces (227 g) block-style cream cheese, softened and cubed
½ cup Monterey Jack cheese
¼ cup queso fresco, crumbled

1. Combine the salsa, chipotle powder, chicken broth, coriander, cumin, garlic powder, sea salt, black pepper, and parsley in the Instant Pot. Stir until well combined. Add the chicken thighs to the pot.
2. Lock the lid. Select Manual mode and set cooking time for 20 minutes on High Pressure.
3. When cooking is complete, allow the pressure to release naturally for 10 minutes and then release the remaining pressure.
4. Open the lid, use a slotted spoon to transfer the chicken thighs to a cutting board, and use two forks to shred the chicken. Return the shredded chicken to the pot. Stir to combine.
5. Select Sauté mode. Bring the soup to a boil and then add the cream cheese. Whisk continuously until the cream cheese is melted.
6. Turn off the pot. Add the Jack cheese and stir until the cheese is melted into the soup.
7. Ladle the soup into bowls. Sprinkle ½ tablespoon queso fresco over each serving. Serve hot.

Per Serving
calories: 286 | fat: 17.8g | protein: 25.1g
carbs: 6.6g | net carbs: 5.4g | fiber: 1.2g

Cayenne Pork Soup

Prep time: 10 minutes | Cook time: 11 minutes | Serves 5

1 cup ground pork
1 teaspoon mustard powder
1 teaspoon cayenne pepper
1 teaspoon coconut oil
2 tablespoons cream
cheese
3 tablespoons heavy cream
4 cups beef broth
½ cup Monterey Jack cheese, shredded

1. In a mixing bowl, combine the ground pork, mustard powder, and cayenne pepper.
2. Melt the coconut oil in the Instant Pot on Sauté mode.
3. Add the ground pork mixture and sauté for 6 minutes.
4. Stir in the cream cheese, heavy cream, and beef broth. Close the lid.
5. Select Manual mode and set cooking time for 5 minutes on High Pressure.
6. When timer beeps, use a quick pressure release and open the lid.
7. Ladle the soup in the bowls. Top the soup with Monterey Jack cheese. Serve warm.

Per Serving
calories: 316 | fat: 23.4g | protein: 23.4g
carbs: 1.6g | net carbs: 1.4g | fiber: 0.2g

Kale and Cauliflower Soup

Prep time: 20 minutes | Cook time: 29 minutes | Serves 5

1 tablespoon olive oil
1 garlic clove, diced
½ cup cauliflower florets
1 cup kale, chopped
2 tablespoons chives, chopped
1 teaspoon sea salt
6 cups beef broth

1. Heat the olive oil in the Instant Pot on Sauté mode for 2 minutes and add the garlic. Sauté for 2 minutes or until fragrant.
2. Add cauliflower, kale, chives, sea salt, and beef broth.
3. Close the lid. Select Manual mode and set cooking time for 5 minutes on High Pressure.
4. When timer beeps, use a quick pressure release and open the lid.
5. Ladle the soup into the bowls. Serve warm.

Per Serving
calories: 80 | fat: 4.5g | protein: 6.5g
carbs: 2.3g | net carbs: 1.8g | fiber: 0.5g

Curried Shrimp and Mushroom Soup

Prep time: 15 minutes | Cook time: 10 minutes | Serves 6

2 tablespoons unsalted butter, divided
½ pound (227 g) medium uncooked shrimp, shelled and deveined
½ medium yellow onion, diced
2 cloves garlic, minced
1 cup sliced fresh white mushrooms
1 tablespoon freshly grated ginger root
4 cups chicken broth
2 tablespoons fish sauce
2½ teaspoons red
curry paste
2 tablespoons lime juice
1 stalk lemongrass, outer stalk removed, crushed, and finely chopped
2 tablespoons coconut aminos
1 teaspoon sea salt
½ teaspoon ground black pepper
1 (13½-ounce / 383-g) can unsweetened, full-fat coconut milk
3 tablespoons chopped fresh cilantro

1. Select the Instant Pot on Sauté mode. Add 1 tablespoon butter.
2. Once the butter is melted, add the shrimp and sauté for 3 minutes or until opaque. Transfer the shrimp to a medium bowl. Set aside.
3. Add the remaining butter to the pot. Once the butter is melted, add the onions and garlic and sauté for 2 minutes or until the garlic is fragrant and the onions are softened.
4. Add the mushrooms, ginger root, chicken broth, fish sauce, red curry paste, lime juice, lemongrass, coconut aminos, sea salt, and black pepper to the pot. Stir to combine.
5. Lock the lid. Select Manual mode and set cooking time for 5 minutes on High Pressure.
6. When cooking is complete, allow the pressure to release naturally for 5 minutes, then release the remaining pressure.
7. Open the lid. Stir in the cooked shrimp and coconut milk.
8. Select Sauté mode. Bring the soup to a boil and then press Keep Warm / Cancel. Let the soup rest in the pot for 2 minutes.
9. Ladle the soup into bowls and sprinkle the cilantro over top. Serve hot.

Per Serving
calories: 237 | fat: 20.0g | protein: 9.1g
carbs: 8.5g | net carbs: 6.3g | fiber: 2.2g

Curried Kale Soup

Prep time: 10 minutes | Cook time: 15 minutes | Serves 3

2 cups kale
1 teaspoon almond butter
1 tablespoon fresh cilantro
½ cup ground chicken
1 teaspoon curry paste
½ cup heavy cream
1 cup chicken stock
½ teaspoon salt

1. Put the kale in the Instant Pot.
2. Add the almond butter, cilantro, and ground chicken. Sauté the mixture for 5 minutes.
3. Meanwhile, mix the curry paste and heavy cream in the Instant Pot until creamy.
4. Add chicken stock and salt, and close the lid.
5. Select Manual mode and set cooking time for 10 minutes on High Pressure.
6. When timer beeps, make a quick pressure release. Open the lid.
7. Serve warm.

Per Serving
calories: 183 | fat: 13.3g | protein: 9.9g
carbs: 7.0g | net carbs: 5.8g | fiber: 1.2g

Pork and Pumpkin Soup with Green Chilies

Prep time: 15 minutes | Cook time: 37 minutes | Serves 4

1½ pounds (680 g) boneless pork shoulder, cut into 1½-inch cubes
½ teaspoon garlic powder
1 teaspoon ground cumin
½ teaspoon sea salt
¼ teaspoon ground black pepper
2 tablespoons butter
1 cup unsweetened

pumpkin purée
1 cup water
2 cups chicken broth
½ cup chopped onion
1 (4.5-ounce / 128-g) can chopped green chilies
1 fresh jalapeño, seeded and ribs removed, minced
4 cups chopped Swiss chard

1. In a large bowl, toss the pork with the garlic powder, cumin, salt, and pepper. Allow it to sit for 20 minutes.
2. Set the Instant Pot to Sauté mode and heat the butter. When it is hot, add the pork shoulder and let brown for 4 minutes, then flip and brown another 4 minutes.
3. Meanwhile, in a bowl, whisk together the pumpkin purée and water.
4. Add the bone broth to the pot. Stir in the pumpkin mixture, onion, chilies, and jalapeño.
5. Secure the lid. Press the Manual button and set cooking time for 30 minutes on High Pressure.
6. When timer beeps, allow the pressure to release naturally for 10 minutes, then release any remaining pressure. Open the lid.
7. Stir in the chard and cook on Keep Warm / Cancel for 3 minutes or until wilted.
Ladle the soup into bowls. Serve hot.

Per Serving
calories: 456 | fat: 23.4g | protein: 44.7g
carbs: 20.3g | net carbs: 13.8g | fiber: 6.5g

Coconut SalmonStew with Tomatillos

Prep time: 15 minutes | Cook time: 12 minutes | Serves 2

10 ounces (283 g) salmon fillet, chopped
2 tomatillos, chopped
½ teaspoon ground turmeric

1 cup coconut cream
1 teaspoon ground paprika
½ teaspoon salt

1. Put all ingredients in the Instant Pot. Stir to mix well.
2. Close the lid. Select Manual mode and set cooking time for 12 minutes on Low Pressure.
3. When timer beeps, use a quick pressure release. Open the lid.
4. Serve warm.

Per Serving
calories: 479 | fat: 37.9g | protein: 30.8g
carbs: 9.6g | net carbs: 5.8g | fiber: 3.8g

Chicken Sausage and Mushroom Soup

Prep time: 10 minutes | Cook time: 15 minutes | Serves 6

2 tablespoons olive oil
12 ounces (340 g) fully cooked chicken sausage, sliced
½ medium onion, chopped
2 cloves garlic, minced
5 cups chicken broth
3 cups roughly chopped curly kale leaves
8 ounces (227 g)

mushrooms, sliced
½ cup peeled and diced rutabaga
2 tablespoons apple cider vinegar
½ teaspoon red pepper flakes
1 teaspoon sea salt
¼ teaspoon ground black pepper
1 cup full-fat coconut milk

1. Set the Instant Pot to Sauté mode. When hot, add the oil and swirl to coat the bottom.
2. Add the sliced sausage and sauté for 4 minutes or until browned.
3. Add the onion and garlic and sauté for 3 minutes or until the onions are translucent and the garlic turns golden.
4. Stir in the mushrooms, rutabaga, kale, broth, vinegar, pepper flakes, salt, and black pepper.
5. Secure the lid. Press the Manual button and set cooking time for 8 minutes on High Pressure.
6. When timer beeps, use a quick pressure release. Open the lid and stir in the milk.
7. Allow the soup to rest for 3 minutes on Keep Warm / Cancel before ladling into serving bowls and serving hot.

Per Serving
calories: 315 | fat: 26.0g | protein: 10.8g
carbs: 12.5g | net carbs: 9.0g | fiber: 3.5g

Lamb and Broccoli Soup with Daikon

Prep time: 10 minutes | Cook time: 25 minutes | Serves 4

7 ounces (198 g) lamb fillet, chopped
1 tablespoon avocado oil
½ cup broccoli, roughly chopped
¼ daikon, chopped
2 bell peppers, chopped
¼ teaspoon ground cumin
5 cups beef broth

1. Sauté the lamb fillet with avocado oil in the Instant Pot for 5 minutes.
2. Add the broccoli, daikon, bell peppers, ground cumin, and beef broth.
3. Close the lid. Select Manual mode and set cooking time for 20 minutes on High Pressure.
4. When timer beeps, use a natural pressure release for 10 minutes, then release any remaining pressure. Open the lid.
5. Serve warm.

Per Serving
calories: 169 | fat: 6.0g | protein: 21.0g
carbs: 6.8g | net carbs: 5.5g | fiber: 1.3g

Italian Leek Soup

Prep time: 10 minutes | Cook time: 15 minutes | Serves 4

4 tablespoons butter
7 ounces (198 g) leek, chopped
½ teaspoon salt
1 teaspoon Italian seasonings
2 cups chicken broth
2 ounces (57 g) Monterey Jack cheese, shredded

1. Heat the butter in the Instant Pot for 4 minutes or until melted.
2. Add the chopped leek, salt, and Italian seasonings.
3. Sauté the leek on Sauté mode for 5 minutes.
4. Pour in the chicken broth and close the lid.
5. Select Manual mode and set cooking time for 10 minutes on High Pressure.
6. When timer beeps, use a quick pressure release. Open the lid.
7. Add the shredded cheese and stir until the cheese is melted.
8. Serve immediately.

Per Serving
calories: 208 | fat: 17.0g | protein: 6.8g
carbs: 7.7g | net carbs: 6.8g | fiber: 0.9g

Coconut Turnip Soup with Celery

Prep time: 15 minutes | Cook time: 15 minutes | Serves 4

3 turnips, chopped
2 ounces (57 g) bell pepper, chopped
2 ounces (57 g) celery, chopped
1 teaspoon ground turmeric
2 cups coconut milk
1 teaspoon ginger paste
1 teaspoon minced garlic
1 cup beef broth

1. Place all ingredients in the Instant Pot and stir to mix well.
2. Close the lid; set Manual mode and set cooking time for 15 minutes at High Pressure.
3. When timer beeps, use a natural pressure release for 10 minutes and open the lid.
4. Ladle the soup into the serving bowls. Serve warm.

Per Serving
calories: 255 | fat: 23.2g | protein: 4.0g
carbs: 11.4g | net carbs: 7.8g | fiber: 3.6g

Sausage, Kale and Cauliflower Soup

Prep time: 15 minutes | Cook time: 13 minutes | Serves 3

1 bacon slice, chopped
6 ounces (170 g) Italian sausages, chopped
2 ounces (57 g) scallions, diced
½ teaspoon garlic
powder
¼ cup cauliflower, chopped
1 cup kale, chopped
3 cups chicken broth
¼ cup heavy cream

1. Heat the the Instant Pot on Sauté mode for 3 minutes.
2. Add chopped bacon and cook for 2 minutes on Sauté mode until curls and buckles.
3. Mix in the Italian sausages, scallions, garlic powder, and cauliflower.
4. Cook for 5 minutes on Sauté mode.
5. Add kale, chicken broth, and heavy cream.
6. Select Manual mode and set cooking time for 6 minutes on High Pressure.
7. When timer beeps, make a quick pressure release. Open the lid.
8. Serve immediately.

Per Serving
calories: 324 | fat: 25.5g | protein: 16.7g
carbs: 6.7g | net carbs: 5.6g | fiber: 1.1g

Pancetta Soup with Jalapeños

Prep time: 10 minutes | Cook time: 10 minutes | Serves 4

3 ounces (85 g) pancetta, chopped
1 teaspoon coconut oil
2 jalapeño peppers, sliced
½ teaspoon garlic powder
½ teaspoon smoked paprika
½ cup heavy cream
2 cups water
½ cup Monterey Jack cheese, shredded

1. Toss the pancetta in the Instant Pot, then add the coconut oil and cook for 4 minutes on Sauté mode. Stir constantly.
2. Add the sliced jalapeños, garlic powder, and smoked paprika. Sauté for 1 more minute.
3. Pour in the heavy cream and water. Add the Monterey Jack cheese and stir to mix well.
4. Close the lid and select Manual mode and set cooking time on High Pressure.
5. When timer beeps, make a quick pressure release. Open the lid.
6. Serve warm.

Per Serving
calories: 234 | fat: 20.0g | protein: 11.8g
carbs: 1.7g | net carbs: 1.3g | fiber: 0.4g

Italian Sausage and Mushroom Soup

Prep time: 10 minutes | Cook time: 22 minutes | Serves 3

1 teaspoon coconut oil
¼ cup cremini mushrooms, sliced
5 ounces (142 g) Italian sausages, chopped
½ jalapeño pepper, sliced
½ teaspoon Italian seasoning
1 teaspoon unsweetened tomato purée
1 cup water
4 ounces (113 g) Mozzarella, shredded

1. Melt the coconut oil in the Instant Pot on Sauté mode.
2. Add the mushrooms and cook for 10 minutes.
3. Add the chopped sausages, sliced jalapeño, Italian seasoning, and unsweetened tomato purée. Pour in the water and stir to mix well.
4. Close the lid and select Manual mode. Set cooking time for 12 minutes on High Pressure.

5. When timer beeps, use a quick pressure release and open the lid.
6. Ladle the soup in the bowls. Top it with Mozzarella. Serve warm.

Per Serving
calories: 289 | fat: 23.2g | protein: 17.7g
carbs: 2.5g | net carbs: 2.3g | fiber: 0.2g

Broccoli and Bacon Soup with Cheddar

Prep time: 6 minutes | Cook time: 10 minutes | Serves 6

3 tablespoons butter
2 stalks celery, diced
½ yellow onion, diced
3 garlic cloves, minced
3½ cups chicken stock
4 cups chopped fresh broccoli florets
3 ounces (85 g) block-style cream cheese, softened and cubed
½ teaspoon ground nutmeg
½ teaspoon sea salt
1 teaspoon ground black pepper
3 cups shredded Cheddar cheese
½ cup shredded Monterey Jack cheese
2 cups heavy cream
4 slices cooked bacon, crumbled
1 tablespoon finely chopped chives

1. Select Sauté mode. Once the Instant Pot is hot, add the butter and heat until the butter is melted.
2. Add the celery, onions, and garlic. Continue sautéing for 5 minutes or until the vegetables are softened.
3. Add the chicken stock and broccoli florets to the pot. Bring the liquid to a boil.
4. Lock the lid,. Select Manual mode and set cooking time for 5 minutes on High Pressure.
5. When cooking is complete, allow the pressure to release naturally for 10 minutes and then release the remaining pressure.
6. Open the lid and add the cream cheese, nutmeg, sea salt, and black pepper. Stir to combine.
7. Select Sauté mode. Bring the soup to a boil and then slowly stir in the Cheddar and Jack cheeses. Once the cheese has melted, stir in the heavy cream.
8. Ladle the soup into serving bowls and top with bacon and chives. Serve hot.

Per Serving
calories: 681 | fat: 59.0g | protein: 27.4g
carbs: 11.6g | net carbs: 10.3g | fiber: 1.3g

Chicken Paprikash with Scallions

Prep time: 10 minutes | Cook time: 18 minutes | Serves 4

1 teaspoon coconut oil	paprika
4 chicken thighs, skinless	½ teaspoon salt
1 bell pepper, chopped	½ teaspoon ground cumin
¼ cup scallions, diced	4 cups chicken broth
1 tablespoon ground	

1. Melt the coconut oil in the Instant Pot on Sauté mode.
2. Add chicken thighs and cook for 4 minutes per side until lightly browned.
3. Stir in the bell pepper, scallions, paprika, salt, and ground cumin.
4. Pour in the chicken broth and close the lid.
5. Select Manual mode and set cooking time for 10 minutes on High Pressure.
6. When timer beeps, perform a quick pressure release. Open the lid.
7. Ladle the paprikash in bowls and serve.

Per Serving
calories: 343 | fat: 13.7g | protein: 47.8g
carbs: 4.7g | net carbs: 3.5g | fiber: 1.2g

Spinach and Artichoke Soup

Prep time: 15 minutes | Cook time: 20 minutes | Serves 4

3 tablespoons salted butter	mustard
8 ounces (227 g) cremini mushrooms, sliced	½ teaspoon garlic powder
1 (6-ounce / 170-g) small jar artichoke hearts packed in water or olive oil, drained, chopped	½ teaspoon kosher salt
	¼ teaspoon ground black pepper
	2 cups chicken broth
	1 cup water
4 ounces (113 g) full-fat cream cheese	2 cups roughly chopped baby spinach
1 teaspoon dried sage	½ cup heavy whipping cream
1 teaspoon dried thyme	½ cup grated Parmesan cheese
1 tablespoon Dijon	

1. Set the Instant Pot to Sauté mode and add the butter. When butter melts, add the mushrooms and sauté for about 8 minutes or until soft.

2. Add the cream cheese to the pot and stir until it is melted. Stir in the sage, thyme, mustard, garlic powder, salt, and black pepper, then mix in the bone broth, water, and artichoke hearts.
3. Secure the lid. Press the Manual button and set cooking time for 5 minutes on High Pressure.
4. When timer beeps, allow the pressure to release naturally for 5 minutes, then release any remaining pressure. Open the lid.
5. Stir in the baby spinach and secure the lid. Allow the spinach to cook for 2 minutes in the soup on Keep Warm / Cancel. Open the lid and stir.
6. Use an immersion blender to blend the soup until smooth and creamy. Stir in the cream.
7. To serve, ladle the soup into bowls and sprinkle with Parmesan cheese. Serve hot.

Per Serving
calories: 261 | fat: 19.7g | protein: 10.5g
carbs: 13.2g | net carbs: 9.8g | fiber: 3.4g

Tomato Beef Chili with Scallions

Prep time: 10 minutes | Cook time: 25 minutes | Serves 2

½ cup ground beef	oil
1 teaspoon dried oregano	2 ounces (57 g) scallions, diced
½ teaspoon chili powder	¼ cup water
1 teaspoon avocado	¼ cup crushed tomatoes

1. Mix the ground beef, dried oregano, chili powder, avocado oil, and scallions in the Instant Pot and cook on Sauté mode for 10 minutes.
2. Add water and crushed tomatoes. Stir the mixture with a spatula until homogenous.
3. Close the lid and select Manual mode. Set cooking time for 15 minutes on High Pressure.
4. When timer beeps, make a quick pressure release. Open the lid.
5. Serve warm.

Per Serving
calories: 94 | fat: 4.6g | protein: 8.0g
carbs: 5.6g | net carbs: 3.2g | fiber: 2.4g

Pork and Mushroom Soup with Eggs

Prep time: 10 minutes | Cook time: 13 minutes | Serves 8

1 pound (454 g) boneless pork center loin chop, thinly sliced
1 cup dried woodear mushrooms
5 cups low-sodium chicken broth
3 tablespoons coconut aminos
1 tablespoon white vinegar
2 tablespoons rice vinegar
½ teaspoon xanthan gum
1 teaspoon salt
2 teaspoons freshly ground black pepper
3 tablespoons water
4 eggs, lightly beaten

1. In the Instant Pot, put the pork, mushrooms, broth, coconut aminos, white vinegar, rice vinegar, xanthan gum, salt, pepper, and water.
2. Lock the lid. Select Soup mode. Set cooking time for 10 minutes at High Pressure.
3. When cooking is complete, let the pressure release naturally for 10 minutes, then release any remaining pressure. Unlock the lid.
4. Turn the Instant Pot on Sauté mode and keep the soup hot.
5. Remove the mushrooms to a cutting board with tongs. Cut into thin slices, then stir them back into the soup.
6. Slowly pour in the eggs. Mix the eggs three times around with chopsticks. Cover the pot and cook for about 1 minute, then serve.

Per Serving
calories: 251 | fat: 15.0g | protein: 19.0g
carbs: 10.0g | net carbs: 10.0g | fiber: 0g

Beef Chili with Roasted Tomatoes

Prep time: 10 minutes | Cook time: 15 minutes | Serves 4

1 tablespoon avocado oil
1 cup chopped onions
1 tablespoon minced garlic
1 pound (454 g) 80% lean ground beef
1 cup canned diced fire-roasted tomatoes, with juices
1 tablespoon chopped
chipotle chiles in adobo sauce
3 teaspoons Mexican red chili powder
2 teaspoons ground cumin
2 teaspoons salt
1 teaspoon dried oregano
½ cup water

1. Preheat the Instant Pot on Sauté mode. Add the oil and heat until shimmering.
2. Add the onions and garlic. Sauté for 30 seconds and add the ground beef.
3. Break up the ground beef with two forks and brown for 4 minutes.
4. Meanwhile, put the tomatoes and chipotle chiles with adobo sauce in a food processor and purée until smooth.
5. In a small bowl, combine the chili powder, cumin, salt, and oregano. When the ground beef is browned, add the chili powder mixture and cook for 30 seconds.
6. Add the tomato and chipotle mixture to the Instant Pot.
7. Lock the lid. Select Manual mode. Set cooking time for 10 minutes on High Pressure.
8. When cooking is complete, let the pressure release naturally for 10 minutes, then release any remaining pressure. Unlock the lid.
9. Mix well and serve.

Per Serving
calories: 433 | fat: 33.0g | protein: 21.0g
carbs: 13.0g | net carbs: 7.0g | fiber: 6.0g

Bok Choy Soup

Prep time: 5 minutes | Cook time: 2 minutes | Serves 1

1 Bok Choy stalk, chopped
¼ teaspoon nutritional yeast
1 cup chicken broth
¼ teaspoon chili flakes
½ teaspoon onion powder

1. Put all ingredients in the Instant Pot. Stir to mix well.
2. Close the lid and select Manual mode. Set cooking time for 2 minutes on High Pressure.
3. When timer beeps, make a quick pressure release. Open the lid.
4. Serve warm.

Per Serving
calories: 58 | fat: 1.7g | protein: 6.9g
carbs: 4.5g | net carbs: 3.2g | fiber: 1.3g

Beef and Veggie Stew

Prep time: 20 minutes | Cook time: 40 minutes | Serves 4

1 pound (454 g) beef chuck roast, cut into 1-inch cubes
2 teaspoons arrowroot powder
1½ tablespoons olive oil
1 cup chopped mushrooms
1 cup chopped zucchini
½ cup sliced turnips
3 ribs celery, sliced
¾ cup unsweetened tomato purée
4 cups beef broth
2 garlic cloves, minced
1 tablespoon dried thyme
1 tablespoon paprika
1 teaspoon dried rosemary
1 teaspoon dried parsley
1 teaspoon garlic powder
1 teaspoon celery seed
1 teaspoon onion powder
2½ teaspoons sea salt
1 teaspoon ground black pepper

1. In a large bowl, combine the chuck roast and arrowroot powder. Toss to coat well.
2. Select Sauté mode and add the olive oil to the pot. Once the oil is hot, add the meat and sauté for 5 minutes or until the meat is browned on all sides.
3. Once the meat is browned, add the mushrooms, zucchini, turnips, celery, tomato purée, beef broth, garlic, thyme, paprika, rosemary, parsley, garlic powder, celery seed, sea salt, black pepper, and onion powder to the pot. Stir well to combine.
4. Lock the lid. Select Meat/Stew and set cooking time for 35 minutes on High Pressure.
5. When cooking is complete, allow the pressure to release naturally for 15 minutes and then release the remaining pressure.
6. Open the lid, stir, and then ladle the stew into serving bowls. Serve hot.

Per Serving
calories: 313 | fat: 15.9g | protein: 35.6g
carbs: 8.9g | net carbs: 6.2g | fiber: 2.7g

Beef and Tomato Chili

Prep time: 15 minutes | Cook time: 35 minutes | Serves 4 to 6

½ tablespoon olive oil
1¼ pounds (567 g) ground beef
½ medium yellow onion, chopped
2 garlic cloves, minced
1 cup diced zucchini
⅔ cup finely chopped cauliflower
1½ cups canned diced tomatoes
1½ tablespoons chili powder
¼ teaspoon coriander powder
4 tablespoons unsweetened tomato purée
2 teaspoons ground cumin
1 teaspoon sea salt
1 teaspoon smoked paprika
⅛ teaspoon cayenne pepper
1 teaspoon garlic powder
⅔ cup water
½ medium avocado, chopped
⅔ cup grated Cheddar cheese
2½ tablespoons full-fat sour cream

1. Select the Instant Pot on Sauté mode. Once the pot is hot, add the olive oil and ground beef and sauté for 6 minutes or until the beef is browned.
2. Add the onions and garlic to the pot. Sauté for 3 minutes or until the garlic becomes fragrant and the onions is softened.
3. Add the zucchini, cauliflower, diced tomatoes (with canning liquid), chili powder, coriander powder, unsweetened tomato purée, cumin, sea salt, paprika, cayenne pepper, garlic powder, and water to the pot. Stir to combine.
4. Lock the lid. Select Manual mode and set cooking time for 25 minutes on High Pressure.
5. When cooking is complete, allow the pressure to release naturally for 10 minutes and then release the remaining pressure.
6. Open the lid and stir. Ladle the chili into serving bowls and top each serving with 2 tablespoons avocado, 2 tablespoons Cheddar cheese, and ½ tablespoon sour cream. Serve hot.

Per Serving
calories: 651 | fat: 42.7g | protein: 48.3g
carbs: 24.0g | net carbs: 15.5g | fiber: 8.5g

Chapter 11 Vegetables

Cheese-Stuffed Zucchini with Scallions

Prep time: 20 minutes | Cook time: 8 minutes | Serves 4

1 large zucchini, cut into four pieces
2 tablespoons olive oil
1 cup Ricotta cheese, room temperature
2 tablespoons scallions, chopped
1 heaping tablespoon fresh parsley, roughly chopped
1 heaping tablespoon

coriander, minced
2 ounces (57 g) Cheddar cheese, preferably freshly grated
1 teaspoon celery seeds
½ teaspoon salt
½ teaspoon garlic pepper

1. Cook your zucchini in the Air Fryer cooking basket for approximately 10 minutes at 350ºF (180ºC). Check for doneness and cook for 2-3 minutes longer if needed.
2. Meanwhile, make the stuffing by mixing the other items.
3. When your zucchini is thoroughly cooked, open them up. Divide the stuffing among all zucchini pieces and bake an additional 5 minutes.

Per Serving
calories: 199 | fat: 16.4g | protein: 9.2g
carbs: 4.5g | net carbs: 4g | fiber: 0.5g

Italian Pepperonata

Prep time: 15 minutes | Cook time: 9 to 10 minutes | Serves 4

1 tablespoon olive oil
½ cup chopped onions
2 green bell peppers, deseeded and chopped
1 red bell pepper, deseeded and chopped
1 yellow bell pepper, deseeded and chopped
1 red chili pepper, deseeded and minced
2 tomatoes, puréed
2 garlic cloves, crushed
¾ cup vegetable broth
¼ cup Italian dry

white wine
1 tablespoon balsamic vinegar
1 teaspoon dried oregano
1 teaspoon dried basil
1 teaspoon paprika
1 teaspoon dried thyme
Sea salt and ground black pepper, to taste
2 tablespoons roughly chopped fresh Italian parsley

1. Press the Sauté button on the Instant Pot and heat the oil. Add the onions to the pot and sauté for 3 minutes, or until tender. Stir in the remaining ingredients, except for the parsley.
2. Close and secure the lid. Select the Manual mode and set the cooking time for 3 minutes at High Pressure. Once cooking is complete, use a quick pressure release. Carefully open the lid.
3. Select the Sauté mode. Let it simmer for 3 to 4 minutes to thicken the cooking liquid.
4. Divide among four serving bowls and garnish with the fresh parsley. Serve immediately.

Per Serving
calories: 94 | fat: 3.9g | protein: 2.3g
carbs: 14.5g | net carbs: 11.6g | fiber: 2.9g

Brussels Sprouts with Peppers

Prep time: 10 minutes | Cook time: 7 minutes | Serves 4

2 tablespoons olive oil
1 white onion, chopped
¾ pound (340 g) Brussels sprouts, trimmed and halved
1 red bell pepper, deseeded and chopped
1 habanero pepper, chopped
1 cup vegetable broth
1 cup water
2 tablespoons

unsweetened tomato purée
1 tablespoon coconut aminos
1 teaspoon fennel seeds
½ teaspoon paprika
2 bay leaves
1 garlic clove, minced
Sea salt and freshly ground black pepper, to taste

1. Press the Sauté button on the Instant Pot and heat the oil. Add the onion to the pot and sauté for 3 minutes, or until tender. Stir in the remaining ingredients.
2. Lock the lid. Select the Manual mode and set the cooking time for 4 minutes on Low Pressure. When the timer goes off, perform a quick pressure release. Carefully open the lid.
3. Remove and discard the bay leaves. Serve warm.

Per Serving
calories: 130 | fat: 7.3g | protein: 4.5g
carbs: 15.1g | net carbs: 10.4g | fiber: 4.7g

Peppery Eggplant with Cheese

Prep time: 35 minutes | Cook time: 5 minutes | Serves 4

1 eggplant, peeled and sliced
2 bell peppers, seeded and sliced
1 red onion, sliced
1 teaspoon fresh garlic, minced
4 tablespoons olive oil
1 teaspoon mustard
1 teaspoon dried
oregano
1 teaspoon smoked paprika
Salt and ground black pepper, to taste
1 tomato, sliced
6 ounces (170 g) halloumi cheese, sliced lengthways

1. Start by preheating your Air Fryer to 370ºF (188ºC). Spritz a baking pan with nonstick cooking spray.
2. Place the eggplant, peppers, onion, and garlic on the bottom of the baking pan. Add the olive oil, mustard, and spices. Transfer to the cooking basket and cook for 14 minutes.
3. Top with the tomatoes and cheese; increase the temperature to 390ºF (199ºC) and cook for 5 minutes more until bubbling. Let it sit on a cooling rack for 10 minutes before serving.
4. Bon appétit!

Per Serving
calories: 306 | fat: 16.1g | protein: 39.6g
carbs: 8.8g | net carbs: 7g | fiber: 1.8g

Vinegary Spinach with Green Olives

Prep time: 15 minutes | Cook time: 2 to 3 minutes | Serves 4

1 tablespoon olive oil
3 cloves garlic, smashed
Bunch scallions, chopped
2 pounds (907 g) spinach, washed
1 cup vegetable broth
1 tablespoon champagne vinegar
½ teaspoon dried dill weed
¼ teaspoon cayenne pepper
Seasoned salt and ground black pepper,
to taste
½ cup almonds, soaked overnight and drained
2 tablespoons green olives, pitted and halved
2 tablespoons water
1 tablespoon extra-virgin olive oil
2 teaspoons lemon juice
1 teaspoon garlic powder
1 teaspoon onion powder

1. Press the Sauté button on the Instant Pot and heat the olive oil. Add the garlic and scallions to the pot and sauté for 1 to 2 minutes, or until fragrant.
2. Stir in the spinach, vegetable broth, vinegar, dill, cayenne pepper, salt and black pepper.
3. Lock the lid. Select the Manual mode and set the cooking time for 1 minute on High Pressure. When the timer goes off, perform a quick pressure release. Carefully open the lid.
4. Stir in the remaining ingredients.
5. Transfer to serving plates and serve immediately.

Per Serving
calories: 239 | fat: 16.9g | protein: 11.1g
carbs: 17.0g | net carbs: 8.7g | fiber: 8.3g

French Ratatouille

Prep time: 15 minutes | Cook time: 13 minutes | Serves 4

1 eggplant, peeled and sliced
2 teaspoons table salt
2 tablespoons olive oil
2 large tomatoes, chopped
1 purple onion, thinly sliced
1 red bell pepper, deseeded and sliced
1 yellow bell pepper, deseeded and sliced
3 garlic cloves, chopped
1 teaspoon hot paprika
⅓ teaspoon dried basil
⅓ teaspoon cayenne pepper
¼ teaspoon tarragon
¼ teaspoon freshly ground black pepper
Sea salt, to taste

1. In a bowl, toss together the eggplant and table salt. Let it sit for 25 to 30 minutes. Drain and rinse the eggplant.
2. Set the Instant Pot to the Sauté mode and heat the oil. Add the eggplant to the pot and sauté for 10 minutes, or until tender. Stir in the remaining ingredients.
3. Close and secure the lid. Select the Manual mode and set the cooking time for 3 minutes at High Pressure. Once cooking is complete, do a quick pressure release. Carefully open the lid.
4. Serve warm.

Per Serving
calories: 141 | fat: 7.5g | protein: 3.3g
carbs: 18.5g | net carbs: 12.0g | fiber: 6.5g

Cheese-Stuffed Pepper with Pickles

Prep time: 20 minutes | Cook time: 15 minutes | Serves 2

1 red bell pepper, top and seeds removed	taste
1 yellow bell pepper, top and seeds removed	1 cup Cottage cheese
	4 tablespoons mayonnaise
Salt and pepper, to	2 pickles, chopped

1. Arrange the peppers in the lightly greased cooking basket. Cook in the preheated Air Fryer at 400ºF (205ºC) for 15 minutes, turning them over halfway through the cooking time.
2. Season with salt and pepper.
3. Then, in a mixing bowl, combine the cream cheese with the mayonnaise and chopped pickles. Stuff the pepper with the cream cheese mixture and serve. Enjoy!

Per Serving
calories: 360 | fat: 27.3g | protein: 20.3g
carbs: 7.6g | net carbs: 6.4g | fiber: 1.2g

Air Fried Mushroom and Spinach

Prep time: 10 minutes | Cook time: 14 minutes | Serves 4

2 tablespoons olive oil	½ cup chopped marinated artichoke hearts
4 large portobello mushrooms, stems removed and gills scraped out	1 cup frozen spinach, thawed and squeezed dry
½ teaspoon salt	
¼ teaspoon freshly ground pepper	½ cup grated Parmesan cheese
4 ounces (113 g) goat cheese, crumbled	2 tablespoons chopped fresh parsley

1. Preheat the air fryer to 400ºF (205ºC).
2. Rub the olive oil over the portobello mushrooms until thoroughly coated. Sprinkle both sides with the salt and black pepper. Place top-side down on a clean work surface.
3. In a small bowl, combine the goat cheese, artichoke hearts, and spinach. Mash with the back of a fork until thoroughly combined. Divide the cheese mixture among the mushrooms and sprinkle with the Parmesan cheese.

4. Air fry for 10 to 14 minutes until the mushrooms are tender and the cheese has begun to brown. Top with the fresh parsley just before serving.

Per Serving
calories: 270 | fat: 23g | protein: 8g
carbs: 11g | net carbs: 7g | fiber: 4g

Asparagus with Lemony Vinaigrette

Prep time: 15 minutes | Cook time: 2 minutes | Serves 2 to 4

Gremolata:

1 cup finely chopped fresh Italian flat-leaf parsley leaves	3 garlic cloves, peeled and grated
	Zest of 2 small lemons

Asparagus:

1½ pounds (680 g) asparagus, trimmed	1 teaspoon Dijon mustard
1 cup water	2 tablespoons extra-virgin olive oil
Lemony Vinaigrette:	
1½ tablespoons fresh lemon juice	Kosher salt and freshly ground black pepper, to taste
1 teaspoon Swerve	

Garnish:
3 tablespoons slivered almonds

1. In a small bowl, stir together all the ingredients for the gremolata.
2. Pour the water into the Instant Pot. Arrange the asparagus in a steamer basket. Lower the steamer basket into the pot.
3. Lock the lid. Select the Steam mode and set the cooking time for 2 minutes on Low Pressure.
4. Meanwhile, prepare the lemony vinaigrette: In a bowl, combine the lemon juice, swerve and mustard and whisk to combine. Slowly drizzle in the olive oil and continue to whisk. Season generously with salt and pepper.
5. When the timer goes off, perform a quick pressure release. Carefully open the lid. Remove the steamer basket from the Instant Pot.
6. Transfer the asparagus to a serving platter. Drizzle with the vinaigrette and sprinkle with the gremolata. Serve the asparagus topped with the slivered almonds.

Per Serving
calories: 277 | fat: 18.8g | protein: 10.9g
carbs: 23.8g | net carbs: 13.4g | fiber: 10.4g

Air Fried Broccoli and Asparagus

Prep time: 25 minutes | Cook time: 22 minutes | Serves 4

½ pound (227g) asparagus, cut into 1½-inch pieces
½ pound (227g) broccoli, cut into 1½-inch pieces

2 tablespoons olive oil
Some salt and white pepper, to taste
½ cup vegetable broth
2 tablespoons apple cider vinegar

1. Place the vegetables in a single layer in the lightly greased cooking basket. Drizzle the olive oil over the vegetables.
2. Sprinkle with salt and white pepper.
3. Cook at 380ºF (193ºC) for 15 minutes, shaking the basket halfway through the cooking time.
4. Add ½ cup of vegetable broth to a saucepan; bring to a rapid boil and add the vinegar. Cook for 5 to 7 minutes or until the sauce has reduced by half.
5. Spoon the sauce over the warm vegetables and serve immediately. Bon appétit!

Per Serving
calories: 181 | fat: 7g | protein: 3g
carbs: 4g | net carbs: 1g | fiber: 3g

Zucchini and Spinach Croquettes

Prep time: 9 minutes | Cook time: 7 minutes | Serves 6

4 eggs, slightly beaten
½ cup almond flour
½ cup goat cheese, crumbled
1 teaspoon fine sea salt
4 garlic cloves, minced
1 cup baby spinach
½ cup Parmesan

cheese grated
1/3 teaspoon red pepper flakes
1 pound (454 g) zucchini, peeled and grated
1/3 teaspoon dried dill weed

1. Thoroughly combine all ingredients in a bowl. Now, roll the mixture to form small croquettes.
2. Air fry at 335ºF (168ºC) for 7 minutes or until golden. Taste, adjust for seasonings and serve warm.

Per Serving
calories: 171 | fat: 10.8g | protein: 3.1g
carbs: 15.9g | net carbs: 14.9g | fiber: 1g

Eggplant and Zucchini Bites with Mint

Prep time: 35 minutes | Cook time: 30 minutes | Serves 8

2 teaspoons fresh mint leaves, chopped
1½ teaspoons red pepper chili flakes
2 tablespoons melted butter
1 pound (454 g)

eggplant, peeled and cubed
1 pound (454 g) zucchini, peeled and cubed
3 tablespoons olive oil

1. Toss all of the above ingredients in a large-sized mixing dish.
2. Roast the eggplant and zucchini bites for 30 minutes at 325ºF (163ºC) in your Air Fryer, turning once or twice.
3. Serve with a homemade dipping sauce.

Per Serving
calories: 110 | fat: 8.3g | protein: 2.6g
carbs: 8.8g | net carbs: 6.3g | fiber: 2.5g

Cauliflower Masala Curry

Prep time: 5 minutes | Cook time: 4 to 5 minutes | Serves 4 to 6

1 tablespoon olive oil
1 teaspoon cumin seeds
1 white onion, diced
1 garlic clove, minced
1 head cauliflower, chopped
1 tablespoon ground

coriander
1 teaspoon ground cumin
½ teaspoon garam masala
½ teaspoon salt
1 cup water

1. Set the Instant Pot to the Sauté mode and heat the olive oil. Add the cumin seeds to the pot and sauté for 30 seconds, stirring constantly. Add the onion and sauté for 2 to 3 minutes, stirring constantly. Add the garlic and sauté for 30 seconds, stirring frequently.
2. Stir in the remaining ingredients.
3. Lock the lid. Select the Manual mode and set the cooking time for 1 minute on High Pressure. When the timer goes off, perform a quick pressure release. Carefully open the lid.
4. Serve immediately.

Per Serving
calories: 101 | fat: 6.3g | protein: 3.7g
carbs: 10.6g | net carbs: 7.7g | fiber: 2.9g

Garlic Squash Noodles with Tomatoes

Prep time: 15 minutes | Cook time: 14 to 16 minutes | Serves 4

1 medium spaghetti squash
1 cup water
2 tablespoons olive oil
1 small yellow onion, diced
6 garlic cloves, minced
2 teaspoons crushed red pepper flakes
2 teaspoons dried oregano
1 cup sliced cherry
tomatoes
1 teaspoon kosher salt
½ teaspoon freshly ground black pepper
1 (14.5-ounce / 411-g) can sugar-free crushed tomatoes
¼ cup capers
1 tablespoon caper brine
½ cup sliced olives

1. With a sharp knife, halve the spaghetti squash crosswise. Using a spoon, scoop out the seeds and sticky gunk in the middle of each half.
2. Pour the water into the Instant Pot and place the trivet in the pot with the handles facing up. Arrange the squash halves, cut side facing up, on the trivet.
3. Lock the lid. Select the Manual mode and set the cooking time for 7 minutes on High Pressure. When the timer goes off, use a quick pressure release. Carefully open the lid.
4. Remove the trivet and pour out the water that has collected in the squash cavities. Using the tines of a fork, separate the cooked strands into spaghetti-like pieces and set aside in a bowl.
5. Pour the water out of the pot. Select the Sauté mode and heat the oil.
6. Add the onion to the pot and sauté for 3 minutes. Add the garlic, pepper flakes and oregano to the pot and sauté for 1 minute.
7. Stir in the cherry tomatoes, salt and black pepper and cook for 2 minutes, or until the tomatoes are tender.
8. Pour in the crushed tomatoes, capers, caper brine and olives and bring the mixture to a boil. Continue to cook for 2 to 3 minutes to allow the flavors to meld.
9. Stir in the spaghetti squash noodles and cook for 1 to 2 minutes to warm everything through.
10. Transfer the dish to a serving platter and serve.

Per Serving
calories: 132 | fat: 9.3g | protein: 2.9g
carbs: 12.7g | net carbs: 7.8g | fiber: 4.9g

Broccoli with Garlic Mayo Sauce

Prep time: 19 minutes | Cook time: 15 minutes | Serves 4

2 tablespoons olive oil
Kosher salt and freshly ground black pepper, to taste
1 pound (454 g) broccoli florets
For the Dipping Sauce:
2 teaspoons dried rosemary, crushed
3 garlic cloves, minced
1/3 teaspoon dried marjoram, crushed
¼ cup sour cream
1/3 cup mayonnaise

1. Lightly grease your broccoli with a thin layer of olive oil. Season with salt and ground black pepper.
2. Arrange the seasoned broccoli in an Air Fryer cooking basket. Bake at 395ºF (202ºC) for 15 minutes, shaking once or twice.
3. In the meantime, prepare the dipping sauce by mixing all the sauce ingredients. Serve warm broccoli with the dipping sauce and enjoy!

Per Serving
calories: 247 | fat: 22g | protein: 4g
carbs: 9g | net carbs: 6g | fiber: 3g

Smoky Zucchini with Basil

Prep time: 5 minutes | Cook time: 4 minutes | Serves 4

1½ tablespoons olive oil
2 garlic cloves, minced
1½ pounds (680 g) zucchinis, sliced
½ cup vegetable broth
1 teaspoon dried basil
½ teaspoon smoked paprika
½ teaspoon dried rosemary
Salt and pepper, to taste

1. Set the Instant Pot to the Sauté mode and heat the olive oil. Add the garlic to the pot and sauté for 1 minute, or until fragrant. Stir in the remaining ingredients.
2. Lock the lid. Select the Manual mode and set the cooking time for 3 minutes on Low Pressure. When the timer goes off, perform a quick pressure release. Carefully open the lid.
3. Serve immediately.

Per Serving
calories: 81 | fat: 5.7g | protein: 2.3g
carbs: 6.9g | net carbs: 4.8g | fiber: 2.1g

Garlic Asparagus with Copoundy Cheese

Prep time: 5 minutes | Cook time: 1 minute | Serves 4

1½ pounds (680 g) fresh asparagus
1 cup water
2 tablespoons olive oil
4 garlic cloves, minced
Sea salt, to taste
¼ teaspoon ground black pepper
½ cup shredded Copoundy cheese

1. Pour the water into the Instant Pot and put the steamer basket in the pot.
2. Place the asparagus in the steamer basket. Drizzle the asparagus with the olive oil and sprinkle with the garlic on top. Season with salt and black pepper.
3. Close and secure the lid. Select the Manual mode and set the cooking time for 1 minute at High Pressure. Once cooking is complete, do a quick pressure release. Carefully open the lid.
4. Transfer the asparagus to a platter and served topped with the shredded cheese.

Per Serving
calories: 151 | fat: 11.3g | protein: 7.4g
carbs: 7.8g | net carbs: 4.1g | fiber: 3.7g

Cauliflower Rice with Cilantro

Prep time: 5 minutes | Cook time: 8 minutes | Serves 4

1 head cauliflower, trimmed, stem removed and cut into medium florets
1 cup water
2 tablespoons avocado oil
1 garlic clove, minced
Juice of 1 lime
⅛ teaspoon fine grind sea salt
4 sprigs fresh cilantro, chopped

1. Pour the water into the Instant Pot and put the trivet in the pot. Place the cauliflower florets in the trivet. Place a steamer basket on the trivet. Add the cauliflower to the steamer basket.
2. Lock the lid. Select the Manual mode and set the cooking time for 2 minutes on High Pressure. When the timer goes off, perform a quick pressure release. Carefully open the lid.
3. Remove the steamer basket and cauliflower from the pot. Place the cauliflower florets in a blender and pulse until it reaches a rice-like texture. Set aside.

4. Pour out the water and wipe the pot dry with a paper towel.
5. Select Sauté mode and heat the avocado oil. Add the garlic to the pot and sauté for 2 minutes, or until fragrant.
6. Add the cauliflower rice to the pot and sauté for 2 additional minutes, or until the rice becomes soft. Stir in the lime juice and sauté for 2 additional minutes.
7. Transfer the cauliflower rice to a serving dish. Season with the sea salt and garnish with the cilantro. Serve hot.

Per Serving
calories: 106 | fat: 7.1g | protein: 3.1g
carbs: 7.4g | net carbs: 4.0g | fiber: 3.4g

Celery Croquettes with Chive Mayo

Prep time: 15 minutes | Cook time: 6 minutes | Serves 4

2 medium-sized celery stalks, trimmed and grated
½ cup of leek, finely chopped
1 tablespoon garlic paste
¼ teaspoon freshly cracked black pepper
1 teaspoon fine sea salt
1 tablespoon fresh dill, finely chopped
1 egg, lightly whisked
¼ cup almond flour
½ cup Parmesan cheese, freshly grated
¼ teaspoon baking powder
2 tablespoons fresh chives, chopped
4 tablespoons mayonnaise

1. Place the celery on a paper towel and squeeze them to remove excess liquid.
2. Combine the vegetables with the other ingredients, except the chives and mayo. Shape the balls using 1 tablespoon of the vegetable mixture.
3. Then, gently flatten each ball with your palm or a wide spatula. Spritz the croquettes with a non - stick cooking oil.
4. Air-fry the vegetable croquettes in a single layer for 6 minutes at 360ºF (182ºC).
5. Meanwhile, mix fresh chives and mayonnaise. Serve warm croquettes with chive mayo. Bon appétit!

Per Serving
calories: 214 | fat: 18g | protein: 7g
carbs: 6.8g | net carbs: 5.2g | fiber: 1.6g

Mushrooms with Teriyaki Sauce

Prep time: 45 minutes | Cook time: 5 minutes | Serves 4

1½ pounds (680 g) button mushrooms
¼ cup coconut milk
¼ cup dry wine
2 tablespoons sesame oil
1 tablespoon coconut aminos

1 teaspoon ginger-garlic paste
1 teaspoon red pepper flakes
Sea salt and ground black pepper, to taste
2 tablespoons roughly chopped fresh chives

1. In a bowl, stir together the mushrooms, coconut milk, wine, sesame oil, coconut aminos and ginger-garlic paste. Cover in plastic and let marinate in the refrigerator for 40 minutes.
2. Place the mushrooms along with the marinade in the Instant Pot. Season with the red pepper flakes, salt and black pepper.
3. Lock the lid. Select the Manual mode and set the cooking time for 5 minutes on High Pressure. When the timer goes off, perform a quick pressure release. Carefully open the lid.
4. Serve topped with the fresh chives.

Per Serving
calories: 139 | fat: 11.1g | protein: 6.3g
carbs: 7.6g | net carbs: 5.2g | fiber: 2.4g

Cheddar Mushrooms with Wine

Prep time: 10 minutes | Cook time: 5 minutes | Serves 4

1 tablespoon olive oil
2 cloves garlic, minced
1 (1-inch) ginger root, grated
16 ounces (454 g) Chanterelle mushrooms, brushed clean and sliced
½ cup unsweetened tomato purée
½ cup water
2 tablespoons dry

white wine
1 teaspoon dried basil
½ teaspoon dried thyme
½ teaspoon dried dill weed
⅓ teaspoon freshly ground black pepper
Kosher salt, to taste
1 cup shredded Cheddar cheese

1. Press the Sauté button on the Instant Pot and heat the olive oil. Add the garlic and grated ginger to the pot and sauté for 1 minute, or until fragrant. Stir in the

remaining ingredients, except for the cheese.
2. Lock the lid. Select the Manual mode and set the cooking time for 5 minutes on Low Pressure. When the timer goes off, perform a quick pressure release. Carefully open the lid..
3. Serve topped with the shredded cheese.

Per Serving
calories: 206 | fat: 13.7g | protein: 9.3g
carbs: 12.3g | net carbs: 7.1g | fiber: 5.2g

Garlic Broccoli with Fresh Basil

Prep time: 10 minutes | Cook time: 4 minutes | Serves 4 to 6

6 cups broccoli florets
1 cup water
1½ tablespoons olive oil
8 garlic cloves, thinly sliced
2 shallots, thinly sliced
½ teaspoon crushed red pepper flakes
Grated zest and juice

of 1 medium lemon
½ teaspoon kosher salt
Freshly ground black pepper, to taste
¼ cup chopped roasted almonds
¼ cup finely slivered fresh basil

1. Pour the water into the Instant Pot. Place the broccoli florets in a steamer basket and lower into the pot.
2. Close and secure the lid. Select the Steam setting and set the cooking time for 2 minutes at Low Pressure. Once the timer goes off, use a quick pressure release. Carefully open the lid.
3. Transfer the broccoli to a large bowl filled with cold water and ice. Once cooled, drain the broccoli and pat dry.
4. Select the Sauté mode on the Instant Pot and heat the olive oil. Add the garlic to the pot and sauté for 30 seconds, tossing constantly. Add the shallots and pepper flakes to the pot and sauté for 1 minute.
5. Stir in the cooked broccoli, lemon juice, salt and black pepper. Toss the ingredients together and cook for 1 minute.
6. Transfer the broccoli to a serving platter and sprinkle with the chopped almonds, lemon zest and basil. Serve immediately.

Per Serving
calories: 127 | fat: 8.2g | protein: 5.1g
carbs: 12.2g | net carbs: 10.6g | fiber: 1.6g

Cauliflower Fritters with Colby Cheese

Prep time: 15 minutes | Cook time: 10 minutes | Serves 8

2 pounds (907 g) cauliflower florets	salt
½ cup scallions, finely chopped	½ teaspoon hot paprika
½ teaspoon freshly ground black pepper, or more to taste	2 cups Colby cheese, shredded
1 tablespoon fine sea	1 cup Parmesan cheese, grated
	¼ cup olive oil

1. Firstly, boil the cauliflower until fork tender. Drain, peel and mash your cauliflower.
2. Thoroughly mix the mashed cauliflower with scallions, pepper, salt, paprika, and Colby cheese. Then, shape the balls using your hands. Now, flatten the balls to make the patties.
3. Roll the patties over grated Parmesan cheese. Drizzle olive oil over them.
4. Next, cook your patties at 360ºF (182ºC) approximately 10 minutes, working in batches. Serve with tabasco mayo if desired. Bon appétit!

Per Serving
calories: 282 | fat: 22g | protein: 13g
carbs: 8g | net carbs: 6g | fiber: 2g

Egg Satarash

Prep time: 10 minutes | Cook time: 5 minutes | Serves 4

2 tablespoons olive oil	1 teaspoon paprika
1 white onion, chopped	½ teaspoon dried oregano
2 cloves garlic	½ teaspoon turmeric
2 ripe tomatoes, puréed	Kosher salt and ground black pepper, to taste
1 green bell pepper, deseeded and sliced	1 cup water
1 red bell pepper, deseeded and sliced	4 large eggs, lightly whisked

1. Press the Sauté button on the Instant Pot and heat the olive oil. Add the onion and garlic to the pot and sauté for 2 minutes, or until fragrant. Stir in the remaining ingredients, except for the eggs.
2. Lock the lid. Select the Manual mode and set the cooking time for 3 minutes on High Pressure. When the timer goes off, perform a quick pressure release. Carefully open the lid.
3. Fold in the eggs and stir to combine. Lock the lid and let it sit in the residual heat for 5 minutes. Serve warm.

Per Serving
calories: 169 | fat: 11.9g | protein: 7.8g
carbs: 8.9g | net carbs: 6.8g | fiber: 2.1g

Spaghetti Squash Noodles with Basil

Prep time: 5 minutes | Cook time: 18 minutes | Serves 4

2 pounds (907 g) spaghetti squash	toasted almonds
1 cup water	¼ cup flat-leaf parsley
3 garlic cloves	3 tablespoons grated Parmesan cheese
1 cup fresh basil leaves	½ teaspoon fine grind sea salt
½ cup olive oil	½ teaspoon ground black pepper
⅓ cup unsalted	

1. Using a knife, pierce all sides of the squash to allow the steam to penetrate during cooking.
2. Pour the water into the Instant Pot and put the trivet in the pot. Place the squash on the trivet.
3. Lock the lid. Select the Manual mode and set the cooking time for 18 minutes at High Pressure. When the timer goes off, use a natural pressure release for 10 minutes, then release any remaining pressure. Carefully open the lid.
4. Remove the trivet and squash from the pot. Set aside to cool for 15 minutes, or until the squash is cool enough to handle.
5. Make the pesto sauce by placing the remaining ingredients in a food processor. Pulse until the ingredients are well combined and form a thick paste. Set aside.
6. Cut the cooled spaghetti squash in half lengthwise. Using a spoon, scoop out and discard the seeds.
7. Using a fork, scrape the flesh of the squash to create the noodles. Transfer the noodles to a large bowl.
8. Divide the squash noodles among 4 serving bowls. Top each serving with the pesto sauce. Serve hot.

Per Serving
calories: 381 | fat: 32.1g | protein: 5.2g
carbs: 18.0g | net carbs: 10.0g | fiber: 8.0g

Green Cabbage in Cream Sauce

Prep time: 10 minutes | Cook time: 13 minutes | Serves 4

1 tablespoon unsalted butter
½ cup diced pancetta
¼ cup diced yellow onion
1 cup chicken broth
1 pound (454 g) green cabbage, finely chopped
1 bay leaf
¹/₃ cup heavy cream
1 tablespoon dried parsley
1 teaspoon fine grind sea salt
¼ teaspoon ground nutmeg
¼ teaspoon ground black pepper

1. Press the Sauté button on the Instant Pot and melt the butter. Add the pancetta and onion to the pot and sauté for about 4 minutes, or until the onion is tender and begins to brown.
2. Pour in the chicken broth. Using a wooden spoon, stir and loosen any browned bits from the bottom of the pot. Stir in the cabbage and bay leaf.
3. Lock the lid. Select the Manual mode and set the cooking time for 4 minutes on High Pressure. When the timer goes off, perform a quick pressure release. Carefully open the lid.
4. Select Sauté mode and bring the ingredients to a boil. Stir in the remaining ingredients and simmer for 5 additional minutes.
5. Remove and discard the bay leaf. Spoon into serving bowls. Serve warm.

Per Serving
calories: 211 | fat: 17.1g | protein: 7.2g
carbs: 7.3g | net carbs: 5.0g | fiber: 2.3g

Mediterranean Zoodles

Prep time: 10 minutes | Cook time: 5 minutes | Serves 2

1 tablespoon olive oil
2 tomatoes, chopped
½ cup water
½ cup roughly chopped fresh parsley
3 tablespoons ground almonds
1 tablespoon fresh rosemary, chopped
1 tablespoon apple
cider vinegar
1 teaspoon garlic, smashed
2 zucchinis, spiralized and cooked
½ avocado, pitted and sliced
Salt and ground black pepper, to taste

1. Add the olive oil, tomatoes, water, parsley, ground almonds, rosemary, apple cider vinegar and garlic to the Instant Pot.
2. Lock the lid. Select the Manual mode and set the cooking time for 5 minutes on High Pressure. When the timer beeps, perform a natural pressure release for 10 minutes, then release any remaining pressure. Carefully open the lid.
3. Divide the cooked zucchini spirals between two serving plates. Spoon the sauce over each serving. Top with the avocado slices and season with salt and black pepper.
4. Serve immediately.

Per Serving
calories: 264 | fat: 20.0g | protein: 7.2g
carbs: 19.6g | net carbs: 10.7g | fiber: 8.9g

Cauliflower and Tomatoes Curry

Prep time: 10 minutes | Cook time: 2 minutes | Serves 4 to 6

1 medium head cauliflower, cut into bite-size pieces
1 (14-ounce / 397-g) can sugar-free diced tomatoes, undrained
1 bell pepper, thinly sliced
1 (14-ounce / 397-g) can full-fat coconut milk
½ to 1 cup water
2 tablespoons red
curry paste
1 teaspoon salt
1 teaspoon garlic powder
½ teaspoon onion powder
½ teaspoon ground ginger
¼ teaspoon chili powder
Freshly ground black pepper, to taste

1. Add all the ingredients, except for the black pepper, to the Instant Pot and stir to combine.
2. Lock the lid. Select the Manual setting and set the cooking time for 2 minutes at High Pressure. Once the timer goes off, use a quick pressure release. Carefully open the lid.
3. Sprinkle the black pepper and stir well. Serve immediately.

Per Serving
calories: 262 | fat: 22.0g | protein: 6.3g
carbs: 16.8g | net carbs: 10.8g | fiber: 6.0g

Cayenne Veggie Kebabs

Prep time: 15 minutes | Cook time: 3 minutes | Serves 5

½ head broccoli, cut into florets
½ head cauliflower, cut into florets
1 red bell pepper, deseeded and diced
1 green bell pepper, deseeded and diced
1 orange bell pepper, deseeded and diced
9 ounces (255 g) button mushrooms
2 cups cherry tomatoes
1 teaspoon ground coriander
1 teaspoon cayenne pepper
Coarse sea salt and ground black pepper, to taste
¼ cup olive oil
1 cup water

1. Pour the water in the Instant Pot and insert the trivet.
2. Thread the broccoli, cauliflower, bell peppers, mushrooms and cherry tomatoes onto small bamboo skewers. Sprinkle with the coriander, cayenne pepper, salt and black pepper. Drizzle with the olive oil. Place the skewers on the trivet.
3. Close and secure the lid. Select the Manual mode and set the cooking time for 3 minutes at High Pressure. Once cooking is complete, use a quick pressure release. Carefully open the lid.
4. Serve immediately.

Per Serving
calories: 140 | fat: 11.4g | protein: 3.6g
carbs: 8.9g | net carbs: 6.5g | fiber: 2.4g

Mozzarella Cauliflower Flatbread

Prep time: 10 minutes | Cook time: 2 hours 30 minutes | Serves 8

½ medium head cauliflower, trimmed, stem removed and cut into florets
3½ tablespoons coconut flour
1½ cups grated Mozzarella cheese, divided
¼ teaspoon fine grind sea salt
2 large eggs, beaten
2 tablespoons heavy cream
2 tablespoons unsalted butter, melted, divided
2 garlic cloves, minced
2 tablespoons fresh basil, cut into ribbons

1. Add the cauliflower to a blender and pulse until it reaches a rice-like texture.
2. In a large bowl, whisk together ⅔ cup of the riced cauliflower, coconut flour, ¾ cup of the Mozzarella cheese and sea salt. Stir in the eggs, heavy cream and 1 tablespoon of the butter.
3. Brush the Instant Pot with the remaining 1 tablespoon of the butter. Add the cauliflower mixture and use a spoon to press the mixture flat into the bottom of the pot. Sprinkle the garlic and the remaining ¾ cup of the Mozzarella cheese on top.
4. Lock the lid. Select the Slow Cook mode and set the cooking time for 2 hours 30 minutes on More.
5. While the flatbread is cooking, preheat the oven broiler to 450ºF (235ºC).
6. Once the cook time is complete, transfer the flatbread to a clean work surface and cut into 8 wedges. Place the wedges on a large baking sheet and transfer to the oven to broil for 2 to 3 minutes, or until the cheese is lightly browned.
7. Remove from the oven and transfer to a serving platter. Sprinkle the basil ribbons on top. Serve warm.

Per Serving
calories: 136 | fat: 10.1g | protein: 6.2g
carbs: 5.3g | net carbs: 2.0g | fiber: 3.3g

Ginger-Garlic Collards in Red Wine

Prep time: 5 minutes | Cook time: 2 minutes | Serves 4

1 pound (454 g) Collards, torn into pieces
¾ cup water
¼ cup dry red wine
1½ tablespoons sesame oil
1 teaspoon ginger-
garlic paste
½ teaspoon fennel seeds
½ teaspoon mustard seeds
Sea salt and ground black pepper, to taste

1. Add all the ingredients to the Instant Pot and stir to combine.
2. Lock the lid. Select the Manual mode and set the cooking time for 2 minutes on High Pressure. When the timer goes off, perform a quick pressure release. Carefully open the lid.
3. Ladle into individual bowls and serve warm.

Per Serving
calories: 86 | fat: 5.9g | protein: 3.7g
carbs: 7.0g | net carbs: 2.2g | fiber: 4.8g

Green Beans and Mushrooms with Scallions

Prep time: 5 minutes | Cook time: 6 to 7 minutes | Serves 4

1 tablespoon olive oil
½ cup chopped scallions
2 cloves garlic, minced
1 cup chopped white mushrooms
¾ pound (340 g)

green beans
1 cup vegetable broth
1 teaspoon crushed red pepper flakes
Sea salt and ground black pepper, to taste

1. Press the Sauté button on the Instant Pot and heat the oil. Add the scallions to the pot and sauté for 2 minutes, or until tender. Add the garlic and mushrooms and continue to sauté for 1 to 2 minutes. Stir in the remaining ingredients.
2. Lock the lid. Select the Manual mode and set the cooking time for 3 minutes on Low Pressure. When the timer goes off, perform a quick pressure release. Carefully open the lid.
3. Serve warm.

Per Serving
calories: 72 | fat: 3.6g | protein: 2.5g
carbs: 9.3g | net carbs: 6.2g | fiber: 3.1g

Blitva in Dry Sherry

Prep time: 5 minutes | Cook time: 3 minutes | Serves 4

2 tablespoons olive oil
1 teaspoon minced garlic
1 pound (454 g) Swiss chard, torn into pieces
1 ripe tomato, puréed

1 cup chopped scallions
¼ cup dry sherry
2 tablespoons dried parsley
¼ teaspoon basil

1. Press the Sauté button on the Instant Pot and heat the oil. Add the garlic to the pot and sauté for 1 minutes, or until fragrant. Stir in the remaining ingredients.
2. Close and secure the lid. Select the Manual mode and set the cooking time for 2 minutes at Low Pressure. Once cooking is complete, do a quick pressure release. Carefully open the lid.
3. Serve immediately.

Per Serving
calories: 101 | fat: 7.1g | protein: 3.0g
carbs: 7.9g | net carbs: 4.8g | fiber: 3.1g

Creamy Broccoli with Turmeric

Prep time: 5 minutes | Cook time: 1 minute | Serves 2

1½ cups shredded broccoli
1 cup water
2 tablespoons cream

cheese
½ teaspoon ground turmeric
½ teaspoon salt

1. Pour the water and insert the trivet in the Instant Pot.
2. Put the shredded broccoli in a bowl and place the bowl on the trivet.
3. Close and secure the lid. Select the Manual mode and set the cooking time for 1 minute at High Pressure. Once cooking is complete, use a quick pressure release. Carefully open the lid.
4. Remove the bowl from the pot and stir in the cream cheese, turmeric and salt.
5. Serve immediately.

Per Serving
calories: 61 | fat: 3.9g | protein: 2.8g
carbs: 5.1g | net carbs: 3.3g | fiber: 1.8g

Balsamic Broccoli with Cottage Cheese

Prep time: 5 minutes | Cook time: 5 minutes | Serves 4

1 pound (454 g) broccoli, cut into florets
1 cup water
2 garlic cloves, minced
1 cup crumbled Cottage cheese
2 tablespoons

balsamic vinegar
1 teaspoon cumin seeds
1 teaspoon mustard seeds
Salt and pepper, to taste

1. Pour the water into the Instant Pot and put the steamer basket in the pot. Place the broccoli in the steamer basket.
2. Close and secure the lid. Select the Manual setting and set the cooking time for 5 minutes at High Pressure. Once the timer goes off, do a quick pressure release. Carefully open the lid.
3. Stir in the remaining ingredients.
4. Serve immediately.

Per Serving
calories: 105 | fat: 3.0g | protein: 9.5g
carbs: 11.9g | net carbs: 8.7g | fiber: 3.2g

Spinach and Cauliflower Medley

Prep time: 10 minutes | Cook time: 3 minutes | Serves 4

1 pound (454 g) cauliflower, cut into florets	2 tablespoons olive oil
	1 tablespoon grated lemon zest
1 yellow onion, peeled and chopped	1 teaspoon Hungarian paprika
1 red bell pepper, deseeded and chopped	Sea salt and ground black pepper, to taste
1 celery stalk, chopped	2 cups spinach, torn into pieces
2 garlic cloves, crushed	

1. Add all the ingredients, except for the spinach, to the Instant Pot.
2. Close and secure the lid. Select the Manual setting and set the cooking time for 3 minutes at High Pressure. Once the timer goes off, use a quick pressure release. Carefully open the lid.
3. Stir in the spinach and lock the lid. Let it sit in the residual heat for 5 minutes, or until wilted.
4. Serve warm.

Per Serving
calories: 114 | fat: 7.3g | protein: 3.4g
carbs: 11.3g | net carbs: 7.5g | fiber: 3.8g

Green Beans with Onion

Prep time: 5 minutes | Cook time: 6 to 7 minutes | Serves 6

6 slices bacon, diced	¼ cup water
1 cup diced onion	1 teaspoon salt
4 cups halved green beans	1 teaspoon freshly ground black pepper

1. Press the Sauté button on the Instant Pot and add the bacon and onion to the pot and sauté for 2 to 3 minutes. Stir in the remaining ingredients.
2. Close and secure the lid. Select the Manual setting and set the cooking time for 4 minutes at High Pressure. Once the timer goes off, use a quick pressure release. Carefully open the lid.
3. Serve immediately.

Per Serving
calories: 166 | fat: 13.1g | protein: 6.2g
carbs: 5.8g | net carbs: 3.0g | fiber: 2.8g

Vinegary Pe-Tsai Cabbage

Prep time: 5 minutes | Cook time: 8 minutes | Serves 4

2 tablespoons sesame oil	vinegar
	1 tablespoon coconut aminos
1 yellow onion, chopped	1 teaspoon finely minced garlic
1 pound (454 g) pe-tsai cabbage, shredded	½ teaspoon salt
	¼ teaspoon Szechuan pepper
¼ cup rice wine	

1. Set the Instant Pot on the Sauté mode and heat the sesame oil. Add the onion to the pot and sauté for 5 minutes, or until tender. Stir in the remaining ingredients.
2. Lock the lid. Select the Manual mode and set the cooking time for 3 minutes on High Pressure. When the timer goes off, perform a quick pressure release. Carefully open the lid.
3. Transfer the cabbage mixture to a bowl and serve immediately.

Per Serving
calories: 96 | fat: 7.1g | protein: 2.2g
carbs: 6.8g | net carbs:4.9 g | fiber: 1.9g

Vinegary Collard Greens with Tomato

Prep time: 5 minutes | Cook time: 20 minutes | Serves 4

1 bunch collard greens, trimmed	purée
	1 tablespoon balsamic vinegar
½ cup chicken stock	
2 tablespoons unsweetened tomato	Pinch of salt and black pepper

1. Add all the ingredients to the Instant Pot and stir to combine.
2. Lock the lid. Select the Manual mode and set the cooking time for 20 minutes at High Pressure. When the timer goes off, use a natural pressure release for 10 minutes, then release any remaining pressure. Carefully open the lid.
3. Divide the dish among plates and serve.

Per Serving
calories: 131 | fat: 2.2g | protein: 6.1g
carbs: 3.8g | net carbs: 2.0g | fiber: 1.8g

Smoky Cauliflower Balls with Olives

Prep time: 10 minutes | Cook time: 2 minutes | Serves 8

1 pound (454 g) cauliflower, cut into florets
1 cup water
1/3 cup coconut cream
3 tablespoons Kalamata olives, pitted
2 teaspoons melted butter
1/3 teaspoon ground black pepper
2 cloves garlic, peeled
Pinch of freshly grated nutmeg
Sea salt, to taste
2 tablespoons smoked paprika powder

1. Pour the water into the Instant Pot and put the steamer basket in the pot. Place the cauliflower florets in the steamer basket.
2. Close and secure the lid. Select the Manual mode and set the cooking time for 2 minutes at High Pressure. Once cooking is complete, do a quick pressure release. Carefully open the lid.
3. In a blender, combine the cooked cauliflower along with the remaining ingredients, except for the smoked paprika powder. Pulse until puréed.
4. Form the cauliflower mixture into balls and roll each ball into the smoked paprika powder. Arrange on the serving platters. Serve immediately.

Per Serving
calories: 67 | fat: 5.2g | protein: 1.8g
carbs: 5.0g | net carbs: 2.9g | fiber: 2.1g

Italian Radish with Rosemary

Prep time: 5 minutes | Cook time: 10 minutes | Serves 2

2 cups roughly chopped radish
2 tablespoons butter
1 teaspoon Italian seasonings
1/4 teaspoon dried rosemary
1/4 cup water

1. Add all the ingredients to the Instant Pot and stir to combine.
2. Select the Sauté mode and sauté for 10 minutes, or until the radish is cooked through, stirring constantly.
3. Transfer to bowls and serve warm.

Per Serving
calories: 129 | fat: 12.5g | protein: 1.0g
carbs: 4.2g | net carbs: 2.4g | fiber: 1.8g

Sesame Eggplants with Keto Teriyaki

Prep time: 5 minutes | Cook time: 4 minutes | Serves 6

2 tablespoons sesame oil
3 eggplants, trimmed and sliced
2 tablespoons keto teriyaki
1/2 teaspoon ground ginger
1/2 teaspoon sesame seeds

1. Press the Sauté button on the Instant Pot and heat the oil for 2 minutes.
2. Meanwhile, sprinkle the eggplant slices with the keto teriyaki, ground ginger and sesame seeds.
3. Arrange the eggplant slices in the pot in one layer and cook for 2 minutes on each side.
4. Transfer the eggplants to plates and serve warm.

Per Serving
calories: 117 | fat: 5.3g | protein: 3.2g
carbs: 17.1g | net carbs: 7.5g | fiber: 9.6g

Garlic Peppers with Cilantro

Prep time: 10 minutes | Cook time: 15 minutes | Serves 4

1 pound (454 g) mixed bell peppers, cut into thick strips
1/2 cup vegetable stock
1 tablespoon cilantro, chopped
3 garlic cloves, minced
Pinch of cayenne pepper
Pinch of salt and black pepper

1. Add all the ingredients to the Instant Pot and stir to combine.
2. Lock the lid. Select the Manual mode and set the cooking time for 15 minutes at High Pressure. When the timer goes off, use a natural pressure release for 10 minutes, then release any remaining pressure. Carefully open the lid.
3. Divide the dish among plates and serve.

Per Serving
calories: 122 | fat: 2.3g | protein: 5.1g
carbs: 3.9g | net carbs: 2.0g | fiber: 1.9g

Ranch Mushrooms with Chives

Prep time: 5 minutes | Cook time: 3 minutes | Serves 2

1 cup sliced cremini mushrooms
2 tablespoons chopped chives
1 tablespoon sesame oil
1 teaspoon ranch seasonings
1 cup water

1. Pour the water and insert the trivet in the Instant Pot.
2. In the mixing bowl, toss together the remaining ingredients.
3. Place the bowl with the mushroom mixture on the trivet.
4. Close and secure the lid. Select the Manual mode and set the cooking time for 3 minutes at High Pressure. Once cooking is complete, use a quick pressure release. Carefully open the lid.
5. Serve immediately.

Per Serving
calories: 71 | fat: 7.0g | protein: 1.1g
carbs: 1.5g | net carbs: 1.3g | fiber: 0.2g

Bell Peppers with Mustard

Prep time: 5 minutes | Cook time: 15 minutes | Serves 4

1 pound (454 g) mixed bell peppers, cut into strips
1 cup chicken stock
½ cup bacon, cooked and chopped
1 tablespoon mustard
Pinch of salt and black pepper

1. Add all the ingredients to the Instant Pot and stir to combine.
2. Lock the lid. Select the Manual mode and set the cooking time for 15 minutes at High Pressure. When the timer goes off, use a natural pressure release for 5 minutes, then release any remaining pressure. Carefully open the lid.
3. Divide the dish among plates and serve.

Per Serving
calories: 152 | fat: 2.3g | protein: 4.1g
carbs: 4.9g | net carbs: 2.0g | fiber: 2.9g

Cauliflower and Mushroom Bowl

Prep time: 10 minutes | Cook time: 5 minutes | Serves 2

½ cup chopped cauliflower
½ cup chopped mushrooms
4 ounces (113 g) bok choy, chopped
1 tablespoon avocado oil
1 tablespoon lemon juice
½ teaspoon salt
1 cup water

1. Pour the water and insert the steamer basket in the Instant Pot.
2. Place the cauliflower, mushrooms and bok choy in the basket.
3. Close and secure the lid. Select the Steam mode and set the cooking time for 5 minutes at High Pressure. Once cooking is complete, use a quick pressure release. Carefully open the lid.
4. Transfer the cooked vegetables to the serving bowls and sprinkle with the avocado oil, lemon juice and salt. Stir to mix well.
5. Serve immediately.

Per Serving
calories: 30 | fat: 1.3g | protein: 2.2g
carbs: 3.6g | net carbs: 2.0g | fiber: 1.6g

Garlic Brussels Sprouts with Onions

Prep time: 10 minutes | Cook time: 20 minutes | Serves 4

1 pound (454 g) Brussels sprouts
2 green onions, chopped
4 garlic cloves, minced
1 cup chicken stock
Pinch of salt and black pepper
1 tablespoon chopped dill

1. Add all the ingredients to the Instant Pot and stir to combine.
2. Lock the lid. Select the Manual mode and set the cooking time for 20 minutes at High Pressure. When the timer goes off, use a natural pressure release for 10 minutes, then release any remaining pressure. Carefully open the lid.
3. Divide the dish among plates and serve.

Per Serving
calories: 143 | fat: 2.3g | protein: 4.2g
carbs: 2.8g | net carbs: 2.0g | fiber: 0.8g

Garlic Cauliflower with Vegan Parmesan

Prep time: 10 minutes | Cook time: 3 minutes | Serves 4

1 pound (454 g) cauliflower, cut into florets	ground black pepper, to taste
1 cup water	Vegan Parmesan:
2 tablespoons sesame oil	½ cup sesame seeds
	½ teaspoon sea salt
1 teaspoon rosemary	½ teaspoon oregano
1 teaspoon dried basil	¼ teaspoon cumin seeds
2 garlic cloves, chopped	¼ teaspoon ground fennel seeds
Kosher salt and freshly	

1. Pour the water into the Instant Pot and put the steamer basket in the pot. Place the cauliflower florets in the steamer basket. Sprinkle with the sesame oil, rosemary, basil, garlic, salt and black pepper.
2. Close and secure the lid. Select the Manual mode and set the cooking time for 3 minutes at Low Pressure. Once cooking is complete, do a quick pressure release. Carefully open the lid.
3. Place the ingredients for the vegan Parmesan in a blender. Pulse until it reaches the texture of granular cheese.
4. Spread the vegan Parmesan over the cooked cauliflower. Serve immediately.

Per Serving
calories: 212 | fat: 18.7g | protein: 6.3g
carbs: 9.0g | net carbs: 4.2g | fiber: 4.8g

Cauliflower Rice with Mushrooms

Prep time: 10 minutes | Cook time: 13 minutes | Serves 4

1 medium head cauliflower, cut into florets	aminos
	1½ tablespoons olive oil
1 cup water	1 large egg, beaten
1½ tablespoons unsalted butter	¼ teaspoon fine grind sea salt
3 garlic cloves, minced	⅛ teaspoon ground black pepper
1 cup sliced fresh white mushrooms	½ tablespoon chopped fresh flat-leaf parsley
1 teaspoon coconut	

1. Place a steamer basket with legs in the inner pot and pour the water in the pot. Place the cauliflower florets in the steamer basket.

2. Lock the lid. Select the Steam mode and set the cooking time for 3 minutes on High Pressure. When the timer goes off, perform a quick pressure release. Carefully open the lid.
3. Transfer the cauliflower florets to a blender. Pulse until it reaches a rice-like texture. Set aside.
4. Remove the steamer basket from the pot. Pour out the water and wipe the pot dry with a paper towel.
5. Select Sauté setting and melt the butter. Add the garlic and mushrooms to the pot and sauté for 4 minutes, or until the mushrooms are tender.
6. Stir in the coconut aminos, olive oil and cauliflower rice. Sauté for 3 minutes.
7. Whisk in the beaten egg and sauté for 3 minutes, or until the egg is thoroughly cooked. Season with the sea salt and black pepper and stir to combine.
8. Transfer the fried rice to serving bowls and sprinkle the parsley on top. Serve hot.

Per Serving
calories: 131 | fat: 9.1g | protein: 5.2g
carbs: 7.1g | net carbs: 5.0g | fiber: 2.1g

Cheese Tomatoes with Basil

Prep time: 5 minutes | Cook time: 3 minutes | Serves 4

8 tomatoes, sliced	virgin olive oil
1 cup water	2 tablespoons snipped fresh basil
½ cup crumbled Halloumi cheese	2 garlic cloves, smashed
2 tablespoons extra-	

1. Pour the water into the Instant Pot and put the trivet in the pot. Place the tomatoes in the trivet.
2. Lock the lid. Select the Manual mode and set the cooking time for 3 minutes on High Pressure. When the timer goes off, perform a quick pressure release. Carefully open the lid.
3. Toss the tomatoes with the remaining ingredients and serve.

Per Serving
calories: 141 | fat: 10.8g | protein: 4.5g
carbs: 8.1g | net carbs: 5.9g | fiber: 2.2g

Chapter 12 Fish and Seafood

Lemon Salmon with Dill

Prep time: 10 minutes | Cook time: 12 minutes | Serves 2

2 (4-ounce / (113 g)) salmon fillets, skin removed
2 tablespoons unsalted butter, melted
½ teaspoon garlic powder
1 medium lemon
½ teaspoon dried dill

1. Place each fillet on a 5-inch × 5-inch square of aluminum foil. Drizzle with butter and sprinkle with garlic powder.
2. Zest half of the lemon and sprinkle zest over salmon. Slice other half of the lemon and lay two slices on each piece of salmon. Sprinkle dill over salmon.
3. Gather and fold foil at the top and sides to fully close packets. Place foil packets into the air fryer basket.
4. Adjust the temperature to 400ºF (205ºC) and set the timer for 12 minutes.
5. Salmon will be easily flaked and have an internal temperature of at least 145ºF (63ºC) when fully cooked. Serve immediately.

Per Serving
calories: 252 | fat: 16g | protein: 20g
carbs: 2g | net carbs: 1g | fiber: 1g

Balsamic Tilapia Fillet

Prep time: 5 minutes | Cook time: 15 minutes | Serves 4

4 tilapia fillets, boneless
2 tablespoons balsamic vinegar
1 teaspoon avocado oil
1 teaspoon dried basil

1. Sprinkle the tilapia fillets with balsamic vinegar, avocado oil, and dried basil.
2. Then put the fillets in the air fryer basket and cook at 365ºF (185ºC) for 15 minutes.

Per Serving
calories: 96 | fat: 1g | protein: 21g
carbs: 1g | net carbs: 0g | fiber: 1g

Salmon Burgers with Avocado

Prep time: 5 minutes | Cook time: 5 minutes | Serves 4

2 tablespoons coconut oil
1 pound (454 g) salmon fillets
1/3 cup finely ground pork rinds
2 tablespoons finely diced onion
2 tablespoons
mayonnaise
½ teaspoon salt
¼ teaspoon chili powder
¼ teaspoon garlic powder
1 egg
1 avocado, pitted
Juice of ½ lime

1. Set your Instant Pot to Sauté. Add and heat the coconut oil.
2. Remove skin from the salmon filets. Finely mince the salmon and add to a large bowl.
3. Stir in the remaining ingredients except the avocado and lime and form 4 patties.
4. Place the burgers into the pot and sear for about 3 to 4 minutes per side, or until the center feels firm and reads at least 145ºF (63ºC) on a meat thermometer.
5. Scoop flesh out of the avocado. In a small bowl, mash the avocado with a fork and squeeze the lime juice over the top.
6. Divide the mash into four sections and place on top of salmon burgers. Serve warm.

Per Serving
calories: 427 | fat: 27.9g | protein: 36.2g
carbs: 3.5g | net carbs: 1g | fiber: 2.5g

Lime Lobster Tails with Basil

Prep time: 10 minutes | Cook time: 6 minutes | Serves 4

4 lobster tails, peeled
2 tablespoons lime juice
½ teaspoon dried basil
½ teaspoon coconut oil, melted

1. Mix lobster tails with lime juice, dried basil, and coconut oil.
2. Put the lobster tails in the air fryer and cook at 380ºF (193ºC) for 6 minutes.

Per Serving
calories: 83 | fat: 1g | protein: 16g
carbs: 1g | net carbs: 1g | fiber: 0g

Vinegary Shrimp with Swiss Chard

Prep time: 10 minutes | Cook time: 10 minutes | Serves 4

1 pound (454 g) shrimp, peeled and deveined
½ teaspoon smoked paprika
½ cup Swiss chard, chopped
2 tablespoons apple cider vinegar
1 tablespoon coconut oil
¼ cup heavy cream

1. Mix shrimps with smoked paprika and apple cider vinegar.
2. Put the shrimps in the air fryer and add coconut oil.
3. Cook the shrimps at 350ºF (180ºC) for 10 minutes.
4. Then mix cooked shrimps with remaining ingredients and carefully mix.

Per Serving
calories: 193 | fat: 8g | protein: 26g
carbs: 2g | net carbs: 1g | fiber: 1g

Parmesan Crab Patties

Prep time: 20 minutes | Cook time: 14 minutes | Serves 3

2 eggs, beaten
1 shallot, chopped
2 garlic cloves, crushed
1 tablespoon olive oil
1 teaspoon yellow mustard
1 teaspoon fresh cilantro, chopped
10 ounces (283 g) crab meat
1 teaspoon smoked paprika
½ teaspoon ground black pepper
Sea salt, to taste
¾ cup Parmesan cheese

1. In a mixing bowl, thoroughly combine the eggs, shallot, garlic, olive oil, mustard, cilantro, crab meat, paprika, black pepper, and salt. Mix until well combined.
2. Shape the mixture into 6 patties. Roll the crab patties over grated Parmesan cheese, coating well on all sides. Place in your refrigerator for 2 hours.
3. Spritz the crab patties with cooking oil on both sides. Cook in the preheated Air Fryer at 360ºF (182ºC) for 14 minutes. Serve on dinner rolls if desired. Bon appétit!

Per Serving
calories: 279 | fat: 15g | protein: 28g
carbs: 6g | net carbs: 5g | fiber: 1g

Lemon Salmon and Avocado Salad

Prep time: 10 minutes | Cook time: 7 minutes | Serves 2

2 (3-ounce / 85-g) salmon fillets
½ teaspoon salt
¼ teaspoon pepper
1 cup water
⅓ cup mayonnaise
Juice of ½ lemon
2 avocados
½ teaspoon chopped fresh dill

1. Season the salmon fillets on all sides with the salt and pepper. Add the water to the Instant Pot and insert a trivet.
2. Arrange the salmon fillets on the trivet, skin-side down.
3. Secure the lid. Select the Steam mode and set the cooking time for 7 minutes at Low Pressure.
4. Once cooking is complete, do a quick pressure release. Carefully open the lid. Set aside to cool.
5. Mix together the mayonnaise and lemon juice in a large bowl. Cut the avocados in half. Remove the pits and dice the avocados. Add the avocados to the large bowl and gently fold into the mixture.
6. Flake the salmon into bite-sized pieces with a fork and gently fold into the mixture.
7. Serve garnished with the fresh dill.

Per Serving
calories: 605 | fat: 50.5g | protein: 21.7g
carbs: 12.5g | net carbs: 3.1g | fiber: 9.4g

Cumin Mussels in Cider Vinegar

Prep time: 10 minutes | Cook time: 2 minutes | Serves 5

2-pounds (907-g) mussels, cleaned, peeled
1 teaspoon onion powder
1 teaspoon ground
cumin
1 tablespoon avocado oil
¼ cup apple cider vinegar

1. Mix mussels with onion powder, ground cumin, avocado oil, and apple cider vinegar.
2. Put the mussels in the air fryer and cook at 395ºF (202ºC) for 2 minutes.

Per Serving
calories: 166 | fat: 4g | protein: 22g
carbs: 8g | net carbs: 7g | fiber: 1g

Vinegary Bluefish in Vermouth

Prep time: 5 minutes | Cook time: 5 minutes | Serves 4

2 teaspoons butter	vinegar
½ yellow onion, chopped	2 teaspoons coconut aminos
1 garlic clove, minced	1 teaspoon chopped fresh tarragon leaves
1 pound (454 g) bluefish fillets	Sea salt and ground black pepper, to taste
¼ cup vermouth	
1 tablespoon rice	

1. Set your Instant Pot to Sauté and melt the butter.
2. Add the onion and sauté for 2 minutes until softened.
3. Add garlic and sauté for 1 minute more or until fragrant. Stir in the remaining ingredients.
4. Lock the lid. Select the Manual mode and set the cooking time for 3 minutes at Low Pressure.
5. When the timer beeps, perform a quick pressure release. Carefully remove the lid.
6. Serve warm.

Per Serving
calories: 190 | fat: 6.8g | protein: 23.0g
carbs: 3.8g | net carbs: 3.5g | fiber: 0.3g

Salmon Patties with Sriracha Mayo

Prep time: 10 minutes | Cook time: 8 minutes | Serves 2

2 (5-ounce / (142 g)) pouches cooked pink salmon	2 tablespoons full-fat mayonnaise
1 large egg	2 teaspoons sriracha
¼ cup ground pork rinds	1 teaspoon chili powder

1. Mix all ingredients in a large bowl and form into four patties. Place patties into the air fryer basket.
2. Adjust the temperature to 400ºF (205ºC) and set the timer for 8 minutes.
3. Carefully flip each patty halfway through the cooking time. Patties will be crispy on the outside when fully cooked.

Per Serving
calories: 319 | fat: 19g | protein: 34g
carbs: 2g | net carbs: 1g | fiber: 1g

Spicy Calamari

Prep time: 10 minutes | Cook time: 6 minutes | Serves 2

10 ounces (284 g) calamari, trimmed	sauce
2 tablespoons keto hot	1 tablespoon avocado oil

1. Slice the calamari and sprinkle with avocado oil.
2. Put the calamari in the air fryer and cook at 400ºF (205ºC) for 3 minutes per side.
3. Then transfer the calamari in the serving plate and sprinkle with hot sauce.

Per Serving
calories: 36 | fat: 2g | protein: 3g
carbs: 2g | net carbs: 1g | fiber: 1g

Garlic Salmon Fillets with Bok Choy

Prep time: 5 minutes | Cook time: 8 minutes | Serves 4

1½ cups water	taste
2 tablespoons unsalted butter	2 cups Bok choy, sliced
4 (1-inch thick) salmon fillets	1 cup chicken broth
½ teaspoon cayenne pepper	3 cloves garlic, minced
Sea salt and freshly ground pepper, to	1 teaspoon grated lemon zest
	½ teaspoon dried dill weed

1. Pour the water into your Instant Pot and insert a trivet.
2. Brush the salmon with the melted butter and season with the cayenne pepper, salt, and black pepper on all sides.
3. Lock the lid. Select the Manual mode and set the cooking time for 3 minutes at Low Pressure.
4. When the timer beeps, perform a quick pressure release. Carefully remove the lid.
5. Add the remaining ingredients.
6. Lock the lid. Select the Manual mode and set the cooking time for 5 minutes at High Pressure.
7. When the timer beeps, perform a quick pressure release. Carefully remove the lid.
8. Serve the poached salmon with the veggies on the side.

Per Serving
calories: 209 | fat: 11.3g | protein: 23.9g
carbs: 2.1g | net carbs: 1.6g | fiber: 0.5g

Parsley Scallops in White Wine

Prep time: 5 minutes | Cook time: 5 minutes | Serves 3

1 tablespoon sesame oil
¾ pound (340 g) scallops
2 garlic cloves, crushed
1 cup chicken broth
¼ cup dry white wine
½ teaspoon paprika
Sea salt, to taste
⅓ teaspoon ground black pepper
2 tablespoons chopped fresh parsley
1 tablespoon fresh lemon juice

1. Set your Instant Pot to Sauté and heat the sesame oil.
2. Add the scallops and sauté for 1 to 2 minutes.
3. Add the garlic and continue to sauté for 30 seconds more. Add the broth, wine, paprika, salt, and pepper.
4. Lock the lid. Select the Manual mode and set the cooking time for 2 minutes at Low Pressure.
5. When the timer beeps, perform a quick pressure release. Carefully remove the lid.
6. Transfer the scallops to a bowl and toss with fresh parsley and lemon juice. Serve immediately.

Per Serving
calories: 131 | fat: 5.4g | protein: 14.6g
carbs: 5.8g | net carbs: 5.4g | fiber: 0.4g

Salmon Steaks with Garlic Yogurt

Prep time: 2 minutes | Cook time: 4 minutes | Serves 4

1 cup water
2 tablespoons olive oil
4 salmon steaks
Garlic Yogurt:
1 (8-ounce / 227-g) container full-fat Greek yogurt
2 cloves garlic, minced
Coarse sea salt and ground black pepper, to taste

2 tablespoons mayonnaise
⅓ teaspoon Dijon mustard

1. Pour the water into the Instant Pot and insert a trivet.
2. Rub the olive oil into the fish and sprinkle with the salt and black pepper on all sides. Put the fish on the trivet.
3. Lock the lid. Select the Manual mode and set the cooking time for 4 minutes at High Pressure.
4. When the timer beeps, perform a quick pressure release. Carefully remove the lid.
5. Meanwhile, stir together all the ingredients for the garlic yogurt in a bowl.
6. Serve the salmon steaks alongside the garlic yogurt.

Per Serving
calories: 128 | fat: 11.2g | protein: 2.5g
carbs:4.9g | net carbs: 4.7g | fiber: 0.2g

Cayenne Haddock

Prep time: 10 minutes | Cook time: 8 minutes | Serves 4

1-pound (454-g) haddock fillet
1 teaspoon cayenne pepper
1 teaspoon salt
1 teaspoon coconut oil
½ cup heavy cream

1. Grease the baking pan with coconut oil.
2. Then put haddock fillet inside and sprinkle it with cayenne pepper, salt, and heavy cream.
3. Put the baking pan in the air fryer basket and cook at 375ºF (190ºC) for 8 minutes.

Per Serving
calories: 190 | fat: 7g | protein: 28g
carbs: 2g | net carbs: 1g | fiber: 1g

Almond-Coated Catfish

Prep time: 10 minutes | Cook time: 12 minutes | Serves 4

2-pound (907-g) catfish fillet
½ cup almond flour
2 eggs, beaten
1 teaspoon salt
1 teaspoon avocado oil

1. Sprinkle the catfish fillet with salt and dip in the eggs.
2. Then coat the fish in the almond flour and put in the air fryer basket. Sprinkle the fish with avocado oil.
3. Cook the fish for 6 minutes per side at 380ºF (193ºC).

Per Serving
calories: 423 | fat: 26g | protein: 41g
carbs: 3g | net carbs: 1g | fiber: 2g

Paprika Tilapia with Pecan

Prep time: 20 minutes | Cook time: 16 minutes | Serves 5

2 tablespoons ground flaxseeds
1 teaspoon paprika
Sea salt and white pepper, to taste
1 teaspoon garlic paste
2 tablespoons extra-virgin olive oil
½ cup pecans, ground
5 tilapia fillets, slice into halves

1. Combine the ground flaxseeds, paprika, salt, white pepper, garlic paste, olive oil, and ground pecans in a Ziploc bag. Add the fish fillets and shake to coat well.
2. Spritz the Air Fryer basket with cooking spray. Cook in the preheated Air Fryer at 400°F (205°C) for 10 minutes; turn them over and cook for 6 minutes more. Work in batches.
3. Serve with lemon wedges, if desired. Enjoy!

Per Serving
calories: 264 | fat: 17g | protein: 6g
carbs: 4g | net carbs: 2g | fiber: 2g

Air Fried Salmon with Pesto

Prep time: 5 minutes | Cook time: 12 minutes | Serves 2

¼ cup pesto
¼ cup sliced almonds, roughly chopped
2 (1½ -inch-thick)
salmon fillets (about 4 ounces each/ 113 g)
2 tablespoons unsalted butter, melted

1. In a small bowl, mix pesto and almonds. Set aside.
2. Place fillets into a 6 -inch round baking dish.
3. Brush each fillet with butter and place half of the pesto mixture on the top of each fillet. Place dish into the air fryer basket.
4. Adjust the temperature to 390°F (199°C) and set the timer for 12 minutes.
5. Salmon will easily flake when fully cooked and reach an internal temperature of at least 145°F (63°C). Serve warm.

Per Serving
calories: 433 | fat: 34g | protein: 23g
carbs: 6g | net carbs: 4g | fiber: 2g

Chili Tilapia with Mustard

Prep time: 5 minutes | Cook time: 20 minutes | Serves 4

4 tilapia fillets, boneless
1 teaspoon chili flakes
1 teaspoon dried
oregano
1 tablespoon avocado oil
1 teaspoon mustard

1. Rub the tilapia fillets with chili flakes, dried oregano, avocado oil, and mustard and put in the air fryer.
2. Cook it for 10 minutes per side at 360°F (182°C).

Per Serving
calories: 103 | fat: 1g | protein: 21g
carbs: 1g | net carbs: 0g | fiber: 1g

Cheese Mussel and Tomato Stew

Prep time: 15 minutes | Cook time: 3 minutes | Serves 6

1½ pounds (680 g) mussels, scrubbed and debearded
1 cup chicken broth
½ cup dry red wine
2 tablespoons olive oil
2 heaping tablespoons chopped green onions
2 tablespoons chopped fresh coriander
½ teaspoon paprika
½ teaspoon dried marjoram
A pinch ground
nutmeg
Sea salt and ground black pepper, to taste
½ (28-ounce / 794-g) can San Marzano tomatoes, crushed
2 cloves garlic, crushed
1 cup shredded Asiago cheese
1 tablespoon chopped fresh dill
1 lemon, sliced

1. Combine all the ingredients except the cheese, dill and lemon in the Instant Pot.
2. Lock the lid. Select the Manual mode and set the cooking time for 3 minutes at Low Pressure.
3. When the timer beeps, perform a quick pressure release. Carefully remove the lid.
4. Sprinkle with the cheese and dill. Serve topped with the lemon slices.

Per Serving
calories: 298 | fat: 16.7g | protein: 28.1g
carbs: 7.5g | net carbs: 6.7g | fiber: 0.8g

Sweet and Sour Tilapia Fillets

Prep time: 5 minutes | Cook time: 14 minutes | Serves 4

2 tablespoons erythritol
1 tablespoon apple cider vinegar
4 tilapia fillets, boneless
1 teaspoon olive oil

1. Mix apple cider vinegar with olive oil and erythritol.
2. Then rub the tilapia fillets with the sweet mixture and put in the air fryer basket in one layer.
3. Cook the fish at 360ºF (182ºC) for 7 minutes per side.

Per Serving
calories: 101 | fat: 2g | protein: 20g
carbs: 0g | net carbs: 0g | fiber: 0g

Coconut-Crusted Salmon

Prep time: 15 minutes | Cook time: 8 minutes | Serves 4

2-pound (907-g) salmon fillet
¼ cup coconut shred
2 eggs, beaten
1 teaspoon coconut oil
1 teaspoon Italian seasonings

1. Cut the salmon fillet into servings.
2. Then sprinkle the fish with Italian seasonings and dip in the eggs.
3. After this, coat every salmon fillet in coconut shred and put it in the air fryer.
4. Cook the fish at 375ºF (190ºC) for 4 minutes per side.

Per Serving
calories: 395 | fat: 22g | protein: 47g
carbs: 2g | net carbs: 1g | fiber: 1g

Parmesan Mackerel Fillet

Prep time: 10 minutes | Cook time: 7 minutes | Serves 2

12 ounces (340 g) mackerel fillet
2 ounces (57 g) Parmesan, grated
1 teaspoon ground coriander
1 tablespoon olive oil

1. Sprinkle the mackerel fillet with olive oil and put it in the air fryer basket.

2. Top the fish with ground coriander and Parmesan.
3. Cook the fish at 390ºF (199ºC) for 7 minutes.

Per Serving
calories: 597 | fat: 43g | protein: 50g
carbs: 1g | net carbs: 1g | fiber: 0g

Coconut Salmon with Cauliflower

Prep time: 10 minutes | Cook time: 25 minutes | Serves 4

1-pound (454-g) salmon fillet, diced
1 cup cauliflower, shredded
1 tablespoon dried cilantro
1 tablespoon coconut oil, melted
1 teaspoon ground turmeric
¼ cup coconut cream

1. Mix salmon with cauliflower, dried cilantro, ground turmeric, coconut cream, and coconut oil.
2. Transfer the salmon mixture in the air fryer and cook the meal at 350ºF (180ºC) for 25 minutes. Stir the meal every 5 minutes to avoid the burning.

Per Serving
calories: 222 | fat: 14g | protein: 23g
carbs: 3g | net carbs: 2g | fiber: 1g

Coconut Mackerel with Cumin

Prep time: 10 minutes | Cook time: 6 minutes | Serves 4

2 pounds (907 g) mackerel fillet
1 cup coconut cream
1 teaspoon ground coriander
1 teaspoon cumin seeds
1 garlic clove, peeled, chopped

1. Chop the mackerel roughly and sprinkle it with coconut cream, ground coriander, cumin seeds, and garlic.
2. Then put the fish in the air fryer and cook at 400ºF (205ºC) for 6 minutes.

Per Serving
calories: 735 | fat: 54g | protein: 55g
carbs: 4g | net carbs: 2g | fiber: 2g

Old Bay Shrimp

Prep time: 5 minutes | Cook time: 6 minutes | Serves 2

8 ounces (227 g) medium shelled and deveined shrimp
2 tablespoons salted butter, melted
1 teaspoon paprika
½ teaspoon garlic powder
¼ teaspoon onion powder
½ teaspoon Old Bay seasoning

1. Toss all ingredients together in a large bowl. Place shrimp into the air fryer basket.
2. Adjust the temperature to 400°F (205°C) and set the timer for 6 minutes.
3. Turn the shrimp halfway through the cooking time to ensure even cooking. Serve immediately.

Per Serving
calories: 192 | fat: 11g | protein: 17g
carbs: 3g | net carbs: 2g | fiber: 1g

Sriacha Shrimp with Mayo

Prep time: 10 minutes | Cook time: 7 minutes | Serves 4

1 pound (454 g) medium shelled and deveined shrimp
2 tablespoons salted butter, melted
½ teaspoon Old Bay seasoning
¼ teaspoon garlic powder
2 tablespoons sriracha
¼ teaspoon powdered erythritol
¼ cup full-fat mayonnaise
⅛ teaspoon ground black pepper

1. In a large bowl, toss shrimp in butter, Old Bay seasoning, and garlic powder. Place shrimp into the air fryer basket.
2. Adjust the temperature to 400°F (205°C) and set the timer for 7 minutes.
3. Flip the shrimp halfway through the cooking time. Shrimp will be bright pink when fully cooked.
4. In another large bowl, mix sriracha, powdered erythritol, mayonnaise, and pepper. Toss shrimp in the spicy mixture and serve immediately.

Per Serving
calories: 143 | fat: 6g | protein: 16g
carbs: 3g | net carbs: 3g | fiber: 0g

Halibut Steaks with Bacon

Prep time: 15 minutes | Cook time: 10 minutes | Serves 4

24 ounces (680 g) halibut steaks (6 ounces / 170 g each fillet)
1 teaspoon avocado
oil
1 teaspoon ground black pepper
4 ounces (113 g) bacon, sliced

1. Sprinkle the halibut steaks with avocado oil and ground black pepper.
2. Then wrap the fish in the bacon slices and put in the air fryer.
3. Cook the fish at 390°F (199°C) for 5 minutes per side.

Per Serving
calories: 266 | fat: 14g | protein: 33g
carbs: 2g | net carbs: 1g | fiber: 1g

Swai Fish Fillets in Port Wine

Prep time: 5 minutes | Cook time: 10 minutes | Serves 4

1 tablespoon butter
1 teaspoon fresh grated ginger
2 garlic cloves, minced
2 tablespoon chopped green onions
1 pound (454 g) swai fish fillets
½ cup port wine
1 teaspoon parsley flakes
½ tablespoon lemon
juice
½ teaspoon chili flakes
½ teaspoon cayenne pepper
½ teaspoon fennel seeds
¼ teaspoon ground bay leaf
Coarse sea salt and ground black pepper, to taste

1. Set your Instant Pot to Sauté and melt the butter.
2. Cook the ginger, garlic, and green onions for 2 minutes until softened. Add the remaining ingredients and gently stir to incorporate.
3. Lock the lid. Select the Manual mode and set the cooking time for 6 minutes at Low Pressure.
4. When the timer beeps, perform a quick pressure release. Carefully remove the lid.
5. Serve warm.

Per Serving
calories: 112 | fat: 3.5g | protein: 17.8g
carbs: 1.7g | net carbs: 1.3g | fiber: 0.4g

Lime Tilapia with Fennel Seeds

Prep time: 15 minutes | Cook time: 10 minutes | Serves 4

2-pound (907-g) tilapia fillet
1 teaspoon fennel seeds
1 tablespoon avocado

oil
½ teaspoon lime zest, grated
1 tablespoon coconut aminos

1. In the shallow bowl, mix fennel seeds with avocado oil, lime zest, and coconut aminos.
2. Then brush the tilapia fillet with fennel seeds and put in the air fryer.
3. Cook the fish at 380ºF (193ºC) for 10 minutes.

Per Serving
calories: 194 | fat: 2g | protein: 42g
carbs: 1g | net carbs: 0g | fiber: 1g

Lime Salmon with Thyme

Prep time: 8 minutes | Cook time: 6 minutes | Serves 4

1½ cups cold water
4 (5-ounce / 142-g) salmon fillets
½ teaspoon fine sea salt
¼ teaspoon ground

black pepper
1 lime, thinly sliced
4 teaspoons extra-virgin olive oil, divided
Fresh thyme leaves

1. Pour the cold water into the Instant Pot and insert a steamer basket.
2. Sprinkle the fish on all sides with the salt and pepper.
3. Take four sheets of parchment paper and place 3 lime slices on each sheet. Top the lime slices with a piece of fish.
4. Drizzle with 1 teaspoon of olive oil and place a few thyme leaves on top. Cover each fillet with the parchment by folding in the edges and folding down the top like an envelope to close tightly.
5. Stack the packets in the steamer basket, seam-side down.
6. Secure the lid. Select the Manual mode and set the cooking time for 6 minutes at Low Pressure.
7. When the timer beeps, perform a natural pressure release for 10 minutes, then release any remaining pressure. Carefully remove the lid.
8. Remove the fish packets from the pot.

9. Serve the fish garnished with the fresh thyme.

Per Serving
calories: 209 | fat: 10.6g | protein: 28.8g
carbs: 2.1g | net carbs: 1.1g | fiber: 1.0g

Mackerel with Bell Pepper

Prep time: 15 minutes | Cook time: 20 minutes | Serves 5

1-pound (454 g) mackerel, trimmed
1 bell pepper, chopped
½ cup spinach, chopped
1 tablespoon avocado

oil
1 teaspoon ground black pepper
1 teaspoon keto tomato paste

1. In the mixing bowl, mix bell pepper with spinach, ground black pepper, and tomato paste.
2. Fill the mackerel with spinach mixture.
3. Then brush the fish with avocado oil and put it in the air fryer.
4. Cook the fish at 365ºF (185ºC) for 20 minutes.

Per Serving
calories: 252 | fat: 16g | protein: 22g
carbs: 2g | net carbs: 1g | fiber: 1g

Rosemary Shrimp Skewers

Prep time: 10 minutes | Cook time: 5 minutes | Serves 5

4-pounds (1.8-kg) shrimps, peeled
1 tablespoon dried rosemary

1 tablespoon avocado oil
1 teaspoon apple cider vinegar

1. Mix the shrimps with dried rosemary, avocado oil, and apple cider vinegar.
2. Then sting the shrimps into skewers and put in the air fryer.
3. Cook the shrimps at 400ºF (205ºC) for 5 minutes.

Per Serving
calories: 437 | fat: 6g | protein: 83g
carbs: 6g | net carbs: 5g | fiber: 1g

Coconut-Coated Sardines

Prep time: 15 minutes | Cook time: 10 minutes | Serves 5

12 ounces (340 g) sardines, trimmed, cleaned
1 cup coconut flour
1 tablespoon coconut oil
1 teaspoon salt

1. Sprinkle the sardines with salt and coat in the coconut flour.
2. Then grease the air fryer basket with coconut oil and put the sardines inside.
3. Cook them at 385ºF (196ºC) for 10 minutes.

Per Serving
calories: 165 | fat: 10g | protein: 17g
carbs: 1g | net carbs: 1g | fiber: 0g

Coconut-Crusted Shrimp

Prep time: 15 minutes | Cook time: 17 minutes | Serves 4

¾ cup unsweetened shredded coconut
¾ cup coconut flour
1 teaspoon garlic powder
¼ teaspoon cayenne pepper
Sea salt, freshly
ground black pepper, to taste
2 large eggs
1 pound (454 g) fresh extra-large or jumbo shrimp, peeled and deveined
Avocado oil spray

1. In a medium bowl, combine the shredded coconut, coconut flour, garlic powder, and cayenne pepper. Season to taste with salt and pepper.
2. In a small bowl, beat the eggs.
3. Pat the shrimp dry with paper towels. Dip each shrimp in the eggs and then the coconut mixture. Gently press the coating to the shrimp to help it adhere.
4. Set the air fryer to 400ºF (205ºC). Spray the shrimp with oil and place them in a single layer in the air fryer basket, working in batches if necessary.
5. Cook the shrimp for 9 minutes, then flip and spray them with more oil. Cook for 8 minutes more, until the center of the shrimp is opaque and cooked through.

Per Serving
calories: 362 | fat: 17g | protein: 35g
carbs: 20g | net carbs: 9g | fiber: 11g

Dill-Lemon Salmon Fillets

Prep time: 3 minutes | Cook time: 5 minutes | Serves 2

2 (3-ounce / 85-g) salmon fillets, 1-inch thick
1 teaspoon chopped fresh dill
½ teaspoon salt
¼ teaspoon pepper
1 cup water
2 tablespoons lemon juice
½ lemon, sliced

1. Season salmon with dill, salt, and pepper.
2. Pour the water into the Instant Pot and insert the trivet. Place the salmon on the trivet, skin-side down. Squeeze lemon juice over fillets and scatter the lemon slices on top.
3. Lock the lid. Select the Steam mode and set the cooking time for 5 minutes at High Pressure.
4. Once cooking is complete, do a quick pressure release. Carefully open the lid.
5. Serve warm.

Per Serving
calories: 129 | fat: 5.3g | protein: 17.9g
carbs: 1.3g | net carbs: 1.0g | fiber: 0.3g

Paprika Salmon Fillets

Prep time: 5 minutes | Cook time: 5 minutes | Serves 2

1 tablespoon avocado oil
2 (3-ounce / 85-g) salmon fillets
1 teaspoon paprika
½ teaspoon salt
¼ teaspoon dried
thyme
¼ teaspoon onion powder
¼ teaspoon pepper
⅛ teaspoon cayenne pepper

1. Drizzle the avocado oil over salmon fillets. Combine the remaining ingredients in a small bowl and rub all over fillets.
2. Press the Sauté button on the Instant Pot. Add the salmon fillets and sear for 2 to 5 minutes until the salmon easily flakes with a fork.
3. Serve warm.

Per Serving
calories: 194 | fat: 11.9g | protein: 18.8g
carbs: 1.0g | net carbs: 0.4g | fiber: 0.6g

Air Fried Crab and Egg Bun

Prep time: 15 minutes | Cook time: 20 minutes | Serves 2

5 ounces (142 g) crab meat, chopped
2 eggs, beaten
2 tablespoons coconut flour
¼ teaspoon baking powder
½ teaspoon coconut aminos
½ teaspoon ground black pepper
1 tablespoon coconut oil, softened

1. In the mixing bowl, mix crab meat with eggs, coconut flour, baking powder, coconut aminos, ground black pepper, and coconut oil.
2. Knead the smooth dough and cut it into pieces.
3. Make the buns from the crab mixture and put them in the air fryer basket.
4. Cook the crab buns at 365ºF (185ºC) for 20 minutes.

Per Serving
calories: 217 | fat: 13g | protein: 15g carbs: 7g | net carbs: 4g | fiber: 3g

Cheese Shrimp

Prep time: 20 minutes | Cook time: 7 minutes | Serves 4

2 egg whites
½ cup coconut flour
1 cup Parmigiano-Reggiano, grated
½ teaspoon celery seeds
½ teaspoon porcini powder
½ teaspoon onion powder
1 teaspoon garlic powder
½ teaspoon dried rosemary
½ teaspoon sea salt
½ teaspoon ground black pepper
1½ pounds (680g) shrimp, deveined

1. Whisk the egg with coconut flour and Parmigiano-Reggiano. Add in seasonings and mix to combine well.
2. Dip your shrimp in the batter. Roll until they are covered on all sides.
3. Cook in the preheated Air Fryer at 390ºF (199ºC) for 5 to 7 minutes or until golden brown. Work in batches. Serve with lemon wedges if desired.

Per Serving
calories: 300 | fat: 11g | protein: 44g carbs: 7g | net carbs: 6g | fiber: 1g

Coconut Mackerel Chowder

Prep time: 5 minutes | Cook time: 8 minutes | Serves 4

1 tablespoon olive oil
1 yellow onion, chopped
1 teaspoon grated ginger
2 garlic cloves, minced
1 pound (454 g) mackerel fillets, sliced
2 cups chicken stock
1½ cups coconut milk
½ cup heavy cream
1 tablespoon butter

1. Set your Instant Pot to Sauté and heat the olive oil.
2. Sauté the onion until softened, about 2 minutes.
3. Sauté the garlic and ginger for 30 to 40 seconds more.
4. Add the remaining ingredients to the Instant Pot and stir until combined.
5. Lock the lid. Select the Manual mode and set the cooking time for 6 minutes at High Pressure.
6. When the timer beeps, perform a quick pressure release. Carefully remove the lid.
7. Serve warm.

Per Serving
calories: 491 | fat: 37.0g | protein: 28.9g carbs: 13.0g | net carbs: 11.5g | fiber: 2.5g

Halibut Steaks with Garlic

Prep time: 2 minutes | Cook time: 5 minutes | Serves 3

1½ cups water
3 halibut steaks
Coarse sea salt, to taste
¼ teaspoon ground black pepper, to taste
4 garlic cloves, crushed

1. Pour the water into the Instant Pot and insert a steamer basket.
2. Put the halibut steaks in the steamer basket and season with salt and black pepper. Scatter with the garlic.
3. Lock the lid. Select the Manual mode and set the cooking time for 5 minutes at High Pressure.
4. When the timer beeps, perform a quick pressure release. Carefully remove the lid.
5. Serve warm.

Per Serving
calories: 289 | fat: 21.3g | protein: 22.1g carbs: 1.5g | net carbs: 1.4g | fiber: 0.1g

Cheddar Shrimp

Prep time: 15 minutes | Cook time: 5 minutes | Serves 4

14 ounces (397 g) shrimps, peeled
1 egg, beaten
½ cup coconut milk
1 cup Cheddar cheese,
shredded
½ teaspoon coconut oil
1 teaspoon ground coriander

1. In the mixing bowl, mix shrimps with egg, coconut milk, Cheddar cheese, coconut oil, and ground coriander.
2. Then put the mixture in the baking ramekins and put in the air fryer.
3. Cook the shrimps at 400ºF (205ºC) for 5 minutes.

Per Serving
calories: 321 | fat: 19g | protein: 32g
carbs: 4g | net carbs: 3g | fiber: 1g

Lemon Butter Scallops

Prep time: 5 minutes | Cook time: 15 minutes | Serves 4

1 pound (454 g) large sea scallops
Sea salt, freshly ground black pepper, to taste
Avocado oil spray
¼ cup (4 tablespoons)
unsalted butter
1 tablespoon freshly squeezed lemon juice
1 teaspoon minced garlic
¼ teaspoon red pepper flakes

1. If your scallops still have the adductor muscles attached, remove them. Pat the scallops dry with a paper towel.
2. Season the scallops with salt and pepper, then place them on a plate and refrigerate for 15 minutes.
3. Spray the air fryer basket with oil, and arrange the scallops in a single layer. Spray the top of the scallops with oil.
4. Set the air fryer to 350°F (180°C) and cook for 6 minutes. Flip the scallops and cook for 6 minutes more, until an instant-read thermometer reads 145° F (63ºC).
5. While the scallops cook, place the butter, lemon juice, garlic, and red pepper flakes in a small ramekin.
6. When the scallops have finished cooking, remove them from the air fryer. Place the ramekin in the air fryer and cook until the butter melts, about 3 minutes. Stir.

7. Toss the scallops with the warm butter and serve.

Per Serving
calories: 203 | fat: 12g | protein: 19g
carbs: 3g | net carbs: 3g | fiber: 0g

Dijon Shrimp with Romaine

Prep time: 10 minutes | Cook time: 4 to 6 minutes | Serves 4

12 ounces (340 g) fresh large shrimp, peeled and deveined
1 tablespoon plus 1 teaspoon freshly squeezed lemon juice, divided
4 tablespoons olive oil or avocado oil, divided
2 garlic cloves, minced, divided
¼ teaspoon sea salt, plus additional to season the marinade
¼ teaspoon freshly
ground black pepper, plus additional to season the marinade
⅓ cup sugar-free mayonnaise
2 tablespoons freshly grated Parmesan cheese
1 teaspoon Dijon mustard
1 tinned anchovy, mashed
12 ounces (340 g) romaine hearts, torn

1. Place the shrimp in a large bowl. Add 1 tablespoon of lemon juice, 1 tablespoon of olive oil, and 1 minced garlic clove. Season with salt and pepper. Toss well and refrigerate for 15 minutes.
2. While the shrimp marinates, make the dressing: In a blender, combine the mayonnaise, Parmesan cheese, Dijon mustard, the remaining 1 teaspoon of lemon juice, the anchovy, the remaining minced garlic clove, ¼ teaspoon of salt, and ¼ teaspoon of pepper. Process until smooth. With the blender running, slowly stream in the remaining 3 tablespoons of oil. Transfer the mixture to a jar; seal and refrigerate until ready to serve.
3. Remove the shrimp from its marinade and place it in the air fryer basket in a single layer. Set the air fryer to 400°F (205ºC) and cook for 2 minutes. Flip the shrimp and cook for 2 to 4 minutes more, until the flesh turns opaque.
4. Place the romaine in a large bowl and toss with the desired amount of dressing. Top with the shrimp and serve immediately.

Per Serving
calories: 329 | fat: 30g | protein: 16g
carbs: 4g | net carbs: 2g | fiber: 2g

Savory Shrimp with Parsley

Prep time: 5 minutes | Cook time: 8 to 10 minutes | Serves 4

1 pound (454 g) fresh large shrimp, peeled and deveined
1 tablespoon avocado oil
2 teaspoons minced garlic, divided
½ teaspoon red pepper flakes
Sea salt, freshly ground black pepper, to taste
2 tablespoons unsalted butter, melted
2 tablespoons chopped fresh parsley

1. Place the shrimp in a large bowl and toss with the avocado oil, 1 teaspoon of minced garlic, and red pepper flakes. Season with salt and pepper.
2. Set the air fryer to 350°F (180°C). Arrange the shrimp in a single layer in the air fryer basket, working in batches if necessary. Cook for 6 minutes. Flip the shrimp and cook for 2 to 4 minutes more, until the internal temperature of the shrimp reaches 120°F (49°C). (The time it takes to cook will depend on the size of the shrimp.)
3. While the shrimp are cooking, melt the butter in a small saucepan over medium heat and stir in the remaining 1 teaspoon of garlic.
4. Transfer the cooked shrimp to a large bowl, add the garlic butter, and toss well. Top with the parsley and serve warm.

Per Serving
calories: 220 | fat: 11g | protein: 28g
carbs: 2g | net carbs: 1g | fiber: 1g

Dijon Crab Cake

Prep time: 10 minutes | Cook time: 14 minutes | Serves 4

Avocado oil spray
⅓ cup red onion, diced
¼ cup red bell pepper, diced
8 ounces (227 g) lump crab meat, picked over for shells
3 tablespoons finely ground blanched almond flour
1 large egg, beaten
1 tablespoon sugar-free mayonnaise
(homemade, here, or store-bought)
2 teaspoons Dijon mustard
⅛ teaspoon cayenne pepper
Sea salt, freshly ground black pepper, to taste
Elevated Tartar Sauce, for serving
Lemon wedges, for serving

1. Spray an air fryer–friendly baking pan with oil. Put the onion and red bell pepper in the pan and give them a quick spray with oil. Place the pan in the air fryer basket. Set the air fryer to 400°F (205°C) and cook the vegetables for 7 minutes, until tender.
2. Transfer the vegetables to a large bowl. Add the crab meat, almond flour, egg, mayonnaise, mustard, and cayenne pepper and season with salt and pepper. Stir until the mixture is well combined.
3. Form the mixture into four 1-inch-thick cakes. Cover with plastic wrap and refrigerate for 1 hour.
4. Place the crab cakes in a single layer in the air fryer basket and spray them with oil.
5. Cook for 4 minutes. Flip the crab cakes and spray with more oil. Cook for 3 minutes more, until the internal temperature of the crab cakes reaches 155°F (68°C).
6. Serve with tartar sauce and a squeeze of fresh lemon juice.

Per Serving
calories: 121 | fat: 8g | protein: 11g
carbs: 3g | net carbs: 2g | fiber: 1g

Buttery Crab Legs with Lemon

Prep time: 3 minutes | Cook time: 7 minutes | Serves 2

1 cup water
2 pounds (907 g) crab legs, rinsed
4 tablespoons butter, melted
1 garlic clove, finely minced
½ lemon, juiced
4 lemon wedges

1. Pour water into Instant Pot and insert a steamer basket. Place the crab legs in the basket.
2. Lock the lid. Select the Steam mode and set the cooking time for 7 minutes at Low Pressure.
3. Once cooking is complete, do a quick pressure release. Carefully open the lid.
4. In a small bowl, stir together the butter and garlic.
5. Squeeze lemon juice into butter or over legs and crack legs open. Serve with the butter sauce and lemon wedges.

Per Serving
calories: 516 | fat: 22.9g | protein: 66.9g
carbs: 0.9g | net carbs: 0.8g | fiber: 0.1g

Coconut-Coated Tilapia

Prep time: 15 minutes | Cook time: 9 minutes | Serves 4

1-pound (454-g) tilapia fillet	paprika
½ cup coconut flour	1 teaspoon dried oregano
2 eggs, beaten	1 teaspoon avocado oil
½ teaspoon ground	

1. Cut the tilapia fillets into fingers and sprinkle with ground paprika and dried oregano.
2. Then dip the tilapia fingers in eggs and coat in the coconut flour.
3. Sprinkle fish fingers with avocado oil and cook in the air fryer at 370ºF (188ºC) for 9 minutes.

Per Serving
calories: 188 | fat: 5g | protein: 26g
carbs: 9g | net carbs: 4g | fiber: 5g

Old Bay Shrimp and Crab Stew

Prep time: 10 minutes | Cook time: 15 minutes | Serves 4

1 tablespoon coconut oil	seasoning
½ medium onion, diced	1 teaspoon salt
2 cloves garlic, minced	4 cups seafood stock
2 stalks celery, chopped	1 pound (454 g) lump crab meat
2 tablespoons butter	1 pound (454 g) shrimp, shelled, deveined, and chopped
1 bay leaf	
2 teaspoons Old Bay	¼ cup heavy cream

1. Set your Instant Pot to Sauté and heat the coconut oil.
2. Sauté the onion for 3 minutes or until translucent. Add garlic and sauté for 30 seconds more.
3. Add the remaining ingredients except the heavy cream to the Instant Pot.
4. Lock the lid. Select the Manual mode and set the cooking time for 10 minutes at Low Pressure.
5. Once cooking is complete, do a quick pressure release. Carefully open the lid.
6. Stir in the heavy cream and serve.

Per Serving
calories: 328 | fat: 15.6g | protein: 28.8g
carbs: 4.1g | net carbs: 3.3g | fiber: 0.8g

Rosemary Scallops

Prep time: 10 minutes | Cook time: 6 minutes | Serves 4

12 ounces (340 g) scallops	½ teaspoon Pink salt
1 tablespoon dried rosemary	1 tablespoon avocado oil

1. Sprinkle scallops with dried rosemary, Pink salt, and avocado oil.
2. Then put the scallops in the air fryer basket in one layer and cook at 400ºF (205ºC) for 6 minutes.

Per Serving
calories: 82 | fat: 1g | protein: 14g
carbs: 3g | net carbs: 2g | fiber: 1g

Lemon Scallops in Port Wine

Prep time: 10 minutes | Cook time: 5 minutes | Serves 5

1 tablespoon olive oil	1 teaspoon smoked paprika
1 brown onion, chopped	Sea salt and ground black pepper, to taste
2 garlic cloves, minced	2 tablespoons fresh lemon juice
½ cup port wine	
½ cup fish stock	½ cup cream cheese, at room temperature
1½ pounds (680 g) scallops, peeled and deveined	2 tablespoons chopped fresh basil, for garnish
1 ripe tomato, crushed	

1. Set your Instant Pot to Sauté and heat the olive oil.
2. Cook the onion and garlic until fragrant for 2 minutes.
3. Add the wine to deglaze the bottom. Add the scallops, fish stock, tomato, salt, black pepper, and paprika.
4. Lock the lid. Select the Manual mode and set the cooking time for 1 minute at Low Pressure.
5. When the timer beeps, perform a quick pressure release. Carefully remove the lid.
6. Drizzle fresh lemon juice over the scallops and top them with cream cheese. Cover and allow to sit in the residual heat for 3 to 5 minutes. Serve warm garnished with fresh basil leaves.

Per Serving
calories: 213 | fat: 10.6g | protein: 19.5g
carbs: 9.8g | net carbs: 8.8g | fiber: 1.0g

Lemon Salmon with Dill

Prep time: 2 minutes | Cook time: 7 minutes | Serves 2

2 (3-ounce / 85-g) salmon fillets
¼ teaspoon garlic powder
1 teaspoon salt
¼ teaspoon pepper
¼ teaspoon dried dill
½ lemon
1 cup water

1. Place each filet of salmon on a square of foil, skin-side down.
2. Season with garlic powder, salt, and pepper and squeeze the lemon juice over the fish.
3. Cut the lemon into four slices and place two on each filet. Close the foil packets by folding over edges.
4. Add the water to the Instant Pot and insert a trivet. Place the foil packets on the trivet.
5. Secure the lid. Select the Steam mode and set the cooking time for 7 minutes at Low Pressure.
6. Once cooking is complete, do a quick pressure release. Carefully open the lid.
7. Check the internal temperature with a meat thermometer to ensure the thickest part of the filets reached at least 145°F (63°C). Salmon should easily flake when fully cooked.
8. Serve immediately.

Per Serving
calories: 128 | fat: 4.9g | protein: 19.1g
carbs: 0.3g | net carbs: 0.2g | fiber: 0.1g

Grouper Fillets with Mushrooms

Prep time: 5 minutes | Cook time: 10 minutes | Serves 4

2 tablespoons butter
½ pound (227 g) smoked turkey sausage, casing removed
1 pound (454 g) cremini mushrooms, sliced
2 garlic cloves, minced
4 grouper fillets
½ cup dry white wine
Sea salt, to taste
½ teaspoon freshly cracked black peppercorns
1 tablespoon fresh lime juice
2 tablespoons chopped fresh cilantro

1. Set your Instant Pot to Sauté and melt the butter.
2. Add the sausage and cook until nicely browned on all sides. Remove the sausage and set aside.
3. Add the mushrooms and cook for about 3 minutes or until fragrant.
4. Add the garlic and continue to sauté for another 30 seconds.
5. Add the fish, wine, salt, and black peppercorns. Return the sausage to the Instant Pot.
6. Lock the lid. Select the Manual mode and set the cooking time for 3 minutes at Low Pressure.
7. When the timer beeps, perform a quick pressure release. Carefully remove the lid.
8. Drizzle with the lime juice and serve garnished with fresh cilantro.

Per Serving
calories: 409 | fat: 13.5g | protein: 61.9g
carbs: 8.7g | net carbs: 7.4g | fiber: 1.3g

Cayenne Shrimp Salad with Chili Mayo

Prep time: 5 minutes | Cook time: 7 minutes | Serves 2

1 pound (454 g) shrimp, peeled and deveined
½ teaspoon Old Bay seasoning
¼ teaspoon pepper
¼ teaspoon salt
⅛ teaspoon cayenne
⅛ teaspoon garlic powder
1 cup water
¼ cup mayonnaise
2 tablespoons chili paste

1. Toss shrimp in a 7-cup glass bowl with Old Bay seasoning, salt, pepper, cayenne, and garlic powder.
2. Pour the water into Instant Pot and insert the trivet. Place the bowl with shrimp on top.
3. Lock the lid. Select the Steam mode and set the cooking time for 7 minutes at Low Pressure.
4. Once cooking is complete, do a quick pressure release. Carefully open the lid.
5. Remove the bowl from the Instant Pot and drain water.
6. In a small bowl, stir together the mayo and chili paste. Add the shrimp and toss to coat. Serve immediately.

Per Serving
calories: 403 | fat: 24.7g | protein: 32.9g
carbs: 8.3g | net carbs: 8.2g | fiber: 0.1g

Stir-Fried Shrimp and Veggies

Prep time: 10 minutes | Cook time: 10 minutes | Serves 4

2 tablespoons coconut oil
1 pound (454 g) medium shrimp, shelled and deveined
2 cups broccoli florets
½ cup diced zucchini
½ cup button mushrooms
¼ cup coconut aminos
2 cloves garlic, minced
⅛ teaspoon red pepper flakes
2 cups cooked cauliflower rice

1. Set your Instant Pot to Sauté and heat the coconut oil.
2. Add shrimp and cook for 5 minutes or until pink. Remove and set aside in a bowl.
3. Add the broccoli florets, zucchini, and mushrooms, coconut aminos, garlic, and red pepper flakes to the Instant Pot. Stir-fry for 3 to 5 minutes until vegetables are softened. Return the shrimp to the pot. Stir well.
4. Divide the cauliflower rice into each bowl and top with a portion of stir-fry. Serve warm.

Per Serving
calories: 176 | fat: 7.9g | protein: 19.7g
carbs: 6.7g | net carbs: 3.4g | fiber: 2.3g

Pesto-Rubbed Salmon with Almonds

Prep time: 5 minutes | Cook time: 12 minutes | Serves 4

1 tablespoon butter
¼ cup sliced almonds
4 (3-ounce / 85-g) salmon fillets
½ cup pesto
¼ teaspoon pepper
½ teaspoon salt
1 cup water

1. Press the Sauté button on the Instant Pot and add the butter and almonds.
2. Sauté for 3 to 5 minutes until they start to soften. Remove and set aside.
3. Brush salmon fillets with pesto and season with salt and pepper.
4. Pour the water into Instant Pot and insert the trivet. Place the salmon fillets on the trivet.
5. Secure the lid. Select the Steam mode and set the cooking time for 7 minutes at High Pressure.
6. Once cooking is complete, do a quick pressure release. Carefully open the lid.
7. Serve the salmon with the almonds sprinkled on top.

Per Serving
calories: 186 | fat: 20.9g | protein: 21.6g
carbs: 4.3g | net carbs: 2.0g | fiber: 1.3g

Halibut, Clam and Bacon Chowder

Prep time: 10 minutes | Cook time: 15 minutes | Serves 6

¼ pound (113 g) meaty bacon, chopped
1 serrano pepper, minced
1 celery with leaves, diced
½ cup diced leeks
3 cups fish stock
½ cup Rose wine
1½ pounds (680 g) halibut fillets, cut into 2-inch pieces
10 ounces (283 g) clams, minced and juice reserved
2 garlic cloves, pressed
Sea salt and ground black pepper, to taste
2 sprigs fresh rosemary
2 sprigs fresh thyme
2 cups heavy cream
2 tablespoons chopped fresh chives

1. Press the Sauté button to heat the Instant Pot.
2. Cook the bacon for about 5 minutes until crisp, stirring occasionally. Remove the bacon and set aside.
3. Add the pepper, celery, and leeks and sauté for an additional 3 minutes or until softened.
4. Add the remaining ingredients except the heavy cream and chives to the Instant Pot and stir well.
5. Lock the lid. Select the Manual mode and set the cooking time for 7 minutes at Low Pressure.
6. When the timer beeps, perform a quick pressure release. Carefully remove the lid.
7. Stir in heavy cream. Press the Sauté button again and let it simmer until heated through.
8. Serve topped with the cooked bacon and fresh chives.

Per Serving
calories: 428 | fat: 32.9g | protein: 24.5g
carbs: 8.1g | net carbs: 7.6g | fiber: 0.5g

Creole Sea Scallops with Parsley

Prep time: 5 minutes | Cook time: 5 minutes | Serves 4

2 teaspoons butter
1½ pounds (680 g) sea scallops
2 garlic cloves, finely chopped
1 (1-inch) piece fresh ginger root, grated
⅔ cup fish stock

⅓ cup dry white wine
1 teaspoon Creole seasoning blend
Coarse sea salt and ground black pepper, to taste
2 tablespoons chopped fresh parsley

1. Set your Instant Pot to Sauté and melt the butter.
2. Cook the sea scallops until browned on all sides, about 2 minutes.
3. Stir in the garlic and ginger and continue sautéing for 1 minute more.
4. Add the remaining ingredients, except for the fresh parsley, into the Instant Pot.
5. Lock the lid. Select the Manual mode and set the cooking time for 1 minute at Low Pressure.
6. When the timer beeps, perform a quick pressure release. Carefully remove the lid.
7. Serve garnished with the fresh parsley.

Per Serving
calories: 149 | fat: 3.1g | protein: 21.7g
carbs: 7.1g | net carbs: 6.8g | fiber: 0.3g

Shrimp and Veggie Salad with Mustard

Prep time: 15 minutes | Cook time: 2 minutes | Serves 4

1 pound (454 g) shrimp, peeled and deveined
Juice of 1 fresh lemon
2 cloves garlic, minced
1 celery stalk, thinly sliced
Sea salt, to taste
½ teaspoon cayenne pepper

¼ teaspoon freshly ground black pepper
1 avocado, pitted and diced
1 cucumber, sliced
2 cups baby spinach
4 tablespoons extra-virgin olive oil
1 tablespoon Dijon mustard

1. Toss the shrimp and fresh lemon juice in the Instant Pot. Add enough water to cover the shrimp.
2. Lock the lid. Select the Manual mode and set the cooking time for 2 minutes at Low Pressure.

3. Once cooking is complete, do a quick pressure release. Carefully open the lid.
4. Allow the shrimp to cool completely. Toss the shrimp with the remaining ingredients and transfer to a salad bowl. Serve immediately.

Per Serving
calories: 332 | fat: 27.8g | protein: 25.2g
carbs: 7.8g | net carbs: 3.4g | fiber: 4.4g

Stir-Fred Shrimp and Asparagus

Prep time: 3 minutes | Cook time: 10 minutes | Serves 2

1 pound (454 g) shrimp, peeled and deveined
½ teaspoon salt
¼ teaspoon pepper
¼ teaspoon dried parsley
¼ teaspoon garlic

powder
6 asparagus spears, cut into bite-sized pieces
1 cup water
2 tablespoons butter
1 cup uncooked cauliflower rice

1. Sprinkle seasoning on shrimp and place in a steamer basket. Add the asparagus to the basket.
2. Pour water into Instant Pot and insert the steamer basket.
3. Lock the lid. Select the Steam mode and set the cooking time for 5 minutes at Low Pressure.
4. Once cooking is complete, do a quick pressure release. Carefully open the lid.
5. Remove steamer basket and pour water out of Instant Pot.
6. Press the Sauté button on the Instant Pot and melt the butter.
7. Add the cauliflower rice and cooked shrimp and asparagus. Stir-fry for 3 to 5 minutes until cauliflower is tender.
8. Serve warm.

Per Serving
calories: 286 | fat: 12.6g | protein: 33.3g
carbs: 6.2g | net carbs: 4.1g | fiber: 2.1g

Buttery Shrimp Scampi

Prep time: 10 minutes | Cook time: 10 minutes | Serves 4

4 tablespoons butter
2 teaspoons finely minced garlic
1 pound (454 g) shrimp, peeled and deveined
1 cup chicken broth
1 tablespoon lemon juice

½ teaspoon salt
¼ cup heavy cream
¼ teaspoon xanthan gum
1 tablespoon chopped fresh parsley
¼ teaspoon red pepper flakes

1. Press the Sauté button on the Instant Pot. Add butter and garlic to pot and sauté for 1 to 3 minutes until fragrant.
2. Add shrimp, broth, lemon juice, and salt to Instant Pot.
3. Lock the lid. Select the Manual mode and set the cooking time for 4 minutes at Low Pressure.
4. Once cooking is complete, do a quick pressure release. Carefully open the lid.
5. Stir in the heavy cream and xanthan gum. Serve garnished with parsley and red pepper flakes.

Per Serving
calories: 246 | fat: 22.6g | protein: 16.9g
carbs: 2.6g | net carbs: 2.3g | fiber: 0.3g

Cajun Shrimp and Crab Stew

Prep time: 10 minutes | Cook time: 5 minutes | Serves 4

2 pounds (907 g) crab legs
½ pound (227 g) large shrimp, shelled and deveined

½ pound (227 g) smoked sausage
2 cups seafood stock
1 tablespoon Cajun seasoning

1. Combine all the ingredients in the Instant Pot.
2. Lock the lid. Select the Steam mode and set the cooking time for 5 minutes at Low Pressure.
3. Once cooking is complete, do a quick pressure release. Carefully open the lid.
4. Serve warm.

Per Serving
calories: 246 | fat: 8.3g | protein: 32.7g
carbs: 5.1g | net carbs: 5.0g | fiber: 0.1g

King Crab Legs with Mushrooms

Prep time: 8 minutes | Cook time: 6 minutes | Serves 6

1 cup water
1½ pounds (680 g) king crab legs, halved
10 ounces (283 g) baby Bella mushrooms

½ stick butter, softened
2 garlic cloves, minced
1 lemon, sliced

1. Pour the water into the Instant Pot and insert a steamer basket. Place the crab legs in the basket.
2. Lock the lid. Select the Manual mode and set the cooking time for 3 minutes at Low Pressure.
3. When the timer beeps, perform a quick pressure release. Carefully remove the lid.
4. Wipe down the Instant Pot with a damp cloth.
5. Set your Instant Pot to Sauté and melt the butter. Cook baby Bella mushrooms with minced garlic for 2 to 3 minutes.
6. Spoon the mushrooms sauce over prepared king crab legs and serve with lemon slices.

Per Serving
calories: 179 | fat: 8.8g | protein: 22.7g
carbs: 2.2g | net carbs: 1.7g | fiber: 0.5g

Steamed Clams with Butter

Prep time: 5 minutes | Cook time: 5 minutes | Serves 4

2 pounds (907 g) clams
1 cup seafood stock

4 tablespoons butter, melted

1. Combine the clams and seafood stock in the Instant Pot.
2. Secure the lid. Select the Steam mode and set the cooking time for 5 minutes at Low Pressure.
3. Once cooking is complete, do a quick pressure release. Carefully open the lid.
4. Serve topped with the melted butter.

Per Serving
calories: 156 | fat: 11.6g | protein: 8.9g
carbs: 2.0g | net carbs: 1.9g | fiber: 0.1g

Chapter 13 Meats

Cumin Short Ribs in Red Wine

Prep time: 20 minutes | Cook time: 10 minutes | Serves 4

1½ pounds (680g) short ribs
1 cup red wine
1 lemon, juiced
1 teaspoon fresh ginger, grated
1 teaspoon salt
1 teaspoon black pepper

1 teaspoon paprika
1 teaspoon chipotle chili powder
1 cup keto tomato paste
1 teaspoon garlic powder
1 teaspoon cumin

1. In a ceramic bowl, place the beef ribs, wine, lemon juice, ginger, salt, black pepper, paprika, and chipotle chili powder. Cover and let it marinate for 3 hours in the refrigerator.
2. Discard the marinade and add the short ribs to the Air Fryer basket. Cook in the preheated Air fry at 380ºF (193ºC) for 10 minutes, turning them over halfway through the cooking time.
3. In the meantime, heat the saucepan over medium heat; add the reserved marinade and stir in the tomato paste, garlic powder, and cumin. Cook until the sauce has thickened slightly.
4. Pour the sauce over the warm ribs and serve immediately. Bon appétit!

Per Serving
calories: 397 | fat: 15g | protein: 35g
carbs: 5g | net carbs: 4g | fiber: 1g

Peppery Beef Parboiled Sausage

Prep time: 35 minutes | Cook time: 30 minutes | Serves 4

2 teaspoons olive oil
2 bell peppers, sliced
1 green bell pepper, sliced
1 serrano pepper, sliced
1 shallot, sliced
Sea salt and pepper, to taste
½ teaspoon dried

thyme
1 teaspoon dried rosemary
½ teaspoon mustard seeds
1 teaspoon fennel seeds
2 pounds (907 g) thin beef parboiled sausage

1. Brush the sides and bottom of the cooking basket with 1 teaspoon of olive oil. Add the peppers and shallot to the cooking basket.
2. Toss them with the spices and cook at 390ºF (199ºC) for 15 minutes, shaking the basket occasionally. Reserve.
3. Turn the temperature to 380ºF (193ºC)
4. Then, add the remaining 1 teaspoon of oil. Once hot, add the sausage and cook in the preheated Air Frye for 15 minutes, flipping them halfway through the cooking time.
5. Serve with reserved pepper mixture. Bon appétit!

Per Serving
calories: 563 | fat: 41g | protein: 35g
carbs: 11g | net carbs: 10g | fiber: 1g

Chuck Kebab with Tahini Sauce

Prep time: 30 minutes | Cook time: 25 minutes | Serves 4

½ cup leeks, chopped
2 garlic cloves, smashed
2 pounds (907 g) ground chuck
Salt, to taste
¼ teaspoon ground black pepper, or more to taste
1 teaspoon cayenne pepper
½ teaspoon ground

sumac
3 saffron threads
2 tablespoons loosely packed fresh continental parsley leaves
4 tablespoons tahini sauce
4 ounces (113 g) baby arugula
1 tomato, cut into slices

1. In a bowl, mix the chopped leeks, garlic, ground chuck, and spices; knead with your hands until everything is well incorporated.
2. Now, mound the beef mixture around a wooden skewer into a pointed-ended sausage.
3. Cook in the preheated Air Fryer at 360ºF (182ºC) for 25 minutes.
4. Serve your kebab with the tahini sauce, baby arugula and tomato. Enjoy!

Per Serving
calories: 354 | fat: 15g | protein: 49g
carbs: 6g | net carbs: 4g | fiber: 2g

Pork Bacon with Mixed Greens

Prep time: 10 minutes | Cook time: 7 minutes | Serves 2

7 ounces (198 g) mixed greens
8 thick slices pork bacon
2 shallots, peeled and diced
Nonstick cooking spray

1. Begin by preheating the air fryer to 345ºF (174ºC).
2. Now, add the shallot and bacon to the Air Fryer cooking basket; set the timer for 2 minutes. Spritz with a nonstick cooking spray.
3. After that, pause the Air Fryer; throw in the mixed greens; give it a good stir and cook an additional 5 minutes. Serve warm.

Per Serving
calories: 259 | fat: 16g | protein: 19g
carbs: 10g | net carbs: 5g | fiber: 5g

Italian Pork Loin in Red Wine

Prep time: 50 minutes | Cook time: 16 minutes | Serves 3

1 teaspoon Celtic sea salt
½ teaspoon black pepper, freshly cracked
¼ cup red wine
2 tablespoons mustard
2 garlic cloves, minced
1 pound (454 g) pork top loin
1 tablespoon Italian herb seasoning blend

1. In a ceramic bowl, mix the salt, black pepper, red wine, mustard, and garlic. Add the pork top loin and let it marinate at least 30 minutes.
2. Spritz the sides and bottom of the cooking basket with a nonstick cooking spray.
3. Place the pork top loin in the basket; sprinkle with the Italian herb seasoning blend.
4. Cook the pork tenderloin at 370ºF (188ºC) for 10 minutes. Flip halfway through, spraying with cooking oil and cook for 5 to 6 minutes more. Serve immediately.

Per Serving
calories: 300 | fat: 9g | protein: 34g
carbs: 2g | net carbs: 1g | fiber: 1g

Paprika Pork Sausage Meatball

Prep time: 20 minutes | Cook time: 10 minutes | Serves 4

1 pound (454 g) pork sausage meat
1 shallot, finely chopped
2 garlic cloves, finely minced
½ teaspoon fine sea salt
¼ teaspoon ground
black pepper, or more to taste
¾ teaspoon paprika
½ cup Parmesan cheese, preferably freshly grated
½ jar no-sugar-added marinara sauce

1. Mix all of the above ingredients, except the marinara sauce, in a large-sized dish, until everything is well incorporated.
2. Shape into meatballs. Air-fry them at 360ºF (182ºC) for 10 minutes; pause the Air Fryer, shake them up and cook for additional 6 minutes or until the balls are no longer pink in the middle.
3. Meanwhile, heat the marinara sauce over a medium flame. Serve the pork sausage meatballs with marinara sauce. Bon appétit!

Per Serving
calories: 409 | fat: 33g | protein: 17g
carbs: 7g | net carbs: 6g | fiber: 1g

Coconut Lamb Sirloin Masala

Prep time: 10 minutes | Cook time: 25 minutes | Serves 3

12 ounces (340 g) lamb sirloin, sliced
1 tablespoon garam masala
1 tablespoon lemon juice
1 tablespoon olive oil
¼ cup coconut cream

1. Sprinkle the sliced lamb sirloin with garam masala, lemon juice, olive oil, and coconut cream in a large bowl. Toss to mix well.
2. Transfer the mixture in the Instant Pot. Cook on Sauté mode for 25 minutes. Flip the lamb for every 5 minutes.
3. When cooking is complete, allow to cool for 10 minutes, then serve warm.

Per Serving
calories: 319 | fat: 19.9g | protein: 32.7g
carbs: 1.2g | net carbs: 0.7g | fiber: 0.5g

Ginger-Garlic Flank Steak

Prep time: 10 minutes | Cook time: 45 minutes | Serves 4

1 tablespoon coconut aminos
1 teaspoon erythritol
¼ teaspoon garlic, minced
1 teaspoon sesame oil
¼ teaspoon ground ginger
1 pound (454 g) flank steak, sliced
¼ cup water

1. In the mixing bowl mix the coconut aminos, erythritol, minced garlic, and ground ginger. Add the flank steak. Toss to coat well.
2. Heat the sesame oil on Sauté mode for 1 minute and add the sliced flank.
3. Cook it for 10 minutes. Flip constantly. Pour in the water and close the lid.
4. Select Manual mode and set cooking time for 35 minutes on High Pressure.
5. When timer beeps, use a natural pressure release for 15 minutes, then release any remaining pressure. Open the lid.
6. Serve warm.

Per Serving
calories: 234 | fat: 10.6g | protein: 31.6g
carbs: 0.9g | net carbs: 0.9g | fiber: 0g

Pork Sausages Pot with Mushrooms

Prep time: 5 minutes | Cook time: 8 minutes | Serves 8

8 pork sausages, casing removed
1 cup cremini mushrooms, chopped
1 ripe tomato, chopped
½ yellow onion, chopped
2 garlic cloves, minced
½ teaspoon dried basil
½ teaspoon dried oregano
½ teaspoon dried rosemary
1 cup chicken broth

1. Add all ingredients to the Instant Pot.
2. Secure the lid. Choose the Manual mode and set cooking time for 8 minutes on High pressure.
3. Once cooking is complete, use a quick pressure release. Carefully remove the lid.
4. Serve immediately.

Per Serving
calories: 410 | fat: 36.2g | protein: 17.3g
carbs: 2.5g | net carbs: 0.9g | fiber: 1.6g

Balsamic London Broil with Mustard

Prep time: 30 minutes | Cook time: 8 to 10 minutes | Serves 8

2 pounds (907 g) London broil
3 large garlic cloves, minced
3 tablespoons balsamic vinegar
3 tablespoons whole-
grain mustard
2 tablespoons olive oil
Sea salt and ground black pepper, to taste
½ teaspoon dried hot red pepper flakes

1. Score both sides of the cleaned London broil.
2. Thoroughly combine the remaining ingredients; massage this mixture into the meat to coat it on all sides. Let it marinate for at least 3 hours.
3. Set the Air Fryer to cook at 400ºF (205ºC); Then cook the London broil for 15 minutes. Flip it over and cook another 10 to 12 minutes. Bon appétit!

Per Serving
calories: 257 | fat: 9g | protein: 41g
carbs: 1g | net carbs: 0g | fiber: 1g

Beef Steaks with Caraway Seeds

Prep time: 16 minutes | Cook time: 10 minutes | Serves 4

$1/3$ cup almond flour
2 eggs
2 teaspoons caraway seeds
4 beef steaks
2 teaspoons garlic
powder
1 tablespoon melted butter
Fine sea salt and cayenne pepper, to taste

1. Generously coat steaks with garlic powder, caraway seeds, salt, and cayenne pepper.
2. In a mixing dish, thoroughly combine melted butter with seasoned crumbs. In another bowl, beat the eggs until they're well whisked.
3. First, coat steaks with the beaten egg; then, coat beef steaks with the buttered crumb mixture.
4. Place the steaks in the Air Fryer cooking basket; cook for 10 minutes at 355ºF (181ºC). Bon appétit!

Per Serving
calories: 474 | fat: 22g | protein: 55g
carbs: 9g | net carbs: 8g | fiber: 1g

Vinegary Skirt Steak with Dill

Prep time: 20 minutes | Cook time: 12 minutes | Serves 5

2 pounds (907 g) skirt steak
2 tablespoons keto tomato paste
1 tablespoon olive oil
1 tablespoon coconut aminos
¼ cup rice vinegar
1 tablespoon fish sauce
Sea salt, to taste
½ teaspoon dried dill
½ teaspoon dried rosemary
¼ teaspoon black pepper, freshly cracked

1. Place all ingredients in a large ceramic dish; let it marinate for 3 hours in your refrigerator.
2. Coat the sides and bottom of the Air Fryer with cooking spray.
3. Add your steak to the cooking basket; reserve the marinade. Cook the skirt steak in the preheated Air Fryer at 400ºF (205ºC) for 12 minutes, turning over a couple of times, basting with the reserved marinade.
4. Bon appétit!

Per Serving
calories: 401 | fat: 21g | protein: 51g
carbs: 2g | net carbs: 1g | fiber: 1g

Beef Flank Steak with Sage

Prep time: 13 minutes | Cook time: 7 minutes | Serves 2

1/3 cup sour cream
½ cup green onion, chopped
1 tablespoon mayonnaise
3 cloves garlic, smashed
1 pound (454 g) beef flank steak, trimmed and cubed
2 tablespoons fresh sage, minced
½ teaspoon salt
1/3 teaspoon black pepper, or to taste

1. Season your meat with salt and pepper; arrange beef cubes on the bottom of a baking dish that fits in your air fryer.
2. Stir in green onions and garlic; air-fry for about 7 minutes at 385ºF (196ºC).
3. Once your beef starts to tender, add the cream, mayonnaise, and sage; air-fry an additional 8 minutes. Bon appétit!

Per Serving
calories: 428 | fat: 20g | protein: 50g
carbs: 7g | net carbs: 6g | fiber: 1g

Vinegary Lamb Shoulder with Turnip

Prep time: 25 minutes | Cook time: 50 minutes | Serves 6

¼ cup apple cider vinegar
½ cup chicken broth
1 tablespoon lemon juice
½ teaspoon lemon zest
½ teaspoon fresh thyme
1 pound (454 g) lamb shoulder, chopped
½ cup turnip, chopped

1. In the mixing bowl, mix the apple cider vinegar, chicken broth, lemon juice, lemon zest, and thyme.
2. Put the lamb shoulder in the Instant Pot. Add the lemon juice mixture and turnip.
3. Close the lid. Select Manual mode and set cooking time for 50 minutes on High Pressure.
4. When the time is over, use a natural pressure release for 20 minutes, then release any remaining pressure. Open the lid.
5. Serve warm.

Per Serving
calories: 150 | fat: 5.7g | protein: 21.8g
carbs: 1.0g | net carbs: 0.8g | fiber: 0.2g

Cayenne Beef Steaks

Prep time: 20 minutes | Cook time: 20 minutes | Serves 4

2 tablespoons coconut aminos
3 heaping tablespoons fresh chives
2 tablespoons olive oil
3 tablespoons dry white wine
4 small-sized beef steaks
2 teaspoons smoked cayenne pepper
½ teaspoon dried basil
½ teaspoon dried rosemary
1 teaspoon freshly ground black pepper
1 teaspoon sea salt, or more to taste

1. Firstly, coat the steaks with the cayenne pepper, black pepper, salt, basil, and rosemary.
2. Drizzle the steaks with olive oil, white wine, and coconut aminos.
3. Finally, roast in an Air Fryer basket for 20 minutes at 335ºF (168ºC). Serve garnished with fresh chives. Bon appétit!

Per Serving
calories: 445 | fat: 23g | protein: 51g
carbs: 11g | net carbs: 10g | fiber: 1g

Dijon Beef Burger

Prep time: 20 minutes | Cook time: 12 minutes | Serves 4

1¼ pounds (567g) lean ground beef
1 tablespoon coconut aminos
1 teaspoon Dijon mustard
A few dashes of liquid smoke
1 teaspoon shallot powder
1 clove garlic, minced
½ teaspoon cumin
powder
¼ cup scallions, minced
1/3 teaspoon sea salt flakes
1/3 teaspoon freshly cracked mixed peppercorns
1 teaspoon celery seeds
1 teaspoon parsley flakes

1. Mix all of the above ingredients in a bowl; knead until everything is well incorporated.
2. Shape the mixture into four patties. Next, make a shallow dip in the center of each patty to prevent them puffing up during air-frying.
3. Spritz the patties on all sides using a non-stick cooking spray. Cook approximately 12 minutes at 360ºF (182ºC).
4. Check for doneness – an instant read thermometer should read 160ºF (71ºC). Bon appétit!

Per Serving
calories: 425 | fat: 25g | protein: 38g
carbs: 10g | net carbs: 8g | fiber: 2g

Lime Pork Loin Roast with Thyme

Prep time: 55 minutes | Cook time: 55 minutes | Serves 6

1½ pounds (680g) boneless pork loin roast, washed
1 teaspoon mustard seeds
1 teaspoon garlic powder
1 teaspoon porcini powder
1 teaspoon shallot
powder
¾ teaspoon sea salt flakes
1 teaspoon red pepper flakes, crushed
2 dried sprigs thyme, crushed
2 tablespoons lime juice

1. Firstly, score the meat using a small knife; make sure to not cut too deep.
2. In a small-sized mixing dish, combine all seasonings in the order listed above; mix to combine well.

3. Massage the spice mix into the pork meat to evenly distribute. Drizzle with lemon juice.
4. Then, set your Air Fryer to cook at 360ºF (182ºC). Place the pork in the Air Fryer basket; roast for 25 to 30 minutes. Pause the machine, check for doneness and cook for 25 minutes more.

Per Serving
calories: 278 | fat: 16g | protein: 31g
carbs: 2g | net carbs: 1g | fiber: 1g

Smoky Beef Steak with Brussels Sprouts

Prep time: 30 minutes | Cook time: 25 minutes | Serves 4

1 pound (454 g) beef chuck shoulder steak
2 tablespoons olive oil
1 tablespoon red wine vinegar
1 teaspoon fine sea salt
½ teaspoon ground black pepper
1 teaspoon smoked paprika
1 teaspoon onion powder
½ teaspoon garlic powder
½ pound (227g) Brussels sprouts, cleaned and halved
½ teaspoon fennel seeds
1 teaspoon dried basil
1 teaspoon dried sage

1. Firstly, marinate the beef with olive oil, wine vinegar, salt, black pepper, paprika, onion powder, and garlic powder. Rub the marinade into the meat and let it stay at least for 3 hours.
2. Air fry at 390ºF (199ºC) for 10 minutes. Pause the machine and add the prepared Brussels sprouts; sprinkle them with fennel seeds, basil, and sage.
3. Turn the machine to 380ºF (193ºC); press the power button and cook for 5 more minutes. Pause the machine, stir and cook for further 10 minutes.
4. Next, remove the meat from the cooking basket and cook the vegetables a few minutes more if needed and according to your taste. Serve with your favorite mayo sauce.

Per Serving
calories: 272 | fat: 14g | protein: 26g
carbs: 6g | net carbs: 3g | fiber: 3g

Beef Sausage with Bell Peppers

Prep time: 35 minutes | Cook time: 20 minutes | Serves 4

4 bell peppers
2 tablespoons olive oil
2 medium-sized tomatoes, halved
4 spring onions
4 beef sausages
1 tablespoon mustard

1. Start by preheating your Air Fryer to 400°F (205°C).
2. Add the bell peppers to the cooking basket. Drizzle 1 tablespoon of olive oil all over the bell peppers.
3. Cook for 5 minutes. Turn the temperature down to 350°F (180°C). Add the tomatoes and spring onions to the cooking basket and cook an additional 10 minutes.
4. Reserve your vegetables.
5. Then, add the sausages to the cooking basket. Drizzle with the remaining tablespoon of olive oil.
6. Cook in the preheated Air Fryer at 380°F (193°C) for 15 minutes, flipping them halfway through the cooking time.
7. Serve sausages with the air-fried vegetables and mustard; serve.

Per Serving
calories: 490 | fat: 42g | protein: 19g
carbs: 9g | net carbs: 7g | fiber: 2g

Smoky Loin Steak with Rosemary Mayo

Prep time: 20 minutes | Cook time: 15 minutes | Serves 4

1 cup mayonnaise
1 tablespoon fresh rosemary, finely chopped
2 tablespoons Worcestershire sauce
Sea salt, to taste
½ teaspoon ground
black pepper
1 teaspoon smoked paprika
1 teaspoon garlic, minced
1½ pounds (680g) short loin steak

1. Combine the mayonnaise, rosemary, Worcestershire sauce, salt, pepper, paprika, and garlic; mix to combine well.
2. Now, brush the mayonnaise mixture over both sides of the steak. Lower the steak onto the grill pan.
3. Grill in the preheated Air Fryer at 390°F (199°C) for 8 minutes. Turn the steaks over and grill an additional 7 minutes.

4. Check for doneness with a meat thermometer. Serve warm and enjoy!

Per Serving
calories: 620 | fat: 50g | protein: 40g
carbs: 3g | net carbs: 2g | fiber: 1g

Beef and Veggie Salad

Prep time: 55 minutes | Cook time: 35 minutes | Serves 6

2 tablespoons Shoyu sauce
1 tablespoon champagne vinegar
⅓ cup dry white wine
1 cup beef broth
1 teaspoon finely grated fresh ginger
1 tablespoon stone-ground mustard
1 teaspoon celery seeds
1½ pounds (680 g) beef rump steak
2 cucumbers, thinly sliced
1 cup cherry tomatoes, halved
1 cup green onions, chopped
1 bunch fresh mint, leaves picked
1 bunch fresh coriander, leaves picked
2 tablespoons fresh chives, chopped
2 tablespoons fresh lemon juice
2 tablespoons extra-virgin olive oil

1. In a mixing dish, combine Shoyu sauce, the vinegar, white wine, broth, fresh ginger, mustard, and celery seeds.
2. Add the beef steak and allow to marinate for at least 40 minutes in the refrigerator.
3. Add the beef steak and marinade to the Instant Pot. Add enough water to cover the beef.
4. Secure the lid. Choose Meat/Stew mode and set cooking time for 35 minutes on High Pressure.
5. Once cooking is complete, use a natural pressure release for 15 minutes, then release any remaining pressure. Carefully remove the lid.
6. Allow the beef to cool completely. Slice into strips and transfer to a large bowl.
7. Add the vegetables, mint, coriander, and fresh chives. Toss to combine.
8. Drizzle with lemon juice and olive oil. Toss to combine and serve chilled.

Per Serving
calories: 346 | fat: 24.8g | protein: 24.2g
carbs: 5.7g | net carbs: 4.1g | fiber: 1.6g

Parmesan Filet Mignon

Prep time: 20 minutes | Cook time: 13 minutes | Serves 4

1 pound (454 g) filet mignon
Sea salt and ground black pepper, to taste
½ teaspoon cayenne pepper
1 teaspoon dried basil
1 teaspoon dried rosemary
1 teaspoon dried thyme
1 tablespoon sesame oil
1 small-sized egg, well-whisked
½ cup Parmesan cheese, grated

1. Season the filet mignon with salt, black pepper, cayenne pepper, basil, rosemary, and thyme. Brush with sesame oil.
2. Put the egg in a shallow plate. Now, place the Parmesan cheese in another plate.
3. Coat the filet mignon with the egg; then, lay it into the Parmesan cheese. Set your Air Fryer to cook at 360ºF (182ºC).
4. Cook for 10 to 13 minutes or until golden. Serve with mixed salad leaves and enjoy!

Per Serving
calories: 315 | fat: 20g | protein: 30g
carbs: 4g | net carbs: 3g | fiber: 1g

Lamb Chops with Lime-Mint Marinade

Prep time: 5 minutes | Cook time: 5 minutes | Serves 2

4 (1-inch-thick) lamb chops
Sprigs of fresh mint, for garnish (optional)
Lime slices, for serving (optional)
Marinade:
2 teaspoons grated lime zest
½ cup lime juice
¼ cup avocado oil
¼ cup chopped fresh mint leaves
4 cloves garlic, roughly chopped
2 teaspoons fine sea salt
½ teaspoon ground black pepper

1. Make the marinade: Place all the ingredients for the marinade in a food processor or blender and purée until mostly smooth with a few small chunks. Transfer half of the marinade to a shallow dish and set the other half aside for serving. Add the lamb to the shallow dish, cover, and place in the refrigerator to marinate for at least 2 hours or overnight.

2. Spray the air fryer basket with avocado oil. Preheat the air fryer to 390°F (199°C).
3. Remove the chops from the marinade and place them in the air fryer basket. Cook for 5 minutes, or until the internal temperature reaches 145°F for medium doneness.
4. Allow the chops to rest for 10 minutes before serving with the rest of the marinade as a sauce. Garnish with fresh mint leaves and serve with lime slices, if desired. Best served fresh.

Per Serving
calories: 692 | fat: 53g | protein: 48g
carbs: 2g | net carbs: 1g | fiber: 1g

Pork Roast with Avocado Mayo

Prep time: 15 minutes | Cook time: 33 minutes | Serves 6

Pork Roast:
1 tablespoon butter
2 pounds (907 g) pork roast
1 cup chicken stock
1 celery rib, chopped
½ cup shallots, chopped
1 tablespoon fish sauce
1 tablespoon coconut aminos
¼ teaspoon ground black pepper
Sea salt, to taste
Avocado Mayo:
½ avocado, pitted and peeled
⅓ cup mayonnaise
1 teaspoon lemon juice
2 garlic cloves, pressed

1. Press the Sauté button to heat up the Instant Pot. Melt the butter and brown pork roast for 3 minutes.
2. Add the pork roast, chicken stock, celery, shallots, fish, sauce, coconut aminos, black pepper, and sea salt to the Instant Pot.
3. Secure the lid. Choose the Manual mode and set cooking time for 30 minutes on High pressure.
4. Once cooking is complete, use a natural pressure release for 15 minutes, then release any remaining pressure. Carefully remove the lid.
5. In the meantime, mix all the ingredients for the mayonnaise in the food processor. Pulse to combine well.
6. Cut pork roast into slices and serve with avocado mayo on the side.

Per Serving
calories: 390 | fat: 22.4g | protein: 42.1g
carbs: 3.0g | net carbs: 0.7g | fiber: 2.3g

Chili Lamb Rack with Pesto

Prep time: 15 minutes | Cook time: 45 minutes | Serves 4

1 pound (454 g) lamb rack
2 tablespoons pesto sauce
1 teaspoon chili powder
1 tablespoon coconut oil
1 cup water

1. Rub the lamb rack with pesto sauce and chili powder. Let sit for 15 minutes to marinate.
2. Heat the coconut oil in the Instant Pot on Sauté mode for 3 minutes.
3. Put the marinated lamb in the hot oil and cook on Sauté mode for 4 minutes on each side. Pour in the water.
4. Close the lid. Select Manual mode and set cooking time for 45 minutes on High Pressure.
5. When timer beeps, use a quick pressure release. Open the lid.
6. Serve immediately.

Per Serving
calories: 256 | fat: 16.8g | protein: 23.9g
carbs: 0.9g | net carbs: 0.5g | fiber: 0.4g

Cheese-Stuffed Pork Meatballs

Prep time: 10 minutes | Cook time: 6 minutes | Serves 5

1½ cups water
1 pound (454 g) ground pork
2 eggs, beaten
1 tablespoon fresh parsley, minced
2 tablespoons green onions, minced
¼ cup heavy cream
¼ teaspoon dried thyme
2 cloves garlic, minced
½ teaspoon dried marjoram
1 teaspoon kosher salt
½ teaspoon ground black pepper
10 (1-inch) cubes provolone cheese

1. Add the water in the Instant Pot and place in the trivet.
2. Combine all ingredients, except the cubes of provolone cheese, in a mixing bowl.
3. Shape the mixture into 10 patties with oiled hands. Place a cube of provolone cheese in the center of each patty, wrap the meat around the cheese, and roll into a ball.

4. Arrange the meatballs in the steamer basket. Place the basket over the trivet.
5. Secure the lid. Choose the Manual mode and set cooking time for 6 minutes at High pressure.
6. Once cooking is complete, use a quick pressure release. Carefully remove the lid.
7. Serve immediately.

Per Serving
calories: 440 | fat: 31.9g | protein: 34.7g
carbs: 2.1g | net carbs: 0.8g | fiber: 1.3g

Pork and Green Salad

Prep time: 10 minutes | Cook time: 30 minutes | Serves 4

1 pound (454 g) pork loin roast
½ cup chicken broth
½ cup water
½ head cabbage, shredded
1 cup baby spinach
1 cup arugula
2 celery with leaves, chopped
4 spring onions, chopped
1 red chili, deseeded and finely chopped
1 teaspoon keto-friendly Thai fish sauce
2 teaspoons coconut aminos
2 teaspoons each sesame oil
Juice of 1 lemon

1. Add pork loin roast, broth and water to the Instant Pot greased with cooking spray.
2. Secure the lid. Choose the Meat/Stew mode and set cooking time for 30 minutes at High pressure.
3. Once cooking is complete, use a natural pressure release for 15 minutes, the release any remaining pressure. Carefully remove the lid.
4. Allow the pork loin roast to cool completely. Shred the meat and transfer to a salad bowl.
5. Add the cabbage, spinach, arugula, celery, spring onions, and chili.
6. Make the dressing by mixing the Thai fish sauce, coconut aminos, sesame oil, and lemon juice. Whisk to combine well and dress the salad.
7. Serve chilled.

Per Serving
calories: 279 | fat: 12.7g | protein: 32.5g
carbs: 8.5g | net carbs: 3.9g | fiber: 4.7g

Classic Lamb Rostelle

Prep time: 20 minutes | Cook time: 30 minutes | Serves 4

1 pound (454 g) lamb loin, slice into strips	black pepper
	1 teaspoon olive oil
½ teaspoon apple cider vinegar	½ teaspoon salt
	1 cup water, for cooking
1 teaspoon ground	

1. Combine the apple cider vinegar, ground black pepper, olive oil, and salt in a bowl. Stir to mix well.
2. Put the lamb strips in the bowl and toss to coat well.
3. Run the lamb strips through four skewers and put in a baking pan.
4. Pour water in the Instant Pot and then insert the trivet.
5. Put the baking pan on the trivet. Close the lid.
6. Select Manual mode and set cooking time for 30 minutes on High Pressure.
7. When timer beeps, use a natural pressure release for 10 minutes, then release any remaining pressure. Open the lid.
8. Serve immediately.

Per Serving
calories: 241 | fat: 12.3g | protein: 30.2g
carbs: 0.4g | net carbs: 0.3g | fiber: 0.1g

Mustard Pork Tenderloin with Ricotta

Prep time: 25 minutes | Cook time: 22 minutes | Serves 4

2 tablespoons olive oil	¼ teaspoon chili powder
2 pounds (907 g) pork tenderloin, cut into serving-size pieces	1 teaspoon dried marjoram
1 teaspoon coarse sea salt	1 tablespoon mustard
	1 cup Ricotta cheese
½ teaspoon freshly ground pepper	1½ cups chicken broth

1. Start by preheating your Air Fryer to 350°F (180°C).
2. Heat the olive oil in a pan over medium-high heat. Once hot, cook the pork for 6 to 7 minutes, flipping it to ensure even cooking.
3. Arrange the pork in a lightly greased casserole dish. Season with salt, black pepper, chili powder, and marjoram.
4. In a mixing dish, thoroughly combine the mustard, cheese, and chicken broth. Pour the mixture over the pork chops in the casserole dish.
5. Bake for another 15 minutes or until bubbly and heated through. Bon appétit!

Per Serving
calories: 433 | fat: 20g | protein: 56g
carbs: 3g | net carbs: 2g | fiber: 1g

Pork Sloppy Joes

Prep time: 15 minutes | Cook time: 30 minutes | Serves 4

Sloppy Joes:

1 tablespoon olive oil	1 tablespoon coconut aminos
1 pound (454 g) lean ground pork	1 teaspoon stone ground mustard
1 tomato, puréed	1 cup vegetable broth
1 cloves garlic, minced	Sea salt and ground black pepper, to taste
½ yellow onion, chopped	

Oopsies:

1 eggs, separated yolks and whites	cheese
¼ teaspoon sea salt	¼ teaspoon baking powder
1 ounce (28 g) cream	

1. Press the Sauté button to heat up the Instant Pot. Heat the oil until sizzling. Brown the ground pork for 3 minutes, crumbling with a fork.
2. Add the remaining ingredients for Sloppy Joes and stir to combine well.
3. Secure the lid. Choose the Manual mode and set cooking time for 5 minutes on High pressure.
4. Once cooking is complete, use a quick pressure release. Carefully remove the lid.
5. To make the oopsies: beat the egg whites with salt until firm peaks form.
6. In another bowl, combine the egg yolks with cream cheese. Add the baking powder and stir well.
7. Fold the egg white mixture into the egg yolk mixture. Divide the mixture into 6 oopsies and transfer them to a baking sheet.
8. Bake in the preheated oven at 300°F (150°C) for about 23 minutes. Serve Sloppy Joes between 2 oopsies.

Per Serving
calories: 524 | fat: 45.0g | protein: 27.8g
carbs: 5.5g | net carbs: 1.9g | fiber: 3.6g

Lamb Kofta Curry with Scallions

Prep time: 15 minutes | Cook time: 20 minutes | Serves 4

1 pound (454 g) ground lamb	1 tablespoon dried cilantro
4 ounces (113 g) scallions, chopped	1 tablespoon coconut oil
1 tablespoon curry powder, divided	1 cup chicken broth
½ teaspoon chili flakes	⅓ cup coconut cream

1. In a mixing bowl, mix the ground lamb, scallions, and ½ tablespoon of curry powder.
2. Add chili flakes and dried cilantro. Stir the mixture until homogenous and shape the mixture into medium size koftas (meatballs).
3. Heat the coconut oil in the Instant Pot on Sauté mode until melted.
4. Put the koftas in the hot oil and cook for 2 minutes on each side.
5. Meanwhile, mix the chicken broth, coconut cream and remaining curry powder in a small bowl.
6. Pour the mixture over the koftas.
7. Select Manual mode and set timer for 12 minutes on High Pressure.
8. When timer beeps, use a natural pressure release for 10 minutes, then release any remaining pressure. Open the lid.
9. Serve warm.

Per Serving
calories: 310 | fat: 17.1g | protein: 34.2g
carbs: 4.4g | net carbs: 2.7g | fiber: 1.7g

Balsamic Beef Sirloin Steak

Prep time: 20 minutes | Cook time: 15 minutes | Serves 4

1¼ pounds (567 g) beef sirloin steak, cut into small-sized strips	2 cloves garlic, crushed
¼ cup balsamic vinegar	1 teaspoon cayenne pepper
1 tablespoon brown mustard	Sea salt flakes and crushed red pepper, to taste
1 tablespoon butter	1 cup sour cream
1 cup beef broth	2½ tablespoons keto tomato paste
1 cup leek, chopped	

1. Place the beef along with the balsamic vinegar and the mustard in a mixing dish; cover and marinate in your refrigerator for about 1 hour.
2. Butter the inside of a baking dish and put the beef into the dish.
3. Add the broth, leeks and garlic. Cook at 380ºF (193ºC) for 8 minutes. Pause the machine and add the cayenne pepper, salt, red pepper, sour cream and tomato paste; cook for additional 7 minutes.
4. Bon appétit!

Per Serving
calories: 418 | fat: 25g | protein: 33g
carbs: 9g | net carbs: 8g | fiber: 1g

Pork and Mushroom Stroganoff

Prep time: 5 minutes | Cook time: 25 minutes | Serves 4

1 tablespoon unsalted butter	1 tablespoon Worcestershire sauce
½ cup diced onion	1 teaspoon salt
1 tablespoon minced garlic	½ teaspoon freshly ground black pepper
1 pound (454 g) pork tips or beef stew meat	½ cup water
1½ cups chopped mushrooms	⅓ cup sour cream
	¼ teaspoon xanthan gum

1. Preheat the Instant Pot on Sauté mode. Add the butter and heat until foaming. Add the onion and garlic and sauté for 5 minutes or until the onion is translucent.
2. Add the beef, mushrooms, Worcestershire sauce, salt, pepper, and water.
3. Lock the lid. Select Manual mode and set cooking time for 20 minutes on High Pressure.
4. When cooking is complete, let the pressure release naturally for 10 minutes, then release any remaining pressure. Unlock the lid.
5. Switch the pot to Sauté mode, then stir in the sour cream.
6. Mix in the xanthan gum a little at a time and keep stirring until the sauce thickens.
7. Serve immediately.

Per Serving
calories: 364 | fat: 28.0g | protein: 23.0g
carbs: 5.0g | net carbs: 4.0g | fiber: 1.0g

Lamb Koobideh with Turmeric

Prep time: 15 minutes | Cook time: 30 minutes | Serves 4

1 pound (454 g) ground lamb	½ teaspoon garlic powder
1 egg, beaten	1 teaspoon chives, chopped
1 tablespoon lemon juice	½ teaspoon ground black pepper
1 teaspoon ground turmeric	1 cup water

1. In a mixing bowl, combine all the ingredients except for water.
2. Shape the mixture into meatballs and press into ellipse shape.
3. Pour the water and insert the trivet in the Instant Pot.
4. Put the prepared ellipse meatballs in a baking pan and transfer on the trivet.
5. Close the lid and select Manual mode. Set cooking time for 30 minutes on High Pressure.
6. When timer beeps, make a quick pressure release. Open the lid.
7. Serve immediately.

Per Serving
calories: 231 | fat: 9.5g | protein: 33.4g
carbs: 1.0g | net carbs: 0.7g | fiber: 0.3g

Beef Meatball Casserole with Pasta Sauce

Prep time: 15 minutes | Cook time: 24 minutes | Serves 6

1 tablespoon olive oil	1½ cups water
For the Meatballs:	
½ pound (227 g) ground beef	cheese, grated
¼ pound (113 g) beef sausage, chopped	2 tablespoons scallions, chopped
¼ pound (113 g) pork rinds, crushed	2 garlic cloves, minced
1 egg	½ teaspoon cayenne pepper
¼ cup Romano	Sea salt and ground black pepper, to taste
For the Casserole:	
2 cups sugar-free pasta sauce	shredded
½ cup full-fat coconut milk	½ cup clotted cream
	A pinch of grated nutmeg
1 cup Swiss cheese,	

1. Mix all ingredients for the meatballs in a large bowl. Shape the mixture into meatballs.
2. Press the Sauté button to heat up the Instant Pot. Then, heat the oil and brown the meatballs for 4 minutes, flipping occasionally.
3. To assemble the casserole, arrange the meatballs in a baking dish greased with cooking spray.
4. Pour ½ of pasta sauce over the meatballs. Mix the cream, milk and nutmeg until well combined; add the cream mixture to the baking dish.
5. Add the remaining half of the pasta sauce to the top. Top with shredded Swiss cheese.
6. Pour the water in the Instant Pot and place the trivet in. Lower the casserole dish onto the trivet.
7. Secure the lid. Choose Manual mode and set cooking time for 20 minutes on High Pressure.
8. Once cooking is complete, use a quick pressure release. Carefully remove the lid.

Per Serving
calories: 436 | fat: 32.8g | protein: 25.9g
carbs: 9.0g | net carbs: 5.3g | fiber: 3.7g

Garlic Pork Tenderloin with Basil

Prep time: 20 minutes | Cook time: 17 minutes | Serves 4

1 pound (454 g) pork tenderloin	½ teaspoon dried oregano
4-5 garlic cloves, peeled and halved	½ teaspoon dried rosemary
1 teaspoon kosher salt	½ teaspoon dried marjoram
⅓ teaspoon ground black pepper	2 tablespoons cooking wine
1 teaspoon dried basil	

1. Rub the pork with garlic halves; add the seasoning and drizzle with the cooking wine. Then, cut slits completely through pork tenderloin. Tuck the remaining garlic into the slits.
2. Wrap the pork tenderloin with foil; let it marinate overnight.
3. Roast at 360ºF (182ºC) for 15 to 17 minutes. Serve warm.

Per Serving
calories: 168 | fat: 4g | protein: 30g
carbs: 2g | net carbs: 1g | fiber: 1g

Cayenne Pork Round Steaks

Prep time: 10 minutes | Cook time: 25 minutes | Serves 2

2 pork round steaks
2 tablespoons avocado oil
½ teaspoon salt
1 teaspoon white

pepper
1 teaspoon cayenne pepper
1 cup water

1. Rub the round steaks with avocado oil, salt, white pepper, and cayenne pepper on a clean work surface. Then wrap it in the foil.
2. Pour in the water and insert the trivet in the Instant Pot. Put the wrapped steaks on the trivet. Close the lid.
3. Select Manual mode and set cooking time for 25 minutes on High Pressure.
4. When the time is over, make a quick pressure release and open the lid.
5. Remove the steaks from the foil. Serve hot.

Per Serving
calories: 334 | fat: 21.0g | protein: 29.4g
carbs: 8.0g | net carbs: 5.9g | fiber: 2.1g

Pork Meatballs with Parmesan Cheese

Prep time: 15 minutes | Cook time: 7 minutes | Serves 3

1 pound (454 g) ground pork
1 tablespoon coconut aminos
1 teaspoon garlic, minced

2 tablespoons spring onions, finely chopped
½ cup pork rinds
½ cup Parmesan cheese, preferably freshly grated

1. Combine the ground pork, coconut aminos, garlic, and spring onions in a mixing dish. Mix until everything is well incorporated.
2. Form the mixture into small meatballs.
3. In a shallow bowl, mix the pork rinds and grated Parmesan cheese. Roll the meatballs over the Parmesan mixture.
4. Cook at 380°F (193°C) for 3 minutes; shake the basket and cook an additional 4 minutes or until meatballs are browned on all sides. Bon appétit!

Per Serving
calories: 539 | fat: 43g | protein: 32g
carbs: 3g | net carbs: 2g | fiber: 1g

Mustard Pork Chop in Vermouth

Prep time: 22 minutes | Cook time: 18 minutes | Serves 6

2 tablespoons vermouth
6 center-cut loin pork chops
½ tablespoon fresh basil, minced
$1/3$ teaspoon freshly

ground black pepper, or more to taste
2 tablespoons whole grain mustard
1 teaspoon fine kosher salt

1. Toss pork chops with other ingredients until they are well coated on both sides.
2. Air-fry your chops for 18 minutes at 405°F (207°C), turning once or twice.
3. Mound your favorite salad on a serving plate; top with pork chops and enjoy.

Per Serving
calories: 393 | fat: 15g | protein: 56g
carbs: 3g | net carbs: 2g | fiber: 1g

Smokey Beef Roast with Jalapeño

Prep time: 20 minutes | Cook time: 45 minutes | Serves 8

2 pounds (907 g) roast beef, at room temperature
2 tablespoons extra-virgin olive oil
1 teaspoon sea salt flakes
1 teaspoon black

pepper, preferably freshly ground
1 teaspoon smoked paprika
A few dashes of liquid smoke
2 jalapeño peppers, thinly sliced

1. Start by preheating the Air Fryer to 330°F (166°C).
2. Then, pat the roast dry using kitchen towels. Rub with extra-virgin olive oil and all seasonings along with liquid smoke.
3. Roast for 30 minutes in the preheated Air Fryer; then, pause the machine and turn the roast over; roast for additional 15 minutes.
4. Check for doneness using a meat thermometer and serve sprinkled with sliced jalapeños. Bon appétit!

Per Serving
calories: 167 | fat: 5g | protein: 26g
carbs: 2g | net carbs: 1g | fiber: 1g

Beef Pho Zoodle Soup

Prep time: 35 minutes | Cook time: 34 minutes | Serves 4

1½ pounds (680 g) oxtails, rinsed
½ pound (227 g) beef brisket, rinsed
1 cinnamon stick
5 whole cloves
⅛ teaspoon ground coriander
2 star anise pods
½ medium onion
2-inch piece fresh ginger, thickly sliced and bruised
10 cups water
½ medium Fuji apple,

peeled and cut into chunks
2 teaspoons sea salt
2 teaspoons sugar-free fish sauce
6 ounces (170 g) sirloin steak
2 large zucchini, spiralized
¼ red onion, thinly sliced
2 scallions, thinly sliced
Lime wedges, for serving

1. Place the oxtails and brisket in a large stockpot and cover with water. Bring the water to a boil over high heat
2. Reduce to a low boil and cook for 15 minutes. Remove the pot from the heat, discard the water, and rinse the oxtails and brisket with warm water until cool enough to handle. Set the beef aside.
3. Set the Instant Pot to Sauté. Once heated, place the cloves, coriander, cinnamon, and star anise in the pot and toast for 3 minutes, stirring constantly.
4. Add the onion and ginger and continue to stir for 1 additional minute or until aromatic.
5. Carefully pour in the water, then add the oxtails, brisket, apple, and salt. Secure the lid. Press the Manual button and set cooking time for 15 minutes at High Pressure.
6. Meanwhile, place the sirloin in the freezer for 20 to 30 minutes.
7. When timer beeps, allow the pressure to release naturally for 20 minutes, then release any remaining pressure.
8. Open the lid. Carefully strain the hot broth from the pot through a fine-mesh sieve. Set the brisket aside and discard the ginger, onion, apple, and spices. Season the strained broth with fish sauce.
9. Remove the sirloin from the freezer and slice thinly. Divide the spiralized zucchini noodles evenly among four large soup bowls. Arrange slices of both raw and cooked beef atop the zucchini noodles, along with slices of red onion and scallion.

10. Gently pour a generous serving of piping hot broth into each bowl directly over top of the raw beef slices and zucchini noodles. Serve immediately along with lime wedges.

Per Serving
calories: 617 | fat: 28.6g | protein: 77.2g
carbs: 9.5g | net carbs: 7.1g | fiber: 2.4g

Pork and Pepper Casserole

Prep time: 50 minutes | Cook time: 30 minutes | Serves 4

2 chili peppers
1 red bell pepper
2 tablespoons olive oil
1 large-sized shallot, chopped
1 pound (454 g) ground pork
2 garlic cloves, minced
2 ripe tomatoes, puréed
1 teaspoon dried marjoram
½ teaspoon mustard seeds
½ teaspoon celery seeds

1 teaspoon Mexican oregano
1 tablespoon fish sauce
2 tablespoons fresh coriander, chopped
Salt and ground black pepper, to taste
2 cups water
1 tablespoon chicken bouillon granules
2 tablespoons sherry wine
1 cup Mexican cheese blend

1. Roast the peppers in the preheated Air Fryer at 395ºF (202ºC) for 10 minutes, flipping them halfway through cook time.
2. Let them steam for 10 minutes; then, peel the skin and discard the stems and seeds. Slice the peppers into halves.
3. Heat the olive oil in a baking pan at 380ºF (193ºC) for 2 minutes; add the shallots and cook for 4 minutes. Add the ground pork and garlic; cook for a further 4 to 5 minutes.
4. After that, stir in the tomatoes, marjoram, mustard seeds, celery seeds, oregano, fish sauce, coriander, salt, and pepper. Add a layer of sliced peppers to the baking pan.
5. Mix the water with the chicken bouillon granules and sherry wine. Add the mixture to the baking pan.
6. Cook in the preheated Air Fryer at 395ºF (202ºC) for 10 minutes. Top with cheese and bake an additional 5 minutes until the cheese has melted. Serve immediately.

Per Serving
calories: 505 | fat: 39g | protein: 28g
carbs: 10g | net carbs: 8g | fiber: 2g

Cumin Lamb Ribs in Cider

Prep time: 20 minutes | Cook time: 35 minutes | Serves 4

1 pound (454 g) lamb ribs, chopped
2 tablespoons coconut aminos
1 teaspoon cumin seeds
¼ cup apple cider vinegar
1 teaspoon ground peppercorn
1 cup water

1. Combine all the ingredients in the Instant Pot. Stir to mix well.
2. Close the lid. Select Manual mode and set cooking time for 35 minutes on High Pressure.
3. When timer beeps, use a natural pressure release for 15 minutes, then release any remaining pressure. Open the lid.
4. Transfer the lamb ribs on a serving plate and baste with hot gravy from the Instant Pot.

Per Serving
calories: 205 | fat: 10.2g | protein: 23.2g
carbs: 2.2g | net carbs: 2.0g | fiber: 0.2g

Lamb Leg with Black Pepper

Prep time: 10 minutes | Cook time: 25 minutes | Serves 3

14 ounces (397 g) lamb leg, roughly chopped
1 teaspoon dried thyme
1 teaspoon ground
black pepper
1 tablespoon sesame oil
¼ cup beef broth
½ cup water

1. Rub the lamb leg with thyme, ground black pepper, and sesame oil on a clean work surface.
2. Put the leg in the Instant Pot, add beef broth and water.
3. Close the lid. Select Manual mode and set cooking time for 25 minutes on High Pressure.
4. When timer beeps, make a quick pressure release. Open the lid.
5. Serve warm.

Per Serving
calories: 292 | fat: 14.4g | protein: 37.7g
carbs: 0.7g | net carbs: 0.4g | fiber: 0.3g

Mozzarella Beef Casserole

Prep time: 15 minutes | Cook time: 3 hours 4 minutes | Serves 6

2 tablespoons olive oil, divided
1 pound (454 g) ground beef
2 cups shredded whole Mozzarella cheese, divided
1 tablespoon Italian seasoning blend, divided
1 teaspoon garlic powder, divided
½ cup unsweetened tomato purée
¼ teaspoon dried oregano
¼ teaspoon sea salt
15 slices pepperoni
2 tablespoons sliced black olives

1. Select Sauté mode. Once the pot is hot, add 1 tablespoon olive oil and crumble the ground beef into the pot. Sauté for 4 minutes until the meat is browned.
2. Place a colander over a large bowl. Transfer the meat to the colander to drain and then transfer the drained meat to a large mixing bowl.
3. To the bowl with the meat, add 1 cup Mozzarella, ½ tablespoon Italian seasoning, and ½ teaspoon garlic powder. Mix until well combined. Set aside.
4. In a small bowl, combine the tomato purée, remaining Italian seasoning, remaining garlic powder, oregano, and sea salt. Mix well. Set aside.
5. Coat the bottom of the Instant Pot with the remaining olive oil. Press the meat mixture into the bottom of the pot.
6. Add the tomato purée mixture to the pot and use a spoon to evenly distribute the sauce over the meat. Add the pepperoni over the sauce. Sprinkle the remaining Mozzarella over and then top with the olives.
7. Lock the lid. Select Slow Cook mode and set cooking time for 3 hours on Normal.
8. When cooking is complete, open the lid and transfer the casserole to a serving platter. Slice into six equal-sized wedges. Serve hot.

Per Serving
calories: 288 | fat: 19.2g | protein: 25.9g
carbs: 2.9g | net carbs: 2.2g | fiber: 0.7g

Cayenne Pork Saag

Prep time: 10 minutes | Cook time: 20 minutes | Serves 4

1/3 cup half-and-half
2 teaspoons garam masala
1 teaspoon minced garlic
1 teaspoon minced fresh ginger
½ teaspoon ground turmeric
½ teaspoon cayenne
1 teaspoon salt
1 pound (454 g) pork shoulder, cut into bite-size cubes

For the Pork Saag:
1 tablespoon peanut oil
1 tablespoon unsweetened tomato purée
¾ cup water
5 ounces (142 g) baby spinach, chopped
Salt, to taste

1. In a large bowl, mix the half-and-half, garam masala, garlic, ginger, turmeric, cayenne, and salt. Add the pork and stir to coat.
2. Marinate the pork for at least 30 minutes in the refrigerator.
3. Preheat the Instant Pot on Sauté mode. Add the peanut oil and heat until shimmering.
4. Add the pork with the marinade, and the tomato purée. Cook for 5 to 10 minutes, or until the pork is lightly seared and the tomato purée has been well incorporated. Pour in the water.
5. Lock the lid. Select Manual mode. Set cooking time for 10 minutes on High Pressure.
6. When cooking is complete, quick release the pressure. Carefully remove the lid and add the spinach. Mix well to incorporate.
7. Lock the lid. Select Manual mode. Set cooking time for 2 minutes on High Pressure.
8. When timer beeps, allow the pressure to release naturally for 5 minutes, then release any remaining pressure. Unlock the lid.
9. Sprinkle with salt and mix to serve.

Per Serving
calories: 335 | fat: 24.0g | protein: 24.0g
carbs: 7.0g | net carbs: 4.0g | fiber: 3.0g

Pomegranate Lamb Fillet

Prep time: 10 minutes | Cook time: 40 minutes | Serves 4

1 teaspoon coconut oil
1 pound (454 g) lamb fillet, chopped
¼ teaspoon ground coriander
1 ounce (28 g) scallions, chopped
¼ cup pomegranate juice
½ cup water

1. Heat the the coconut oil on Sauté mode for 2 minutes.
2. Add lamb fillet and cook for 5 minutes.
3. Stir in the ground coriander, scallions, and pomegranate juice. Add water. Close the lid.
4. Select Manual mode and set cooking time for 32 minutes on High Pressure.
5. When timer beeps, make a quick pressure release. Open the lid.
6. Serve warm.

Per Serving
calories: 232 | fat: 9.5g | protein: 32.0g
carbs: 2.8g | net carbs: 2.6g | fiber: 0.2g

Beef Steak Cubes with Red Pepper

Prep time: 10 minutes | Cook time: 35 minutes | Serves 6

1 pound (454 g) beef sirloin steak, cut into cubes
3 tablespoons coconut aminos
3 tablespoons sesame
oil
1 teaspoon red pepper flakes
½ teaspoon minced garlic

1. Drizzle the beef cubes with coconut aminos and sesame oil. Sprinkle with red pepper flake and minced garlic.
2. Let the meat stand for 10 minutes to marinate. Add the beef bites to the Instant Pot and close the lid.
3. Cook the meal for 35 minutes on Sauté mode. Flip every 5 minutes to avoid burning.
4. When cooking is complete, serve immediately.

Per Serving
calories: 209 | fat: 11.6g | protein: 23.0g
carbs: 1.8g | net carbs: 1.7g | fiber: 0.1g

Cumin Veal Meatloaf with Mustard

Prep time: 20 minutes | Cook time: 25 minutes | Serves 4

1 pound (454 g) ground veal
¼ cup coconut flour
2 eggs, beaten
1 tablespoon mustard
1 teaspoon salt
1 teaspoon ground cumin
1 teaspoon olive oil
1 cup water, for cooking

1. In a mixing bowl, combine the veal, coconut flour, eggs, mustard, salt, and ground cumin.
2. Brush a baking pan with olive oil. Put the ground veal mixture in the pan and press with a spatula.
3. Pour the water in the Instant Pot and insert the trivet.
4. Put the pan of meatloaf on the trivet. Close the lid.
5. Select Manual mode and set cooking time for 25 minutes on High Pressure.
6. When timer beeps, use a natural pressure release for 15 minutes, then release any remaining pressure. Open the lid.
7. Serve warm.

Per Serving
calories: 281 | fat: 13.6g | protein: 32.2g
carbs: 6.4g | net carbs: 2.9g | fiber: 3.5g

Buttery Beef Steak with Nutmeg

Prep time: 10 minutes | Cook time: 7 hours | Serves 4

½ cup butter, softened
1 pound (454 g) beef steak
1 teaspoon ground nutmeg
½ teaspoon salt

1. Heat the butter in the Instant Pot on Sauté mode.
2. When the butter is melted, add beef steak, ground nutmeg, and salt.
3. Close the lid and select Slow Cook mode and set cooking time for 7 hours on Less.
4. When cooking is complete, allow to cool for half an hour and serve warm.

Per Serving
calories: 417 | fat: 30.3g | protein: 34.7g
carbs: 0.3g | net carbs: 0.2g | fiber: 0.1g

Chili Pork Stew

Prep time: 10 minutes | Cook time: 35 minutes | Serves 4

½ teaspoon ground coriander
2 cups beef broth
½ teaspoon cocoa powder
1 teaspoon Ancho chili powder
1 pound (454 g) pork shoulder, boneless, chopped

1. Put ground coriander, beef broth, and cocoa powder in the Instant Pot.
2. Stir the mixture until the beef broth turns color into chocolate.
3. Add the Ancho chili powder and pork shoulder.
4. Close the lid. Select Meat/Stew mode and set cooking time for 35 minutes on High Pressure.
5. When the timer beeps, use a natural pressure release for 15 minutes, then release any remaining pressure. Open the lid.
6. Serve warm.

Per Serving
calories: 351 | fat: 25.0g | protein: 28.9g
carbs: 0.6g | net carbs: 0.5g | fiber: 0.1g

Simple Smoked Sausages with Kale

Prep time: 5 minutes | Cook time: 4 minutes | Serves 4

4 smoked sausages
6 cups chopped kale
¼ cup water

1. Place the sausages in the Instant Pot. Top with the kale and pour in the water.
2. Lock the lid. Select Manual mode. Set cooking time for 4 minutes on High Pressure.
3. When cooking is complete, let the pressure release naturally for 5 minutes, then release any remaining pressure. Unlock the lid.
4. Serve immediately.

Per Serving
calories: 259 | fat: 6.0g | protein: 11.0g
carbs: 11.0g | net carbs: 9.0g | fiber: 2.0g

Pork and Beef Meatloaf

Prep time: 10 minutes | Cook time: 30 minutes | Serves 6

1½ cups water
1½ pounds (680 g) ground pork
½ pound (227 g) ground chuck
2 eggs, whisked
½ teaspoon ground bay leaf
1 teaspoon brown mustard
½ teaspoon sea salt
½ teaspoon ground black pepper
1 teaspoon red pepper flakes, crushed
²/₃ cup cream cheese
6 thin slices bacon
¹/₃ cup tomatillo salsa

1. Add the water in the Instant Pot and place in the trivet.
2. In a mixing dish, combine ground meat, eggs, ground bay leaf, brown mustard, salt, black pepper, red pepper flakes, and cream cheese.
3. Shape the mixture into the meatloaf. Place the meatloaf in a baking pan.
4. Arrange bacon slices over the meatloaf, overlapping. Top with tomatillo salsa.
5. Secure the lid. Choose the Manual mode and set cooking time for 30 minutes at High pressure.
6. Once cooking is complete, use a quick pressure release. Carefully remove the lid.
7. Serve immediately.

Per Serving
calories: 468 | fat: 35.7g | protein: 33.6g
carbs: 1.6g | net carbs: 1.2g | fiber: 0.4g

Cayenne Pork Chops with Sauerkraut

Prep time: 10 minutes | Cook time: 15 minutes | Serves 4

1 tablespoon coconut oil
½ teaspoon ground coriander
½ teaspoon cayenne pepper
4 pork chops, chopped
1 cup sauerkraut

1. Melt the coconut oil in the Instant Pot on Sauté mode.
2. Add the ground coriander, cayenne pepper, and chopped pork chops.
3. Cook the pork on Sauté mode for 7 minutes on each side.
4. Transfer the cooked pork in the bowl, add sauerkraut and mix well.
5. Serve immediately.

Per Serving
calories: 297 | fat: 23.8g | protein: 18.4g
carbs: 1.9g | net carbs: 0.7g | fiber: 1.2g

Garlic Pork Shank with Cauliflower

Prep time: 15 minutes | Cook time: 58 minutes | Serves 6

2 pounds (907 g) pork shank, cubed
Sea salt, to taste
2 teaspoons coconut oil
1 leek, sliced
1 cup chicken stock
4 cloves garlic, sliced
½ teaspoon cumin powder
½ teaspoon porcini powder
½ teaspoon oregano
½ teaspoon basil
4 cups cauliflower, broken into small florets
¼ teaspoon red pepper flakes, crushed
½ teaspoon salt
¼ teaspoon ground black pepper

1. Season the pork shank with sea salt.
2. Press the Sauté button to heat up the Instant Pot. Melt the coconut oil. Once hot, cook pork shank for 5 minutes or until browned on all sides.
3. Add leeks, chicken stock, garlic, cumin powder, porcini powder, oregano, and basil to the Instant Pot.
4. Secure the lid. Choose the Meat/Stew mode and set cooking time for 50 minutes on High pressure.
5. Once cooking is complete, use a natural pressure release for 20 minutes, then release any remaining pressure. Carefully remove the lid. Reserve the cooked meat.
6. Add the remaining ingredients to the Instant Pot.
7. Secure the lid. Choose the Manual mode and set cooking time for 3 minutes at Low pressure.
8. Once cooking is complete, use a natural pressure release for 5 minutes, then release any remaining pressure. Carefully remove the lid.
9. Serve the cooked cauliflower with reserved pork shank.

Per Serving
calories: 342 | fat: 20.1g | protein: 32.7g
carbs: 6.6g | net carbs: 1.9g | fiber: 4.7g

Chili Beef Goulash

Prep time: 10 minutes | Cook time: 35 minutes | Serves 4

1 teaspoon coconut oil
1 pound (454 g) beef sirloin, chopped
1 teaspoon chili flakes
2 celery stalks, chopped
1 bell pepper, chopped
1 cup water

1. Put the coconut oil and chopped beef sirloin in the Instant Pot.
2. Cook on Sauté mode for 5 minutes. Stir constantly and add chili flakes.
3. Add the celery stalk, bell pepper and water.
4. Close the lid. Select Manual mode and set cooking time for 30 minutes on High Pressure.
5. When timer beeps, make a quick pressure release. Open the lid.
6. Serve immediately.

Per Serving
calories: 231 | fat: 8.3g | protein: 34.8g
carbs: 2.5g | net carbs: 1.9g | fiber: 0.6g

Pork Shank with Radish

Prep time: 15 minutes | Cook time: 44 minutes | Serves 6

1½ pounds (680 g) pork shank
Seasoned salt and ground black pepper, to taste
1 tablespoons za'atar
1 tablespoon olive oil
1 medium leek, sliced
1 turnip, chopped
1 radish, chopped
1 celery with leaves,
chopped
2 garlic cloves, smashed
1 tablespoon coconut aminos
½ teaspoon mustard powder
1 cup beef bone broth
1 tablespoon flaxseed meal
1 tablespoon water

1. Season the pork shank with salt and black pepper. Sprinkle with za'atar on all sides.
2. Press the Sauté button to heat up the Instant Pot. Heat the olive oil. Once hot, sear the pork shank for 3 minute per side. Remove the pork from the pot and reserve.
3. Sauté leeks in the pot for 3 minutes.
4. Add the turnip, radish, celery with leaves, garlic, coconut aminos, mustard powder, and broth.
5. Put the pork shank back to the Instant Pot.
6. Secure the lid. Choose the Meat/Stew mode and set cooking time for 35 minutes on High pressure.

7. Once cooking is complete, use a natural pressure release for 15 minutes, then release any remaining pressure. Carefully remove the lid. Transfer the pork and vegetables to a platter.
8. Mix flaxseed meal with water to make the slurry. Add to the Instant Pot. Press the Sauté button again and bring the cooking liquid to a boil.
9. Serve the pork and vegetables with the thickened cooking liquid.

Per Serving
calories: 328 | fat: 18.1g | protein: 30.6g
carbs: 9.0g | net carbs: 2.6g | fiber: 6.4g

Pork Cutlets with Mushroom Sauce

Prep time: 10 minutes | Cook time: 15 minutes | Serves 4

2 teaspoons olive oil
4 pork cutlets
Seasoned salt, to taste
½ teaspoon ground black pepper
½ teaspoon cayenne pepper
1 cup porcini mushrooms, thinly sliced
½ cup scallions, chopped
1 teaspoon roasted garlic paste
1 bay leaf
1 cup chicken broth
1 tablespoon arrowroot powder
1 tablespoon water
½ cup heavy cream

1. Press the Sauté button to heat up the Instant Pot; add the olive oil.
2. Sear the pork cutlets for 5 minutes or until browned on both sides. Season with salt, black pepper, and cayenne pepper.
3. Add the mushrooms, scallions, garlic paste, bay leaf, and broth to the Instant Pot.
4. Secure the lid. Choose the Manual mode and set cooking time for 10 minutes on High pressure.
5. Once cooking is complete, use a quick pressure release. Carefully remove the lid.
6. Whisk the arrowroot powder with water in a small mixing bowl to make the slurry. Ad the slurry with heavy cream to the cooking liquid.
7. Press the Sauté button to bring the cooking liquid to a boil. Serve the sauce over pork cutlets.

Per Serving
calories: 412 | fat: 25.4g | protein: 41.5g
carbs: 2.1g | net carbs: 0.8g | fiber: 1.3g

Pork, Spinach and Almond Rolls

Prep time: 15 minutes | Cook time: 21 minutes | Serves 4

¼ cup spinach
2 ounces (57 g) Parmesan cheese, grated
¼ cup almonds, chopped
12 ounces (340 g)

pork fillet, cut into 4 fillets
1 tablespoon avocado oil
5 tablespoons beef broth

1. Put the spinach in a food processor. Pulse until smooth.
2. Mix the Parmesan with spinach and chopped almonds in a bowl. Arrange four pork fillets on a clean work surface.
3. Sprinkle the spinach mixture over the fillets and roll the fillets up.
4. Heat the avocado oil on Sauté mode in the Instant Pot.
5. Place the pork rolls in the hot oil and cook for 3 minutes on each side.
6. Add the broth and close the lid.
7. Select Manual mode and set cooking time for 15 minutes on High Pressure. Flip the rolls on another side every 5 minutes to avoid burning.
8. When timer beeps, perform a natural pressure release for 5 minutes, then release any remaining pressure. Open the lid.
9. Serve immediately.

Per Serving
calories: 286 | fat: 17.4g | protein: 29.9g
carbs: 2.1g | net carbs: 1.2g | fiber: 0.9g

Buttery Ham with Cumin Seeds

Prep time: 10 minutes | Cook time: 7 minutes | Serves 6

1 cup water
3 tablespoons erythritol
½ cup butter

½ teaspoon cumin seeds
1 pound (454 g) ham

1. Pour the water in the Instant Pot and insert the trivet.
2. In a mixing bowl, mix the erythritol, butter, and cumin seeds.
3. Brush the ham with the sweet mixture and transfer to the Instant Pot.
4. Add the remaining sweet mixture. Close the lid.

5. Select Manual mode and set cooking time for 7 minutes on High Pressure.
6. When timer beeps, use a quick pressure release and open the lid.
7. Slice the ham and serve.

Per Serving
calories: 260 | fat: 21.9g | protein: 12.7g
carbs: 3.0g | net carbs: 2.0g | fiber: 1.0g

Parmesan Pork Meatballs in Tomato Sauce

Prep time: 15 minutes | Cook time: 8 minutes | Serves 6

2 pounds (907 g) lean ground pork
¼ cup pork rinds, crushed
1 egg
1 cup grated Parmesan cheese
1 teaspoon garlic paste
2 tablespoons scallions, chopped
1 teaspoon shallot powder
½ teaspoon dried basil

½ teaspoon dried sage, crushed
1 teaspoon red pepper flakes, crushed
Salt and ground black pepper, to taste
¼ cup beef bone broth
1 tablespoon sesame oil
2 cups unsweetened tomato purée
4 ounces (113 g) Mozzarella cheese, slices

1. In a mixing bowl, combine the ground pork, pork rinds, egg, Parmesan cheese, garlic paste, scallions, shallot powder, basil, sage, red pepper, salt, black pepper, and beef bone broth. Mix to combine well. Shape the mixture into 2-inch meatballs.
2. Press the Sauté button to heat up the Instant Pot. Heat the oil until sizzling. Sear the meatballs until browned.
3. Pour the tomato purée over the meatballs.
4. Secure the lid. Choose the Manual mode and set cooking time for 8 minutes at High pressure.
5. Once cooking is complete, use a quick pressure release. Carefully remove the lid.
6. Top the meatballs with Mozzarella slices and cook for 2 more minutes on Sauté mode until Mozzarella is golden. Serve hot

Per Serving
calories: 356 | fat: 17.2g | protein: 44.7g
carbs: 5.6g | net carbs: 1.5g | fiber: 4.1g

Pork Fillet and Tomato Salad

Prep time: 10 minutes | Cook time: 15 minutes | Serves 4

10 ounces (283 g) pork fillet
½ teaspoon chicken seasonings
1 tablespoon olive oil
⅓ cup water
1 tomato, chopped
⅓ cup black olives, sliced
1 cup lettuce, chopped

1. Slice the pork fillet and sprinkle with chicken seasonings.
2. Place the fillet slices in the Instant Pot, then add olive oil and cook on Sauté mode for 5 minutes. Stir constantly.
3. When the meat is light browned, add water and close the lid.
4. Select Meat/Stew mode and set cooking time for 10 minutes on High Pressure.
5. Meanwhile, in the salad bowl, mix the tomato, black olives, and lettuce.
6. Top the salad with the cooked pork slices. Toss and serve.

Per Serving
calories: 213 | fat: 13.8g | protein: 20.0g
carbs: 1.7g | net carbs: 1.1g | fiber: 0.6g

Parmesan Pork Cutlets in Red Wine

Prep time: 20 minutes | Cook time: 15 minutes | Serves 2

1 cup water
1 cup red wine
1 tablespoon sea salt
2 pork cutlets
¼ cup almond meal
¼ cup flaxseed meal
½ teaspoon baking powder
1 teaspoon shallot powder
½ teaspoon porcini powder
Sea salt and ground black pepper, to taste
1 egg
¼ cup yogurt
1 teaspoon brown mustard
⅓ cup Parmesan cheese, grated

1. In a large ceramic dish, combine the water, wine and salt. Add the pork cutlets and put for 1 hour in the refrigerator.
2. In a shallow bowl, mix the almond meal, flaxseed meal, baking powder, shallot powder, porcini powder, salt, and ground pepper. In another bowl, whisk the eggs with yogurt and mustard.
3. In a third bowl, place the grated Parmesan cheese.
4. Dip the pork cutlets in the seasoned flour mixture and toss evenly; then, in the egg mixture. Finally, roll them over the grated Parmesan cheese.
5. Spritz the bottom of the cooking basket with cooking oil. Add the breaded pork cutlets and cook at 395ºF (202ºC) and for 10 minutes.
6. Flip and cook for 5 minutes more on the other side. Serve warm.

Per Serving
calories: 450 | fat: 26g | protein: 41g
carbs: 9g | net carbs: 7g | fiber: 2g

Pork and Cauliflower Vindaloo

Prep time: 10 minutes | Cook time: 16 minutes | Serves 6

1 tablespoon olive oil
2 pounds (907 g) pork loin, sliced into strips
1 head cauliflower, broken into florets
1 teaspoon oyster sauce
2 tablespoons coconut aminos
3 cloves, whole
1 teaspoon brown mustard seeds
1 teaspoon ground cardamom
2 garlic cloves, minced
½ teaspoon mixed peppercorns
1 teaspoon cayenne pepper
Sea salt, to taste
1 cup water
2 tablespoons fresh cilantro, roughly chopped

1. Press the Sauté button to heat up the Instant Pot. Heat the oil and sear the pork loin for 4 minutes, stirring periodically.
2. Add the remaining ingredients, except for fresh cilantro.
3. Secure the lid. Choose the Meat/Stew mode and set cooking time for 12 minutes at High pressure.
4. Once cooking is complete, use a natural pressure release for 5 minutes, then release any remaining pressure. Carefully remove the lid.
5. Serve topped with fresh cilantro.

Per Serving
calories: 354 | fat: 19.3g | protein: 39.8g
carbs: 3.3g | net carbs: 1.1g | fiber: 2.2g

Greek Pork Meatball

Prep time: 15 minutes | Cook time: 25 minutes | Serves 4

1 pound (454 g) ground pork	½ teaspoon ground black pepper
1 egg white	½ teaspoon cayenne pepper
1 teaspoon dill	
½ cup green onions, chopped	1 tablespoon olive oil
1 teaspoon garlic paste	4 cups beef bone broth
2 tablespoons parsley, finely chopped	1 tablespoon butter
	2 eggs
1 tablespoon cilantro, finely chopped	2 tablespoons freshly squeezed lemon juice
1 teaspoon basil	½ cup feta cheese, sliced
Sea salt, to taste	

1. In a mixing bowl, combine ground pork, egg white, dill, green onions, garlic paste, parsley, cilantro, basil, salt, black pepper, and cayenne pepper. Roll the mixture into meatballs.
2. Press the Sauté button to heat up the Instant Pot. Once hot, add the oil. Sear the meatballs for 4 minutes or until no longer pink in center.
3. Add broth and butter. Secure the lid. Choose the Soup mode and set cooking time for 20 minutes at High pressure.
4. Once cooking is complete, use a quick pressure release. Carefully remove the lid.
5. In a small mixing dish, whisk two eggs with lemon juice. Add the mixture to the hot soup.
6. Press the Sauté button and let it simmer for a couple of minutes more or until heated through.
7. Serve garnished with feta cheese.

Per Serving
calories: 525 | fat: 37.5g | protein: 40.0g
carbs: 3.9g | net carbs: 1.8g | fiber: 2.1g

Paprika Smoked Sausages with Cabbage

Prep time: 15 minutes | Cook time: 20 minutes | Serves 2

6 ounces (170 g) smoked sausages, chopped	powder
	1 teaspoon ground paprika
1 teaspoon avocado oil	1 cup white cabbage, shredded
½ teaspoon chili	1 cup chicken stock

1. Put the smoked sausages and avocado oil in the Instant Pot and cook on Sauté mode for 5 minutes. Stir constantly.
2. Add the chili powder, ground paprika, and shredded cabbage. Mix the well.
3. Add chicken stock. Close the lid.
4. Select Manual mode mode and set cooking time for 15 minutes on High Pressure.
5. When timer beeps, make a quick pressure release. Open the lid.
6. Stir and serve.

Per Serving
calories: 310 | fat: 25.0g | protein: 17.6g
carbs: 3.5g | net carbs: 1.9g | fiber: 1.6g

Pork Tenderloin with Bay

Prep time: 5 minutes | Cook time: 23 minutes | Serves 4

2 teaspoons peanut oil	2 bay leaves
2 pounds (907 g) pork tenderloin	1 teaspoon mixed peppercorns
1 cup beef bone broth	

1. Massage the peanut oil into the pork.
2. Press the Sauté button to heat up the Instant Pot. Heat the oil and sear the meat for 3 minute on both sides.
3. Add the broth, bay leaves and mixed peppercorns to the Instant Pot.
4. Secure the lid. Choose the Meat/Stew mode and set cooking time for 20 minutes at High pressure.
5. Once cooking is complete, use a natural pressure release for 10 minutes, then release any remaining pressure. Carefully remove the lid.
6. Discard the bay leaves and serve warm.

Per Serving
calories: 351 | fat: 10.4g | protein: 60.0g
carbs: 1.0g | net carbs: 0.7g | fiber: 0.3g

Pork and Shrimp Cabbage Shumai

Prep time: 25 minutes | Cook time: 10 minutes | Makes 16 shumais

8 large outer cabbage leaves
For Filling:

10 ounces (283 g) ground pork
½ pound (227 g) shrimp, peeled, deveined, and finely chopped
2 dried shiitake mushrooms, soaked to rehydrate, minced
1 large egg
1 tablespoon coconut vinegar

1 tablespoon coconut aminos
1 scallion, white and light-green parts only, minced
1 teaspoon grated fresh ginger
1 teaspoon sesame oil
Pinch of ground black pepper
1 cup water

For Dipping Sauce:

2 tablespoons coconut vinegar
¼ cup coconut aminos
2 teaspoons sesame

oil
½ teaspoon red pepper flakes

1. Bring a large pot of water to a boil. Prepare a large bowl of ice water.
2. Blanch the cabbage by boiling the leaves for 1 minute, then dunking them in a bowl of ice water.
3. Halve each leaf lengthwise and remove the tough center rib. Blot any excess moisture from the leaves with a clean kitchen towel and set aside.
4. In a bowl, combine the pork, shrimp, mushrooms, egg, vinegar, coconut aminos, scallion, ginger, sesame oil, and pepper and stir in one direction until the mixture comes together in a ball. Toss the mixture between the hands a few times to help the filling set.
5. Place about 1 tablespoon of filling in the center of one piece of cabbage wrapper. Fold the wrapper in the left and right sides, then fold the bottom edge up over the filling snugly. Roll the wrap away from you. Set the wraps on a plate, seam side down. Continue until all the filling is used.
6. Pour the water into the Instant Pot. Place the trivet inside. Place a steaming basket atop the trivet. Arrange the cabbage rolls inside the basket, seam side down.
7. Secure the lid. Press the Manual button and set cooking time for 9 minutes on High Pressure.
8. Meanwhile, in a bowl, whisk together the vinegar, coconut aminos, sesame oil, and pepper flakes.
9. When timer beeps, quick release the pressure. Open the lid. Use tongs to transfer the cabbage shumais to a serving plate.
10. Serve the cabbage shumais warm with sauce.

Per Serving (1 shumai)
calories: 89 | fat: 5.1g | protein: 8.7g
carbs: 1.9g | net carbs: 1.5g | fiber: 0.4g

Pork and Lettuce Salad

Prep time: 15 minutes | Cook time: 30 minutes | Serves 6

2 tablespoons grapeseed oil, divided
4 pork chops
½ teaspoon garlic powder
1 teaspoon shallot powder
1 teaspoon dried parsley flakes
½ teaspoon sea salt

¼ teaspoon ground black pepper
½ teaspoon paprika
1 cup water
1 cup winter squash, diced
1 head Iceberg lettuce
1 cucumber, sliced
3 ounces (85 g) feta cheese, crumbled

1. Press the Sauté button to heat up the Instant Pot. Heat 1 tablespoon of the grapeseed oil and brown pork chops for 2 minutes per side.
2. Add the garlic powder, shallot powder, parsley flakes, salt, black pepper, paprika, and water.
3. Secure the lid. Choose the Manual mode and set cooking time for 8 minutes on High pressure.
4. Once cooking is complete, use a quick pressure release. Carefully remove the lid.
5. Meanwhile, preheat the oven to 400ºF (205ºC). Toss winter squash with remaining 1 tablespoon oil. Bake for 18 minutes on a lightly greased baking sheet in the oven. Allow it to cool completely.
6. Add cooked squash to a salad bowl, then toss with Iceberg lettuce and cucumber.
7. Scatter crumbled feta cheese over the top. Top with pork chops and serve.

Per Serving
calories: 481 | fat: 29.0g | protein: 29.0g
carbs: 9.0g | net carbs: 5.2g | fiber: 3.8g

Chapter 14 Poultry

Rosemary Chicken Thighs in Wine

Prep time: 20 minutes | Cook time: 18 minutes | Serves 4

½ cup full-fat sour cream
1 teaspoon ground cinnamon
½ teaspoon whole grain mustard
1½ tablespoons mayonnaise
1 pound (454 g) chicken thighs, boneless, skinless, and cut into pieces
1½ tablespoons olive oil
2 heaping tablespoons fresh rosemary, minced
½ cup white wine
3 cloves garlic, minced
½ teaspoon smoked paprika
Salt and freshly cracked black pepper, to taste

1. Firstly, in a mixing dish, combine chicken thighs with olive oil and white wine; stir to coat.
2. After that, throw in the garlic, smoked paprika, ground cinnamon, salt, and black pepper; cover and refrigerate for 1 to 3 hours.
3. Set the Air Fryer to cook at 375ºF (190ºC). Roast the chicken thighs for 18 minutes, turning halfway through and working in batches.
4. To make the sauce, combine the sour cream, whole grain mustard, mayonnaise and rosemary. Serve the turkey with the mustard/rosemary sauce and enjoy!

Per Serving
calories: 362 | fat: 27g | protein: 8g
carbs: 17g | net carbs: 16g | fiber: 1g

Vinegary Chicken with Tomatoes

Prep time: 25 minutes | Cook time: 10 minutes | Serves 4

4 medium-sized skin-on chicken drumsticks
1½ teaspoons herbs de Provence
Salt and pepper, to taste
1 tablespoon rice vinegar
2 tablespoons olive oil
2 garlic cloves, crushed
12 ounces (340 g) crushed canned tomatoes
1 small-size leek, thinly sliced
2 slices smoked bacon, chopped

1. Sprinkle the chicken drumsticks with herbs de Provence, salt and pepper; then, drizzle them with rice vinegar and olive oil.
2. Cook in the baking pan at 360ºF (182ºC) for 8 to 10 minutes.
3. Pause the Air Fryer; stir in the remaining ingredients and continue to cook for 15 minutes longer; make sure to check them periodically. Bon appétit!

Per Serving
calories: 296 | fat: 13g | protein: 34g
carbs: 7g | net carbs: 5g | fiber: 2g

Chive Chicken with Cauliflower

Prep time: 15 minutes | Cook time: 28 minutes | Serves 6

2 handful fresh Italian parsley, roughly chopped
½ cup fresh chopped chives
2 sprigs thyme
6 chicken drumsticks
1½ small-sized head cauliflower, broken into large-sized florets
2 teaspoons mustard powder
⅓ teaspoon porcini powder
1½ teaspoons berbere spice
⅓ teaspoon sweet paprika
½ teaspoon shallot powder
1 teaspoon granulated garlic
1 teaspoon freshly cracked pink peppercorns
½ teaspoon sea salt

1. Simply combine all items for the berbere spice rub mix. After that, coat the chicken drumsticks with this rub mix on all sides. Transfer them to the baking dish.
2. Now, lower the cauliflower onto the chicken drumsticks. Add thyme, chives and Italian parsley and spritz everything with a pan spray. Transfer the baking dish to the preheated Air Fryer.
3. Next step, set the timer for 28 minutes; roast at 355ºF (181ºC), turning occasionally. Bon appétit!

Per Serving
calories: 234 | fat: 12g | protein: 2g
carbs: 9g | net carbs: 7g | fiber: 2g

Chicken Breasts in White Wine

Prep time: 30 minutes | Cook time: 28 minutes | Serves 4

½ teaspoon grated fresh ginger
⅓ cup coconut milk
½ teaspoon sea salt flakes
3 medium-sized boneless chicken breasts, cut into small pieces
1½ tablespoons sesame oil
3 green garlic stalks, finely chopped
½ cup dry white wine
½ teaspoon fresh thyme leaves, minced
⅓ teaspoon freshly cracked black pepper

1. Warm the sesame oil in a deep sauté pan over a moderate heat. Then, sauté the green garlic until just fragrant.
2. Remove the pan from the heat and pour in the coconut milk and the white wine. After that, add the thyme, sea salt, fresh ginger, and freshly cracked black pepper. Scrape this mixture into a baking dish.
3. Stir in the chicken chunks.
4. Cook in the preheated Air Fryer for 28 minutes at 335°F (168°C). Serve on individual plates and eat warm.

Per Serving
calories: 471 | fat: 28g | protein: 12g
carbs: 31g | net carbs: 31g | fiber: 0g

Curried Chicken Fillets with Bacon

Prep time: 10 minutes | Cook time: 13 minutes | Serves 2

4 rashers smoked bacon
2 chicken fillets
½ teaspoon coarse sea salt
¼ teaspoon black pepper, preferably freshly ground
1 teaspoon garlic, minced
1 (2-inch) piece ginger, peeled and minced
1 teaspoon black mustard seeds
1 teaspoon mild curry powder
½ cup coconut milk
½ cup Parmesan cheese, grated

1. Start by preheating your Air Fryer to 400°F (205°C). Add the smoked bacon and cook in the preheated Air Fryer for 5 to 7 minutes. Reserve.
2. In a mixing bowl, place the chicken fillets, salt, black pepper, garlic, ginger, mustard seeds, curry powder, and milk. Let it marinate in your refrigerator about 30 minutes.
3. In another bowl, place the grated Parmesan cheese.
4. Dredge the chicken fillets through the Parmesan mixture and transfer them to the cooking basket. Reduce the temperature to 380°F (193°C) and cook the chicken for 6 minutes.
5. Turn them over and cook for a further 6 minutes. Repeat the process until you have run out of ingredients.
6. Serve with reserved bacon. Enjoy!

Per Serving
calories: 612 | fat: 44g | protein: 16g
carbs: 38g | net carbs: 37g | fiber: 1g

Chicken Wings with Pepper Sauce

Prep time: 10 minutes | Cook time: 30 minutes | Serves 6

12 chicken wings
1½ ounces (43 g) butter, melted
1 teaspoon onion powder
½ teaspoon cumin powder
1 teaspoon garlic paste

For the Sauce:
2 ounces (57 g) piri piri peppers, stemmed and chopped
1 tablespoon pimiento, seeded and minced
1 garlic clove, chopped
2 tablespoons fresh lemon juice
⅓ teaspoon sea salt
½ teaspoon tarragon

1. Steam the chicken wings using a steamer basket that is placed over a saucepan with boiling water; reduce the heat.
2. Now, steam the wings for 10 minutes over a moderate heat. Toss the wings with butter, onion powder, cumin powder, and garlic paste.
3. Let the chicken wings cool to room temperature. Then, refrigerate them for 45 to 50 minutes.
4. Roast in the preheated Air Fryer at 330°F (166°C) for 25 to 30 minutes; make sure to flip them halfway through.
5. While the chicken wings are cooking, prepare the sauce by mixing all of the sauce ingredients in a food processor. Toss the wings with prepared Piri Piri Sauce and serve.

Per Serving
calories: 517 | fat: 21g | protein: 4g
carbs: 12g | net carbs: 11g | fiber: 1g

Parmesan Chicken Burgers

Prep time: 10 minutes | Cook time: 15 minutes | Serves 4

1 palmful dried basil
1/3 cup Parmesan cheese, grated
2 teaspoons dried marjoram
1/3 teaspoon ancho chili powder
2 teaspoons dried parsley flakes
1/2 teaspoon onion powder
Toppings, to serve

1/3 teaspoon porcini powder
1 teaspoon sea salt flakes
1 pound (454 g) chicken meat, ground
2 teaspoons cumin powder
1/3 teaspoon red pepper flakes, crushed
1 teaspoon freshly cracked black pepper

1. Generously grease an Air Fryer cooking basket with a thin layer of olive oil.
2. In a mixing dish, combine chicken meat with all seasonings. Shape into 4 patties and coat them with grated Parmesan cheese.
3. Cook chicken burgers in the preheated Air Fryer for 15 minutes at 345°F (174°C), working in batches, flipping them once.
4. Serve with toppings of choice. Bon appétit!

Per Serving
calories: 234 | fat: 12g | protein: 6g
carbs: 12g | net carbs: 11g | fiber: 1g

Chicken and Veggie Kebabs

Prep time: 15 minutes | Cook time: 20 minutes | Serves 5

1/4 diced red onion
1/2 diced zucchini
1/2 diced red pepper
1/2 diced green pepper
1/2 diced yellow pepper
1 teaspoon BBQ seasoning
1 tablespoon chicken seasoning
2 tablespoons coconut

aminos
5 grape tomatoes
16 ounces (454 g) 1-inch cubed chicken breasts
Salt and pepper, to taste
Nonstick cooking oil spray

1. Pat dry the chicken breasts then combine the BBQ seasoning, chicken seasoning, salt, pepper and coconut aminos together.
2. Generously coat the chicken cubes with the mixture then set aside to marinate for about an hour.
3. Sew the marinated chicken cubes onto the wooden skewers.

4. Alternatively layer the chicken cubes with onions, zucchini, pepper and top each skewer with a grape tomato.
5. Spray the layered skewers with the cooking oil then line the fryer basket with parchment paper and fit in a small grill rack.
6. Place the skewers on the grill rack then air fry at 350°F (180°C) for 10 minutes.
7. Flip the skewers over and fry for an additional 10 minutes.
8. Allow the chicken to cool for a bit then serve and enjoy with any sauce of choice.

Per Serving
calories: 255 | fat: 12g | protein: 25g
carbs: 6g | net carbs: 5g | fiber: 1g

Chicken Breasts with Asiago Cheese

Prep time: 10 minutes | Cook time: 10 minutes | Serves 4

2 ounces (57 g) Asiago cheese, cut into sticks
1/3 cup keto tomato paste
1/2 teaspoon garlic paste
2 chicken breasts, cut in half lengthwise
1/2 cup green onions, chopped
1 tablespoon chili

sauce
1/2 cup roasted vegetable stock
1 tablespoon sesame oil
1 teaspoon salt
2 teaspoons unsweetened cocoa
1/2 teaspoon sweet paprika, or more to taste

1. Sprinkle chicken breasts with the salt and sweet paprika; drizzle with chili sauce. Now, place a stick of Asiago cheese in the middle of each chicken breast.
2. Then, tie the whole thing using a kitchen string; give a drizzle of sesame oil.
3. Transfer the stuffed chicken to the cooking basket. Add the other ingredients and toss to coat the chicken.
4. Afterward, cook for about 11 minutes at 395°F (202°C). Serve the chicken on two serving plates, garnish with fresh or pickled salad and serve immediately. Bon appétit!

Per Serving
calories: 390 | fat: 12g | protein: 2g
carbs: 8g | net carbs: 7g | fiber: 1g

Turkey Breasts with Mustard Sauce

Prep time: 13 minutes | Cook time: 18 minutes | Serves 4

½ teaspoon cumin powder
2 pounds (907 g) turkey breasts, quartered
2 cloves garlic, smashed
½ teaspoon hot paprika
2 tablespoons melted butter
1 teaspoon fine sea salt
Freshly cracked mixed peppercorns, to taste
Fresh juice of 1 lemon

For the Mustard Sauce:
1½ tablespoons mayonnaise
1½ cups Greek yogurt
½ tablespoon yellow mustard

1. Grab a medium-sized mixing dish and combine together the garlic and melted butter; rub this mixture evenly over the surface of the turkey.
2. Add the cumin powder, followed by paprika, salt, peppercorns, and lemon juice. Place in your refrigerator at least 55 minutes.
3. Set your Air Fryer to cook at 375ºF (190ºC). Roast the turkey for 18 minutes, turning halfway through; roast in batches.
4. In the meantime, make the mustard sauce by mixing all ingredients for the sauce. Serve warm roasted turkey with the mustard sauce. Bon appétit!

Per Serving
calories: 471 | fat: 23g | protein: 16g
carbs: 34g | net carbs: 33g | fiber: 1g

Chicken Nuggets with Sesame Seeds

Prep time: 10 minutes | Cook time: 12 minutes | Serves 4

⅛ teaspoon sea salt
¼ cup coconut flour
½ teaspoon ground ginger
1 teaspoon sesame oil
1 pound (454 g) chicken breast,
boneless & skinless
4 large egg whites
6 tablespoons toasted sesame seeds
Nonstick cooking oil spray

For the Dip:
½ teaspoon monk fruit
½ teaspoon ground ginger
1 tablespoon water
1 teaspoon sriracha
2 teaspoons rice
vinegar
2 tablespoons almond butter
4 teaspoons coconut aminos

1. Chop the chicken breast into 1-inch nuggets then pat dry and place in a medium sized mixing bowl.
2. Pour in the sesame oil, salt and massage into the chicken nuggets.
3. Pour the ground ginger and coconut flour into a large ziploc bag then add in the coated chicken nuggets and shake around to coat.
4. Transfer the chicken nuggets into a bowl filled with the egg whites and toss around until covered in the whites.
5. Shake off excess white from the nuggets then cover with the sesame seeds.
6. Heat the fryer up 400°F (205ºC) for 10 minutes then coat the basket with oil and add in the covered chicken nuggets and fry for 6 minutes.
7. Flip the chicken nuggets over and cook until crispy for 6 extra minutes.
8. In the meantime, combine all the sauce ingredients together until mixed.
9. Serve the fried nuggets along with the sauce and enjoy as desired.

Per Serving
calories: 293 | fat: 14g | protein: 33g
carbs: 8g | net carbs: 6g | fiber: 2g

Cheese Chicken and Veggies

Prep time: 25 minutes | Cook time: 22 minutes | Serves 4

3 eggs, whisked
½ teaspoon dried marjoram
⅓ cup Fontina cheese, grated
1 teaspoon sea salt
⅓ teaspoon red pepper flakes, crushed
2 cups leftover keto vegetables
½ red onion, thinly sliced
2 cups cooked chicken, shredded or chopped
3 cloves garlic, finely minced

1. Simply mix all of the above ingredients, except for cheese, with a wide spatula.
2. Scrape the mixture into a previously greased baking dish.
3. Set your Air Fryer to cook at 365ºF (185ºC) for 22 minutes. Air-fry until everything is bubbling. Serve warm topped with grated Fontina cheese. Bon appétit!

Per Serving
calories: 361 | fat: 29g | protein: 1g
carbs: 24g | net carbs: 23g | fiber: 1g

Smoky Chicken Thighs

Prep time: 20 minutes | Cook time: 15 minutes | Serves 4

¼ cup full-fat Greek yogurt
½ teaspoon cayenne pepper
½ teaspoon ground cinnamon
½ teaspoon ground black pepper
1 teaspoon kosher salt
1 teaspoon ground cumin
1 tablespoon juiced

lime
1 tablespoon avocado oil
1 teaspoon smoked paprika
1 tablespoon keto tomato paste
1 tablespoon minced garlic
1 pound (454 g) chicken thighs, boneless & skinless

1. Using a large mixing bowl, add in the tomato paste, garlic, oil, juiced lime, cumin, salt, black pepper, cinnamon, paprika, cayenne pepper, yogurt and mix until combined.
2. Add the chicken pieces into the mixing bowl and toss until combined, then set aside to marinate for an hour.
3. Arrange the marinated chicken in the fryer basket then cook for 10 minutes at 370°F (188°C).
4. Flip the chicken over and cook for an additional 5 minutes.
5. Serve and enjoy as desired.

Per Serving
calories: 298 | fat: 23g | protein: 20g
carbs: 4g | net carbs: 3g | fiber: 1g

Paprika Chicken with Scallions

Prep time: 20 minutes | Cook time: 18 minutes | Serves 4

¹/₃ teaspoon paprika
¹/₃ cup scallions, peeled and chopped
3 cloves garlic, peeled and minced
1 teaspoon ground black pepper, or to taste
½ teaspoon fresh basil, minced

1½ cups chicken, minced
1½ tablespoons coconut aminos
½ teaspoon grated fresh ginger
½ tablespoon chili sauce
1 teaspoon salt

1. Thoroughly combine all ingredients in a mixing dish. Then, form into 4 patties.
2. Cook in the preheated Air Fryer for 18 minutes at 355°F (181°C).

3. Garnish with toppings of choice. Bon appétit!

Per Serving
calories: 366 | fat: 9g | protein: 11g
carbs: 34g | net carbs: 33g | fiber: 1g

Greek Chicken Salad with Feta Cheese

Prep time: 10 minutes | Cook time: 14 minutes | Serves 4

4 bone-in, skin-on chicken thighs
1 teaspoon fine sea salt
¾ teaspoon ground black pepper
2 tablespoons unsalted butter
2 cloves garlic, minced
¼ cup red wine
Greek Salad:
2 cups Greek olives, pitted
1 medium tomato, diced
1 medium cucumber, diced
¼ cup diced red

vinegar
2 tablespoons lemon or lime juice
2 teaspoons Dijon mustard
½ teaspoon dried oregano leaves
½ teaspoon dried basil leaves

onions
2 tablespoons extra-virgin olive oil
4 sprigs fresh oregano
1 cup crumbled feta cheese, for garnish

1. Sprinkle the chicken thighs on all sides with the salt and pepper.
2. Set your Instant Pot to Sauté and melt the butter.
3. Add the chicken thighs to the Instant Pot, skin-side down. Add the garlic and sauté for 4 minutes until golden brown.
4. Turn the chicken thighs over and stir in the vinegar, lemon juice, mustard, oregano, and basil.
5. Secure the lid. Select the Manual mode and set the cooking time for 10 minutes at High Pressure.
6. Once cooking is complete, do a quick pressure release. Carefully open the lid.
7. Meanwhile, toss all the salad ingredients except the cheese in a large serving dish. When the chicken is finished, take ¼ cup of the liquid from the Instant Pot and stir into the salad.
8. Place the chicken on top of the salad and serve garnished with the cheese.

Per Serving
calories: 581 | fat: 44.3g | protein: 38.5g
carbs: 7.3g | net carbs: 6.0g | fiber: 1.3g

Garlic Hens with Cilantro

Prep time: 20 minutes | Cook time: 20 minutes | Serves 4

¼ cup fish sauce
1 teaspoon turmeric
1 tablespoon coconut aminos
1 chopped jalapeño peppers
1 cup chopped cilantro leaves
2 tablespoon stevia
2 teaspoon ground

coriander
2 tablespoon lemongrass paste
2 halved whole cornish game hens, with the giblets removed
8 minced garlic cloves
Salt and black pepper, to taste

1. Using a high speed blender, add in the turmeric, salt, coriander, pepper, lemongrass paste, sugar, garlic, cilantro, fish sauce and incorporate together.
2. Add in the broiler chicken and toss together until fully coated with the mixture then set aside to marinate for an hour.
3. Transfer the marinated broiler into the fryer basket and air fry for 10 minutes at 400°F (205°C).
4. Flip the broiler over then cook for an extra 10 minutes.
5. Serve and enjoy as desired.

Per Serving
calories: 222 | fat: 9g | protein: 14g
carbs: 4g | net carbs: 3g | fiber: 1g

Ginger-Garlic Chicken Breast

Prep time: 10 minutes | Cook time: 15 minutes | Serves 4

For the Chicken:
1 teaspoon turmeric
1 diced large onion
1 tablespoon avocado oil
1 teaspoons garam masala
1 teaspoons smoked paprika
1 teaspoons ground fennel seeds
1 pound (454 g)

chicken breast, boneless and skinless
2 teaspoons minced ginger
2 teaspoons minced garlic cloves
Nonstick cooking oil spray
Salt and cayenne pepper, to taste

Topping:
¼ cup chopped cilantro

2 teaspoons juiced lime

1. Make slight piercing all over the chicken breast then set aside.

2. Using a large mixing bowl add in all the remaining ingredients and combine together.
3. Add the pierced chicken breast into the bowl then set aside for an hour to marinate.
4. Transfer the marinated chicken and veggies into the fryer basket then coat with the cooking oil spray.
5. Cook for 15 minutes at 360°F (182°C) then serve and enjoy with a garnish of cilantro topped with the juiced lime.

Per Serving
calories: 305 | fat: 23g | protein: 19g
carbs: 6g | net carbs: 5g | fiber: 1g

Cumin Chicken Drumsticks with Oregano

Prep time: 5 minutes | Cook time: 25 minutes | Serves 4

¼ cup juiced lemon
½ teaspoon cayenne pepper
½ teaspoon coriander seeds
½ teaspoon whole black peppercorns
1 teaspoon turmeric
1 teaspoon kosher salt
1 teaspoon cumin

seeds
1 teaspoon parsley, dried
1 teaspoon oregano, dried
1½ pounds (680g) chicken drumsticks
2 tablespoons coconut oil

1. Using a high speed blender, add in the peppercorns, kosher salt, cayenne pepper, coriander seeds, parsley, oregano, cumin, turmeric and blend together until smooth.
2. Transfer the blended spices into a mixing bowl, then add in the oil, juiced lemon and incorporate together.
3. Add in the drumsticks then toss to coat and allow to marinate for an hour.
4. Arrange the drumsticks in the fryer basket with the skin side up and air fry for 15 minutes at 390°F (199°C).
5. Flip the chicken drumstick over then fry for an extra 10 minutes.
6. Serve and enjoy as desired.

Per Serving
calories: 253 | fat: 17g | protein: 20g
carbs: 2g | net carbs: 1g | fiber: 1g

Cilantro Chicken Legs with Mayo Sauce

Prep time: 5 minutes | Cook time: 20 minutes | Serves 4

4 chicken legs, bone-in, skinless
2 garlic cloves, peeled and halved
½ teaspoon coarse sea salt
½ teaspoon crushed
Dipping Sauce:
¾ cup mayonnaise
2 tablespoons stone ground mustard
For Garnish:
¼ cup roughly chopped fresh cilantro

red pepper flakes
¼ teaspoon ground black pepper, or more to taste
1 tablespoon olive oil
¼ cup chicken broth

1 teaspoon fresh lemon juice
½ teaspoon Sriracha

1. Rub the chicken legs with the garlic. Sprinkle with salt, red pepper flakes, and black pepper.
2. Set your Instant Pot to Sauté and heat the olive oil.
3. Add the chicken legs and brown for 4 to 5 minutes. Add a splash of chicken broth to deglaze the bottom of the pot.
4. Pour the remaining chicken broth into the Instant Pot and mix well.
5. Lock the lid. Select the Manual mode and set the cooking time for 14 minutes at High Pressure.
6. Meanwhile, whisk together all the sauce ingredients in a small bowl.
7. When the timer beeps, perform a natural pressure release for 10 minutes, then release any remaining pressure. Carefully remove the lid.
8. Sprinkle the cilantro on top for garnish and serve with the prepared dipping sauce.

Per Serving
calories: 487 | fat: 42.9g | protein: 22.7g
carbs: 2.2g | net carbs: 1.5g | fiber: 0.7g

Bacon-Wrapped Turkey Breast

Prep time: 20 minutes | Cook time: 13 minutes | Serves 12

1½ small-sized turkey breast, chop into 12 pieces
12 thin slices Asiago cheese

Paprika, to taste
Fine sea salt and ground black pepper, to taste
12 rashers bacon

1. Lay out the bacon rashers; place 1 slice of Asiago cheese on each bacon piece.
2. Top with turkey, season with paprika, salt, and pepper, and roll them up; secure with a cocktail stick.
3. Air-fry at 365ºF (185ºC) for 13 minutes. Bon appétit!

Per Serving
calories: 568 | fat: 34g | protein: 5g
carbs: 30g | net carbs: 29g | fiber: 1g

Cheese Chicken with Mushroom Sauce

Prep time: 8 minutes | Cook time: 14 minutes | Serves 4

2 tablespoons unsalted butter or coconut oil
2 cloves garlic, minced
¼ cup diced onions
2 cups sliced button or cremini mushrooms
4 boneless, skinless chicken breast halves
½ cup chicken broth
¼ cup heavy cream
1 teaspoon fine sea salt

1 teaspoon dried tarragon leaves
½ teaspoon dried thyme leaves
½ teaspoon ground black pepper
2 bay leaves
½ cup grated Parmesan cheese
Fresh thyme leaves, for garnish

1. Set your Instant Pot to Sauté and melt the butter.
2. Add the garlic, onions, and mushrooms and sauté for 4 minutes, stirring often, or until the onions are softened.
3. Add the remaining ingredients except the Parmesan cheese and thyme leaves to the Instant Pot and stir to combine.
4. Lock the lid. Select the Manual mode and set the cooking time for 10 minutes at High Pressure.
5. When the timer beeps, perform a natural pressure release for 10 minutes, then release any remaining pressure. Carefully remove the lid.
6. Discard the bay leaves and transfer the chicken to a serving platter.
7. Add the Parmesan cheese to the Instant Pot with the sauce and stir until the cheese melts.
8. Pour the mushroom sauce from the pot over the chicken. Serve garnished with the fresh thyme leaves.

Per Serving
calories: 278 | fat: 17.3g | protein: 27.5g
carbs: 5.1g | net carbs: 4.1g | fiber: 1.0g

Turkey and Bell Pepper Meatballs

Prep time: 10 minutes | Cook time: 10 minutes | Serves 4

1 red bell pepper, seeded and coarsely chopped	85% lean ground turkey
2 cloves garlic, coarsely chopped	1 egg, lightly beaten
¼ cup chopped fresh parsley	½ cup grated Parmesan cheese
1½ pounds (680g)	1 teaspoon salt
	½ teaspoon freshly ground black pepper

1. Preheat the air fryer to 400°F (205°C).
2. In a food processor fitted with a metal blade, combine the bell pepper, garlic, and parsley. Pulse until finely chopped. Transfer the vegetables to a large mixing bowl.
3. Add the turkey, egg, Parmesan, salt, and black pepper. Mix gently until thoroughly combined. Shape the mixture into 1¼-inch meatballs.
4. Working in batches if necessary, arrange the meatballs in a single layer in the air fryer basket; coat lightly with olive oil spray. Pausing halfway through the cooking time to shake the basket, air fry for 7 to 10 minutes, until lightly browned and a thermometer inserted into the center of a meatball registers 165°F (74°C).

Per Serving
calories: 410 | fat: 27g | protein: 38g
carbs: 4g | net carbs: 3g | fiber: 1g

Chicken and Cauliflower Soup with Sage

Prep time: 5 minutes | Cook time: 13 minutes | Serves 4

1½ tablespoons olive oil	½ pound (227 g) cauliflower, broken into small florets
4 chicken thighs	4 cups chicken broth
1 teaspoon minced garlic	½ cup heavy cream
1 leek, chopped	3 ounces (85 g) mild blue cheese, crumbled
1 tablespoon chopped sage	

1. Set your Instant Pot to Sauté and heat the olive oil.
2. Add the chicken thighs and brown each side for 2 to 3 minutes. Remove and set aside.
3. Add the garlic and leek to the Instant Pot and sauté for about 2 minutes until softened.
4. Add the cooked chicken thighs, sage, cauliflower, and broth to the pot. Stir well.
5. Lock the lid. Select the Manual mode and set the cooking time for 6 minutes at High Pressure.
6. When the timer beeps, perform a natural pressure release for 10 minutes, then release any remaining pressure. Carefully remove the lid.
7. Shred the chicken with two forks and discard the bones, then return to the Instant Pot.
8. Add the heavy cream and blue cheese and stir until the cheese is melted.
9. Ladle the chicken mixture into four bowls and serve immediately.

Per Serving
calories: 203 | fat: 14.6g | protein: 9.3g
carbs: 9.1g | net carbs: 7.3g | fiber: 1.8g

Rosemary Chicken Drumettes

Prep time: 15 minutes | Cook time: 22 minutes | Serves 3

¹⁄₃ cup almond meal	1 teaspoon rosemary
½ teaspoon ground white pepper	1 whole egg + 1 egg white
1 teaspoon seasoning salt	6 chicken drumettes
1 teaspoon garlic paste	1 heaping tablespoon fresh chives, chopped

1. Start by preheating your Air Fryer to 390°F (199°C).
2. Mix the almond meal with white pepper, salt, garlic paste, and rosemary in a small-sized bowl.
3. In another bowl, beat the eggs until frothy.
4. Dip the chicken into the flour mixture, then into the beaten eggs; coat with the flour mixture one more time.
5. Cook the chicken drumettes for 22 minutes. Serve warm, garnished with chives.

Per Serving
calories: 319 | fat: 11g | protein: 4g
carbs: 22g | net carbs: 21g | fiber: 1g

Mustard Turkey Breasts with Cayenne

Prep time: 1 hour | Cook time: 53 minutes | Serves 4

½ teaspoon dried thyme
1½ pounds (680g) turkey breasts
½ teaspoon dried sage
3 whole star anise
1½ tablespoons olive oil
1½ tablespoons hot mustard
1 teaspoon smoked cayenne pepper
1 teaspoon fine sea salt

1. Set your Air Fryer to cook at 365ºF (185ºC).
2. Brush the turkey breast with olive oil and sprinkle with seasonings.
3. Cook at 365ºF (185ºC) for 45 minutes, turning twice. Now, pause the machine and spread the cooked breast with the hot mustard.
4. Air-fry for 6 to 8 more minutes. Let it rest before slicing and serving. Bon appétit!

Per Serving
calories: 321 | fat: 17g | protein: 3g
carbs: 21g | net carbs: 20g | fiber: 1g

Paprika Turkey Breast

Prep time: 5 minutes | Cook time: 45 to 55 minutes | Serves 10

1 tablespoon sea salt
1 teaspoon paprika
1 teaspoon onion powder
1 teaspoon garlic powder
½ teaspoon freshly
ground black pepper
4 pounds (1.8 kg) bone-in, skin-on turkey breast
2 tablespoons unsalted butter, melted

1. In a small bowl, combine the salt, paprika, onion powder, garlic powder, and pepper.
2. Sprinkle the seasonings all over the turkey. Brush the turkey with some of the melted butter.
3. Set the air fryer to 350ºF (180ºC). Place the turkey in the air fryer basket, skin-side down, and cook for 25 minutes.
4. Flip the turkey and brush it with the remaining butter. Continue cooking for another 20 to 30 minutes, until an instant-read thermometer reads 160ºF.
5. Remove the turkey breast from the air fryer. Tent a piece of aluminum foil over the turkey, and allow it to rest for about 5 minutes before serving.

Per Serving
calories: 278 | fat: 14g | protein: 34g
carbs: 2g | net carbs: 1g | fiber: 1g

Chicken Cordon Bleu with Cream Sauce

Prep time: 12 minutes | Cook time: 15 minutes | Serves 6

4 boneless, skinless chicken breast halves, butterflied
4 (1-ounce / 28-g) slices Swiss cheese
Sauce:
1½ ounces (43 g) cream cheese (3 tablespoons)
¼ cup chicken broth
1 tablespoon unsalted
8 (1-ounce / 28-g) slices ham
1 cup water
Chopped fresh flat-leaf parsley, for garnish
butter
¼ teaspoon ground black pepper
¼ teaspoon fine sea salt

1. Lay the chicken breast halves on a clean work surface. Top each with a slice of Swiss cheese and 2 slices of ham. Roll the chicken around the ham and cheese, then secure with toothpicks. Set aside.
2. Whisk together all the ingredients for the sauce in a small saucepan over medium heat, stirring until the cream cheese melts and the sauce is smooth.
3. Place the chicken rolls, seam-side down, in a casserole dish. Pour half of the sauce over the chicken rolls. Set the remaining sauce aside.
4. Pour the water into the Instant Pot and insert the trivet. Place the dish on the trivet.
5. Lock the lid. Select the Manual mode and set the cooking time for 15 minutes at High Pressure.
6. When the timer beeps, perform a natural pressure release for 10 minutes, then release any remaining pressure. Carefully remove the lid.
7. Remove the chicken rolls from the Instant Pot to a plate. Pour the remaining sauce over them and serve garnished with the parsley.

Per Serving
calories: 314 | fat: 13.6g | protein: 46.2g
carbs: 1.7g | net carbs: 1.7g | fiber: 0g

Rosemary Turkey with Celery

Prep time: 50 minutes | Cook time: 45 minutes | Serves 6

2½ pounds (1.1kg) turkey breasts
1 tablespoon fresh rosemary, chopped
1 teaspoon sea salt
½ teaspoon ground black pepper
1 onion, chopped
1 celery stalk, chopped

1. Start by preheating your Air Fryer to 360ºF (182ºC). Spritz the sides and bottom of the cooking basket with a nonstick cooking spray.
2. Place the turkey in the cooking basket. Add the rosemary, salt, and black pepper. Cook for 30 minutes in the preheated Air Fryer.
3. Add the onion and celery and cook an additional 15 minutes. Bon appétit!

Per Serving
calories: 316 | fat: 14g | protein: 41g
carbs: 2g | net carbs: 1g | fiber: 1g

Turkey with Mustard Gravy

Prep time: 50 minutes | Cook time: 20 minutes | Serves 6

2 teaspoons butter, softened
1 teaspoon dried sage
2 sprigs rosemary, chopped
1 teaspoon salt
¼ teaspoon freshly ground black pepper,
or more to taste
1 whole turkey breast
2 tablespoons turkey broth
2 tablespoons whole-grain mustard
1 tablespoon butter

1. Start by preheating your Air Fryer to 360ºF (182ºC).
2. To make the rub, combine 2 tablespoons of butter, sage, rosemary, salt, and pepper; mix well to combine and spread it evenly over the surface of the turkey breast.
3. Roast for 20 minutes in an Air Fryer cooking basket. Flip the turkey breast over and cook for a further 15 to 16 minutes. Now, flip it back over and roast for 12 minutes more.
4. While the turkey is roasting, whisk the other ingredients in a saucepan. After that, spread the gravy all over the turkey breast.
5. Let the turkey rest for a few minutes before carving. Bon appétit!

Per Serving
calories: 384 | fat: 8g | protein: 131g
carbs: 2g | net carbs: 1g | fiber: 1g

Turkey with Cauliflower-Mushroom Gravy

Prep time: 5 minutes | Cook time: 25 minutes | Serves 6

2 pounds (907 g) turkey breasts, boneless and skinless
½ teaspoon smoked paprika
¼ teaspoon mustard powder
Salt and ground black pepper, to taste
1 head cauliflower, broken into small florets
1 cup chopped
scallions
2 cloves garlic, crushed
1 celery with leaves, chopped
1 bay leaf
1½ cups water
1 tablespoon butter
6 ounces (170 g) cremini mushrooms, chopped
Olive oil spray

1. Spray the bottom of the Instant Pot with olive oil spray.
2. Place turkey breasts into the Instant Pot. Sprinkle them with the paprika, mustard powder, salt, and black pepper.
3. Top with the cauliflower, scallions, garlic, and celery. Sprinkle with the bay leaf. Pour in the water.
4. Lock the lid. Select the Poultry mode and set the cooking time for 20 minutes at High Pressure.
5. When the timer beeps, perform a natural pressure release for 10 minutes, then release any remaining pressure. Carefully open the lid.
6. Remove the turkey from the pot to a platter and set aside. Transfer the cooking liquid along with vegetables to a food processor and pulse until smoothly puréed.
7. Set your Instant Pot to Sauté and melt the butter. Add the mushrooms and sauté for about 4 minutes until slightly tender. Stir in puréed vegetables and continue cooking, or until the sauce thickens. Spoon the mushroom gravy over the turkey breasts and serve.

Per Serving
calories: 284 | fat: 13.1g | protein: 35.4g
carbs: 4.8g | net carbs: 3.0g | fiber: 1.8g

Spicy Turkey with Peppers

Prep time: 40 minutes | Cook time: 36 minutes | Serves 4

½ medium-sized leek, chopped
½ red onion, chopped
2 garlic cloves, minced
1 jalapeño pepper, seeded and minced
1 bell pepper, seeded and chopped
2 tablespoons olive oil
1 pound (454 g) ground turkey, 85% lean 15% fat
2 cups tomato purée
2 cups chicken stock
½ teaspoon black peppercorns
Salt, to taste
1 teaspoon chili powder
1 teaspoon mustard seeds
1 teaspoon ground cumin

1. Start by preheating your Air Fryer to 365ºF (185ºC).
2. Place the leeks, onion, garlic and peppers in a baking pan; drizzle olive oil evenly over the top. Cook for 4 to 6 minutes.
3. Add the ground turkey. Cook for 6 minutes more or until the meat is no longer pink.
4. Now, add the tomato purée, 1 cup of chicken stock, black peppercorns, salt, chili powder, mustard seeds, and cumin to the baking pan. Cook for 24 minutes, stirring every 7 to 10 minutes.
5. Bon appétit!

Per Serving
calories: 271 | fat: 15g | protein: 6g
carbs: 11g | net carbs: 10g | fiber: 1g

Cheese Chicken Drumsticks in Wine

Prep time: 3 minutes | Cook time: 23 minutes | Serves 5

1 tablespoon olive oil
5 chicken drumsticks
½ cup chicken stock
¼ cup unsweetened coconut milk
¼ cup dry white wine
2 garlic cloves, minced
1 teaspoon shallot powder
½ teaspoon marjoram
½ teaspoon thyme
6 ounces (170 g) ricotta cheese
4 ounces (113 g) Cheddar cheese
½ teaspoon cayenne pepper
¼ teaspoon ground black pepper
Sea salt, to taste

1. Set your Instant Pot to Sauté and heat the olive oil until sizzling.
2. Add the chicken drumsticks and brown each side for 3 minutes.

3. Stir in the chicken stock, milk, wine, garlic, shallot powder, marjoram, thyme.
4. Lock the lid. Select the Manual mode and set the cooking time for 15 minutes at High Pressure.
5. When the timer beeps, perform a natural pressure release for 10 minutes, then release any remaining pressure. Carefully remove the lid.
6. Shred the chicken with two forks and return to the Instant Pot.
7. Set your Instant Pot to Sauté again and add the remaining ingredients and stir well.
8. Cook for another 2 minutes, or until the cheese is melted. Taste and add more salt, if desired. Serve immediately.

Per Serving
calories: 413 | fat: 24.3g | protein: 41.9g
carbs: 4.6g | net carbs: 4.0g | fiber: 0.6g

Turkey Egg Cups

Prep time: 15 minutes | Cook time: 22 minutes | Serves 6

1½ pounds (680g) ground turkey
6 whole eggs, well beaten
1/3 teaspoon smoked paprika
2 egg whites, beaten
Tabasco sauce, for drizzling
2 tablespoons sesame oil
2 leeks, chopped
3 cloves garlic, finely minced
1 teaspoon ground black pepper
½ teaspoon sea salt

1. Warm the oil in a pan over moderate heat; then, sweat the leeks and garlic until tender; stir periodically.
2. Next, grease 6 oven safe ramekins with pan spray. Divide the sautéed mixture among six ramekins.
3. In a bowl, beat the eggs and egg whites using a wire whisk. Stir in the smoked paprika, salt and black pepper; whisk until everything is thoroughly combined. Divide the egg mixture among the ramekins.
4. Air-fry approximately 22 minutes at 345ºF (174ºC). Drizzle Tabasco sauce over each portion and serve.

Per Serving
calories: 298 | fat: 15g | protein: 6g
carbs: 25g | net carbs: 24g | fiber: 1g

Ginger Turkey Drumsticks Curry

Prep time: 25 minutes | Cook time: 23 minutes | Serves 2

1 tablespoon red curry paste
½ teaspoon cayenne pepper
1½ tablespoons minced ginger
2 turkey drumsticks
¼ cup coconut milk
1 teaspoon kosher salt, or more to taste
⅓ teaspoon ground pepper, to more to taste

1. First of all, place turkey drumsticks with all ingredients in your refrigerator; let it marinate overnight.
2. Cook turkey drumsticks at 380ºF (193ºC) for 23 minutes; make sure to flip them over at half-time. Serve with the salad on the side.

Per Serving
calories: 298 | fat: 16g | protein: 12g
carbs: 25g | net carbs: 22g | fiber: 3g

Prosciutto-Wrapped Chicken Breast

Prep time: 5 minutes | Cook time: 15 minutes | Serves 5

1½ cups water
5 chicken breast halves, butterflied
2 garlic cloves, halved
1 teaspoon marjoram
Sea salt, to taste
½ teaspoon red pepper flakes
¼ teaspoon ground black pepper, or more to taste
10 strips prosciutto

1. Pour the water into the Instant Pot and insert the trivet.
2. Rub the chicken breast halves with garlic. Sprinkle with marjoram, salt, red pepper flakes, and black pepper. Wrap each chicken breast into 2 prosciutto strips and secure with toothpicks. Put the chicken on the trivet.
3. Lock the lid. Select the Poultry mode and set the cooking time for 15 minutes at High Pressure.
4. When the timer beeps, perform a natural pressure release for 10 minutes, then release any remaining pressure. Carefully remove the lid.
5. Remove the toothpicks and serve warm.

Per Serving
calories: 550| fat: 28.6g | protein: 68.5g
carbs: 1.0g | net carbs: 0.8g | fiber: 0.2g

Parmesan Turkey Meatballs

Prep time: 15 minutes | Cook time: 10 minutes | Serves 8

1 cup Parmesan cheese, grated
1½ cups water
14 ounces (397 g) ground turkey
2 small eggs, beaten
1 teaspoon ground ginger
2½ tablespoons olive oil
1 cup chopped fresh parsley
2 tablespoons almond meal
¾ teaspoon salt
1 heaping teaspoon fresh rosemary, finely chopped
½ teaspoon ground allspice

1. Mix all of the above ingredients in a bowl. Knead the mixture with your hands.
2. Then, take small portions and gently roll them into balls.
3. Now, preheat your Air Fryer to 380ºF (193ºC). Air fry for 8 to 10 minutes in the Air Fryer basket. Serve on a serving platter with skewers and eat with your favorite dipping sauce.

Per Serving
calories: 185 | fat: 13g | protein: 14g
carbs: 3g | net carbs: 2g | fiber: 1g

Lemon Turkey Breasts with Basil

Prep time: 1 hour | Cook time: 58 minutes | Serves 4

2 tablespoons olive oil
2 pounds (907 g) turkey breasts, bone-in, skin-on
Coarse sea salt and ground black pepper,
to taste
1 teaspoon fresh basil leaves, chopped
2 tablespoons lemon zest, grated

1. Rub olive oil on all sides of the turkey breasts; sprinkle with salt, pepper, basil, and lemon zest.
2. Place the turkey breasts skin side up on a parchment-lined cooking basket.
3. Cook in the preheated Air Fryer at 330ºF (166ºC) for 30 minutes. Now, turn them over and cook an additional 28 minutes.
4. Serve with lemon wedges, if desired. Bon appétit!

Per Serving
calories: 416 | fat: 22g | protein: 49g
carbs: 0g | net carbs: 0g | fiber: 0g

Parmesan Chicken Wings

Prep time: 5 minutes | Cook time: 12 minutes | Serves 4

2 pounds (907 g) chicken wings, patted dry
1 teaspoon seasoned salt
½ teaspoon garlic powder

½ teaspoon pepper
1 cup water
3 tablespoons butter
1 teaspoon lemon pepper
¼ cup grated Parmesan cheese

1. Season the chicken wings with the salt, garlic powder, and pepper.
2. Pour the water into the Instant Pot and insert the trivet. Arrange the wings on the trivet.
3. Secure the lid. Select the Manual mode and set the cooking time for 10 minutes at High Pressure.
4. Once cooking is complete, do a quick pressure release. Carefully open the lid.
5. Remove the chicken wings and set aside on a plate.
6. For crispy wings, you can place them on a foil-lined baking sheet and broil for 3 to 5 minutes, or until the skin is crispy.
7. Pour the water out of the Instant Pot. Set your Instant Pot to Sauté and melt the butter.
8. Stir in the lemon pepper and return the wings to the pot, tossing to coat. Scatter with the cheese and serve warm.

Per Serving
calories: 538 | fat: 39.6g | protein: 41.9g
carbs: 1.1g | net carbs: 1.0g | fiber: 0.1g

Chicken Wingettes with Cayenne Peppers

Prep time: 5 minutes | Cook time: 6 minutes | Serves 6

12 chicken wingettes
10 fresh cayenne peppers, trimmed and chopped
3 garlic cloves, minced
1½ cups white vinegar
Dipping Sauce:
½ cup sour cream
½ cup mayonnaise
½ cup cilantro, chopped

1 teaspoon sea salt
1 teaspoon onion powder
½ teaspoon black pepper
2 tablespoons olive oil

2 cloves garlic, minced
1 teaspoon smoked paprika

1. In a large bowl, toss the chicken wingettes, cayenne peppers, garlic, white vinegar, salt, onion powder, and black pepper. Cover and marinate for 1 hour in the refrigerator.
2. When ready, transfer the chicken wingettes to the Instant Pot, along with the marinade and olive oil.
3. Lock the lid. Select the Manual mode and set the cooking time for 6 minutes at High Pressure.
4. Meanwhile, thoroughly combine all the sauce ingredients in a mixing bowl.
5. When the timer beeps, perform a quick pressure release. Carefully remove the lid.
6. Serve the chicken warm alongside the dipping sauce.

Per Serving
calories: 298 | fat: 22.8g | protein: 10.9g
carbs: 11.1g | net carbs: 9.6g | fiber: 1.5g

Buffalo Chicken Wings with Bacon

Prep time: 5 minutes | Cook time: 12 minutes | Serves 4

2 pounds (907 g) chicken wings, patted dry
1 teaspoon seasoned salt
¼ teaspoon pepper
½ teaspoon garlic powder

¼ cup buffalo sauce
¾ cup chicken broth
⅓ cup blue cheese crumbles
¼ cup cooked bacon crumbles
2 stalks green onion, sliced

1. Season the chicken wings with salt, pepper, and garlic powder.
2. Pour the buffalo sauce and broth into the Instant Pot. Stir in the chicken wings.
3. Lock the lid. Select the Manual mode and set the cooking time for 12 minutes at High Pressure.
4. Once cooking is complete, do a quick pressure release. Carefully open the lid. Gently stir to coat wings with the sauce.
5. If you prefer crispier wings, you can broil them for 3 to 5 minutes until the skin is crispy.
6. Remove the chicken wings from the pot to a plate. Brush them with the leftover sauce and serve topped with the blue cheese, bacon, and green onions.

Per Serving
calories: 536 | fat: 37.3g | protein: 47.1g
carbs: 1.0g | net carbs: 0.8g | fiber: 0.2g

Roasted Turkey Sausage with Cauliflower

Prep time: 45 minutes | Cook time: 28 minutes | Serves 4

1 pound (454 g) ground turkey
1 teaspoon garlic pepper
1 teaspoon garlic powder
1/3 teaspoon dried oregano
1/2 teaspoon salt
1/3 cup onions, chopped
1/2 head cauliflower, broken into florets
1/3 teaspoon dried basil
1/2 teaspoon dried thyme, chopped

1. In a mixing bowl, thoroughly combine the ground turkey, garlic pepper, garlic powder, oregano, salt, and onion; stir well to combine. Spritz a nonstick skillet with pan spray; form the mixture into 4 sausages.
2. Then, cook the sausage over medium heat until they are no longer pink, approximately 12 minutes.
3. Arrange the cauliflower florets at the bottom of a baking dish. Sprinkle with thyme and basil; spritz with pan spray. Top with the turkey sausages.
4. Roast for 28 minutes at 375°F (190°C), turning once halfway through. Eat warm.

Per Serving
calories: 289 | fat: 25g | protein: 11g
carbs: 3g | net carbs: 2g | fiber: 1g

Chicken Cacciatore with Tomatoes

Prep time: 5 minutes | Cook time: 22 minutes | Serves 4 to 5

6 tablespoons coconut oil
5 chicken legs
1 bell pepper, diced
1/2 onion, chopped
1 (14-ounce / 397-g) can sugar-free or low-sugar diced tomatoes
1/2 teaspoon dried basil
1/2 teaspoon dried parsley
1/2 teaspoon kosher salt
1/2 teaspoon freshly ground black pepper
1/2 cup filtered water

1. Press the Sauté button on the Instant Pot and melt the coconut oil.
2. Add the chicken legs and sauté until the outside is browned.
3. Remove the chicken and set aside.
4. Add the bell pepper, onion, tomatoes, basil, parsley, salt, and pepper to the Instant Pot and cook for about 2 minutes.

5. Pour in the water and return the chicken to the pot.
6. Lock the lid. Select the Manual mode and set the cooking time for 18 minutes at High Pressure.
7. Once cooking is complete, do a quick pressure release. Carefully open the lid. Serve warm.

Per Serving
calories: 346 | fat: 24.5g | protein: 26.8g
carbs: 5.0g | net carbs: 3.4g | fiber: 1.6g

Creamy Cheese Chicken Drumsticks

Prep time: 5 minutes | Cook time: 25 minutes | Serves 4

2 pounds (907 g) chicken drumsticks (about 8 pieces)
1 teaspoon salt
1 teaspoon dried parsley
1/2 teaspoon garlic powder
1/2 teaspoon dried oregano
1/4 teaspoon pepper
1 cup water
1 stick butter
2 ounces (57 g) cream cheese, softened
1/2 cup grated Parmesan cheese
1/2 cup chicken broth
1/4 cup heavy cream
1/8 teaspoon pepper

1. Sprinkle the salt, parsley, garlic powder, oregano, and pepper evenly over the chicken drumsticks.
2. Pour the water into the Instant Pot and insert the trivet. Arrange the drumsticks on the trivet.
3. Secure the lid. Select the Manual mode and set the cooking time for 15 minutes at High Pressure.
4. Once cooking is complete, do a quick pressure release. Carefully open the lid.
5. Transfer the drumsticks to a foil-lined baking sheet and broil each side for 3 to 5 minutes, or until the skin begins to crisp.
6. Meanwhile, pour the water out of the Instant Pot. Set your Instant Pot to Sauté and melt the butter.
7. Add the remaining ingredients to the Instant Pot and whisk to combine. Pour the sauce over the drumsticks and serve warm.

Per Serving
calories: 788 | fat: 55.8g | protein: 53.7g
carbs: 3.4g | net carbs: 3.3g | fiber: 0.1g

Curried Chicken Drumsticks with Thyme

Prep time: 5 minutes | Cook time: 20 minutes | Serves 4

1½ pounds (680 g) chicken drumsticks
1 tablespoon Jamaican curry powder
1 teaspoon salt
1 cup chicken broth
½ medium onion, diced
½ teaspoon dried thyme

1. Sprinkle the salt and curry powder over the chicken drumsticks.
2. Place the chicken drumsticks into the Instant Pot, along with the remaining ingredients.
3. Secure the lid. Select the Manual mode and set the cooking time for 20 minutes at High Pressure.
4. Once cooking is complete, do a quick pressure release. Carefully open the lid. Serve warm.

Per Serving
calories: 290 | fat: 14.6g | protein: 31.8g
carbs: 1.6g | net carbs: 1.3g | fiber: 0.3g

Basil Chicken Fillets with Cheese Sauce

Prep time: 5 minutes | Cook time: 10 minutes | Serves 4

1 tablespoon olive oil
1 pound (454 g) chicken fillets
½ teaspoon dried basil
Cheese Sauce:
3 teaspoons butter, at room temperature
1/3 cup grated Gruyère cheese
1/3 cup Neufchâtel cheese, at room temperature
1/3 cup heavy cream
Salt and freshly ground black pepper, to taste
1 cup chicken broth

3 tablespoons unsweetened coconut milk
1 teaspoon shallot powder
½ teaspoon granulated garlic

1. Set your Instant Pot to Sauté and heat the olive oil until sizzling.
2. Add the chicken and sear each side for 3 minutes. Sprinkle with the basil, salt, and black pepper.
3. Pour the broth into the Instant Pot and stir well.

4. Lock the lid. Select the Manual mode and set the cooking time for 6 minutes at High Pressure.
5. When the timer beeps, perform a natural pressure release for 10 minutes, then release any remaining pressure. Carefully remove the lid.
6. Transfer the chicken to a platter and set aside.
7. Clean the Instant Pot. Press the Sauté button and melt the butter.
8. Add the cheeses, heavy cream, milk, shallot powder, and garlic, stirring until everything is heated through.
9. Pour the cheese sauce over the chicken and serve.

Per Serving
calories: 317 | fat: 20.6g | protein: 30.2g
carbs: 1.5g | net carbs: 1.4g | fiber: 0.1g

Turkey Breasts with Pesto Sauce

Prep time: 5 minutes | Cook time: 26 minutes | Serves 6

2 pounds (907 g) turkey breasts
Sea salt and ground black pepper, to taste
1 teaspoon paprika
1 tablespoon olive oil
1 cup water
Pesto Sauce:
1/3 cup olive oil
½ cup fresh basil leaves
1/3 cup grated Parmesan cheese
2 tablespoons pine nuts, toasted
1 garlic clove, halved
Salt and ground black pepper, to taste

1. Season the turkey breasts on both sides with salt, black pepper, and paprika.
2. Set your Instant Pot to Sauté and heat the olive oil.
3. Add the turkey breasts and sear each side for 2 to 3 minutes. Pour in the water.
4. Secure the lid. Select the Poultry mode and set the cooking time for 20 minutes at High Pressure.
5. Meanwhile, place all the ingredients for the pesto sauce into a food processor. Pulse until everything is well combined.
6. When the timer beeps, perform a quick pressure release. Carefully remove the lid.
7. Spoon the pesto sauce onto the turkey breasts and serve.

Per Serving
calories: 395 | fat: 26.7g | protein: 35.3g
carbs: 2.1g | net carbs: 1.7g | fiber: 0.4g

BBQ Chicken Wings

Prep time: 5 minutes | Cook time: 12 minutes | Serves 4

1 pound (454 g) chicken wings	powder
1 teaspoon salt	1 cup sugar-free barbecue sauce,
½ teaspoon pepper	divided
¼ teaspoon garlic	1 cup water

1. Toss the chicken wings with the salt, pepper, garlic powder, and half of barbecue sauce in a large bowl until well coated.
2. Pour the water into the Instant Pot and insert the trivet. Place the wings on the trivet.
3. Secure the lid. Select the Manual mode and set the cooking time for 12 minutes at High Pressure.
4. Once cooking is complete, do a quick pressure release. Carefully open the lid.
5. Transfer the wings to a serving bowl and toss with the remaining sauce. Serve immediately.

Per Serving
calories: 239 | fat: 15.2g | protein: 20.2g
carbs: 4.2g | net carbs: 4.1g | fiber: 0.1g

Mustard Chicken Livers with Rosemary

Prep time: 5 minutes | Cook time: 15 minutes | Serves 8

2 tablespoons olive oil	marjoram
1 pound (454 g) chicken livers	½ teaspoon red pepper flakes
2 garlic cloves, crushed	½ teaspoon ground black pepper
½ cup chopped leeks	¼ teaspoon dried dill weed
1 tablespoon poultry seasonings	Salt, to taste
1 teaspoon dried rosemary	1 cup water
½ teaspoon paprika	1 tablespoon stone ground mustard
½ teaspoon dried	

1. Set your Instant Pot to Sauté and heat the olive oil.
2. Add the chicken livers and sauté for about 3 minutes until no longer pink.
3. Add the remaining ingredients except the mustard to the Instant Pot and stir to combine.

4. Lock the lid. Select the Manual mode and set the cooking time for 10 minutes at High Pressure.
5. When the timer beeps, perform a quick pressure release. Carefully remove the lid.
6. Transfer the cooked mixture to a food processor, along with the mustard. Pulse until the mixture is smooth. Serve immediately.

Per Serving
calories: 112 | fat: 6.9g | protein: 10.3g
carbs: 2.1g | net carbs: 1.7g | fiber: 0.4g

Sesame Chicken Thighs with Lime

Prep time: 5 minutes | Cook time: 24 minutes | Serves 4

1 pound (454 g) boneless, skinless chicken thighs, cut into bite-sized pieces and patted dry	½ cup chicken broth
	½ cup coconut aminos
	⅓ cup Swerve
	2 tablespoons toasted sesame oil
Fine sea salt, to taste	1 tablespoon lime juice
2 tablespoons avocado oil or coconut oil	¼ teaspoon peeled and grated fresh ginger
1 clove garlic, smashed to a paste	
For Garnish:	
Sesame seeds	Sliced green onions

1. Season all sides of chicken thighs with salt.
2. Set your Instant Pot to Sauté and heat the avocado oil.
3. Add the chicken thighs and sear for about 4 minutes, or until lightly browned on all sides.
4. Remove the chicken and set aside.
5. Add the remaining ingredients to the Instant Pot and cook for 10 minutes, stirring occasionally, or until the sauce is reduced and thickened.
6. Return the chicken thighs to the pot and cook for 10 minutes, stirring occasionally, or until the chicken is cooked through.
7. Sprinkle the sesame seeds and green onions on top for garnish and serve.

Per Serving
calories: 359 | fat: 29.3g | protein: 20.5g
carbs: 3.1g | net carbs: 3.0g | fiber: 1.0g

Chicken Legs with Salsa Sauce

Prep time: 5 minutes | Cook time: 16 minutes | Serves 5

5 chicken legs, skinless and boneless
½ teaspoon sea salt
Salsa Sauce:

1 cup puréed tomatoes	2 tablespoons minced
1 cup onion, chopped	fresh cilantro
1 jalapeño, chopped	3 teaspoons lime juice
2 bell peppers, deveined and chopped	1 teaspoon granulated garlic

1. Press the Sauté button to heat your Instant Pot.
2. Add the chicken legs and sear each side for 2 to 3 minutes until evenly browned. Season with sea salt.
3. Thoroughly combine all the ingredients for the salsa sauce in a mixing bowl. Spoon the salsa mixture evenly over the browned chicken legs.
4. Lock the lid. Select the Manual mode and set the cooking time for 10 minutes at High Pressure.
5. When the timer beeps, perform a natural pressure release for 10 minutes, then release any remaining pressure. Carefully remove the lid. Serve warm.

Per Serving
calories: 357 | fat: 11.6g | protein: 52.4g
carbs: 8.6g | net carbs: 7.0g | fiber: 1.6g

Mustard Chicken Legs with Pancetta

Prep time: 10 minutes | Cook time: 20 minutes | Serves 5

5 chicken legs, boneless, skin-on	1 tablespoon yellow mustard
2 garlic cloves, halved	1 teaspoon curry paste
Sea salt, to taste	4 strips pancetta, chopped
½ teaspoon smoked paprika	1 shallot, peeled and chopped
¼ teaspoon ground black pepper	1 cup vegetable broth
2 teaspoons olive oil	

1. Rub the chicken legs with the garlic halves. Sprinkle with salt, paprika, and black pepper.
2. Set your Instant Pot to Sauté and heat the olive oil.

3. Add the chicken legs and brown for 4 to 5 minutes. Add a splash of chicken broth to deglaze the bottom of the pot.
4. Spread the chicken legs with mustard and curry paste.
5. Add the pancetta strips, shallot, and remaining vegetable broth to the Instant Pot.
6. Lock the lid. Select the Manual mode and set the cooking time for 14 minutes at High Pressure.
7. When the timer beeps, perform a natural pressure release for 10 minutes, then release any remaining pressure. Carefully remove the lid.
8. Serve warm.

Per Serving
calories: 479 | fat: 26.5g | protein: 53.1g
carbs: 4.3g | net carbs: 3.2g | fiber: 1.1g

Paprika Turkey Breasts with Basil

Prep time: 2 minutes | Cook time: 38 minutes | Serves 6

6 turkey breast tenderloins	½ teaspoon dried basil
4 cloves garlic, halved	½ teaspoon dried marjoram
2 tablespoons olive oil, divided	Sea salt, to taste
½ teaspoon paprika	¼ teaspoon ground black pepper, or more to taste
½ teaspoon dried oregano	1 cup water

1. Rub the turkey with the garlic halves. Massage 1 tablespoon of olive oil into the turkey and sprinkle with paprika, oregano, basil, marjoram, salt, and black pepper.
2. Set your Instant Pot to Sauté and heat the remaining 1 tablespoon of olive oil.
3. Add the turkey and brown each side for 3 to 4 minutes. Pour in the water.
4. Secure the lid. Select the Manual mode and set the cooking time for 30 minutes at High Pressure.
5. When the timer beeps, perform a natural pressure release for 15 minutes, then release any remaining pressure. Carefully remove the lid.
6. Serve warm.

Per Serving
calories: 258 | fat: 7.3g | protein: 50.1g
carbs: 0.6g | net carbs: 0.3g | fiber: 0.2g

Turkey, Onion and Tomato Soup

Prep time: 10 minutes | Cook time: 18 minutes | Serves 4

2 teaspoons coconut oil
2 garlic cloves, finely chopped
2 onions, chopped
3 turkey thighs
4 cups vegetable broth
2 tomatoes, chopped
1 celery stalk with leaves, chopped
1 teaspoon dried basil
½ teaspoon freshly grated ginger
½ teaspoon dried rosemary
1 bay leaf
¼ teaspoon crushed red pepper flakes
¼ teaspoon freshly ground black pepper
Sea salt, to taste
¼ cup finely minced fresh parsley

1. Set your Instant Pot to Sauté and melt the coconut oil.
2. Add the garlic and onions and cook for 3 minutes until softened.
3. Add the remaining ingredients except the parsley to the Instant Pot and stir well.
4. Lock the lid. Select the Manual mode and set the cooking time for 15 minutes at High Pressure.
5. When the timer beeps, perform a quick pressure release. Carefully remove the lid.
6. Remove the turkey thighs from the pot. Shred the meat and discard the bones, then return to the Instant Pot.
7. Stir in the fresh parsley and serve warm.

Per Serving
calories: 433 | fat: 26.6g | protein: 40.6g
carbs: 6.9g | net carbs: 4.9g | fiber: 2.0g

Turkey and Cucumber Salad

Prep time: 5 minutes | Cook time: 20 minutes | Serves 6

1½ cups water
2 pounds (907 g) turkey breasts, boneless and skinless
½ teaspoon crushed red pepper flakes
½ teaspoon black pepper
Salt, to taste
2 sprigs thyme
2 garlic cloves, pressed
1 sprig sage
1 leek, sliced
1 cucumber, chopped
½ cup finely diced celery
½ cup mayonnaise
1½ tablespoons Dijon mustard

1. Pour the water into the Instant Pot and insert the trivet.
2. Season the turkey breasts with red pepper flakes, black pepper, and salt. Place the turkey breasts on the trivet. Scatter the thyme, garlic, and sage on top.
3. Lock the lid. Select the Poultry mode and set the cooking time for 20 minutes at High Pressure.
4. When the timer beeps, perform a natural pressure release for 10 minutes, then release any remaining pressure. Carefully remove the lid.
5. Allow the turkey to cool completely, then slice it into strips. Transfer to a salad bowl.
6. Add the remaining ingredients to the bowl and gently toss until well combined. Serve immediately or serve chilled.

Per Serving
calories: 325 | fat: 17.4g | protein: 35.3g
carbs: 4.1g | net carbs: 3.2g | fiber: 0.9g

Sesame Turkey Legs with Scallions

Prep time: 5 minutes | Cook time: 40 minutes | Serves 6

3 tablespoons sesame oil
2 pounds (907 g) turkey legs
Sea salt and ground black pepper, to taste
A bunch of scallions, roughly chopped
1½ cups turkey broth

1. Set your Instant Pot to Sauté and heat the sesame oil.
2. Add the turkey legs and brown for 4 to 5 minutes. Season with salt and black pepper to taste.
3. Stir in the scallions and broth.
4. Lock the lid. Select the Manual mode and set the cooking time for 35 minutes at High Pressure.
5. When the timer beeps, perform a natural pressure release for 10 minutes, then release any remaining pressure. Carefully remove the lid.
6. Serve warm.

Per Serving
calories: 342 | fat: 19.5g | protein: 37.9g
carbs: 1.2g | net carbs: 1.0g | fiber: 0.2g

Basil Chicken Thighs with Oregano

Prep time: 10 minutes | Cook time: 15 minutes | Serves 4

4 bone-in chicken thighs
2 cloves garlic, minced
1 teaspoon salt
½ teaspoon dried oregano
¼ teaspoon pepper
¼ teaspoon dried parsley
¼ teaspoon dried basil
1 cup water

1. Place all the ingredients except the water into a large bowl and toss to evenly coat.
2. Pour the water into the Instant Pot and insert the trivet. Arrange the chicken thighs on the trivet.
3. Secure the lid. Select the Manual mode and set the cooking time for 15 minutes at High Pressure.
4. Once cooking is complete, do a quick pressure release. Carefully open the lid.
5. Serve warm.

Per Serving
calories: 432 | fat: 29.3g | protein: 32.3g
carbs: 1.1g | net carbs: 0.9g | fiber: 0.2g

Chicken Thighs in Vinegar Sauce

Prep time: 6 minutes | Cook time: 21 minutes | Serves 6

2 pounds (907 g) bone-in, skin-on chicken thighs
½ cup chicken broth
1/3 cup coconut aminos
¼ cup coconut vinegar or apple cider vinegar
6 cloves garlic, minced
3 tablespoons Swerve
2 shallots, minced
½ teaspoon ground black pepper
¼ teaspoon cayenne pepper
2 bay leaves

1. Combine all the ingredients in the Instant Pot.
2. Secure the lid. Select the Manual mode and set the cooking time for 10 minutes at High Pressure.
3. Once cooking is complete, do a quick pressure release. Carefully open the lid.
4. Transfer the chicken thighs to a rimmed baking sheet.
5. Strain the remaining sauce from the Instant Pot into a saucepan and cook over medium-high heat for about 8 minutes, stirring frequently, until the sauce is reduced by half.

6. Brush both sides of the chicken thighs with the sauce.
7. Place the baking sheet in the oven and broil for 2 to 3 minutes, or until the chicken is slightly charred and crispy.
8. Cool for 5 minutes and serve the chicken thighs with the sauce.

Per Serving
calories: 321 | fat: 21.4g | protein: 25.3g
carbs: 5.1g | net carbs: 2.1g | fiber: 3.0g

Rosemary Hens with Garlic

Prep time: 12 minutes | Cook time: 33 minutes | Serves 4

4 cloves garlic, minced
1 teaspoon lemon pepper
½ teaspoon dried basil
½ teaspoon fine sea salt
Leaves from 1 sprig fresh rosemary
2 (1-pound / 454-g) Cornish game hens, skin removed and patted dry
½ cup chicken broth
1 small onion, cut into thick slices

1. Combine the garlic, lemon pepper, basil, salt, and rosemary in a small bowl. Rub the mixture all over the hens.
2. Place the broth and onion into the Instant Pot. Place the hens on top of the onion slices, breast-side down.
3. Lock the lid. Select the Manual mode and set the cooking time for 25 minutes at High Pressure.
4. When the timer beeps, perform a natural pressure release for 10 minutes, then release any remaining pressure. Carefully remove the lid.
5. Transfer the hens to a rimmed baking sheet, breast-side up.
6. Preheat the oven to 425ºF (220ºC).
7. Roast in the preheated oven for 8 minutes, or until the skin is crispy and golden brown.
8. Remove from the oven and place on a cutting board to rest for 10 minutes before slicing to serve.

Per Serving
calories: 614 | fat: 42.4g | protein: 51.4g
carbs: 4.1g | net carbs: 3.7g | fiber: 0.4g

Cheese Turkey with Mayo

Prep time: 5 minutes | Cook time: 26 minutes | Serves 8

2 pounds (907 g) turkey breasts
2 garlic cloves, halved
Sea salt and ground black pepper, to taste
1 teaspoon paprika
1 tablespoon butter
10 slices Colby cheese, shredded
1 cup grated Romano cheese, divided
²/₃ cup mayonnaise
¹/₃ cup sour cream

1. Rub the turkey breasts with the garlic halves. Season with salt, black pepper, and paprika.
2. Set your Instant Pot to Sauté and melt the butter.
3. Add the turkey breasts and sear each side for 2 to 3 minutes.
4. Meanwhile, thoroughly combine the Colby cheese, ½ cup of Romano cheese, mayonnaise, and sour cream in a mixing bowl.
5. Spread this mixture over turkey breasts. Scatter the remaining ½ cup of Romano cheese on top.
6. Secure the lid. Select the Manual mode and set the cooking time for 20 minutes at High Pressure.
7. When the timer beeps, perform a quick pressure release. Carefully remove the lid.
8. Cool for 5 minutes before serving.

Per Serving
calories: 475 | fat: 33.5g | protein: 39.3g
carbs: 3.1g | net carbs: 2.9g | fiber: 0.2g

Turkey Meatballs in Hot Sauce

Prep time: 5 minutes | Cook time: 25 minutes | Serves 5

1 pound (454 g) ground turkey
¼ cup hot sauce, or more to taste
2 tablespoons coconut oil
1 teaspoon finely grated ginger
½ teaspoon dried basil
½ teaspoon chili powder
½ teaspoon kosher salt
½ teaspoon freshly ground black pepper
1 cup filtered water

1. Shape the ground turkey into 1½ inch meatballs with your hands and place in a greased dish in a single layer.
2. Whisk together the hot sauce, oil, ginger, basil, chili powder, salt, and pepper in a small bowl until combined. Sprinkle evenly over the meatballs.
3. Pour the water into the Instant Pot and insert the trivet. Using a sling, put the dish with the meatballs on the trivet.
4. Lock the lid. Select the Manual mode and set the cooking time for 25 minutes at High Pressure.
5. When the timer beeps, perform a natural pressure release for 10 minutes, then release any remaining pressure. Carefully remove the lid.
6. Cool for 5 minutes and serve warm.

Per Serving
calories: 208 | fat: 10.5g | protein: 26.9g
carbs: 0.7g | net carbs: 0.5g | fiber: 0.2g

Turkey Breasts with Mushrooms

Prep time: 10 minutes | Cook time: 15 minutes | Serves 6

3 teaspoons butter
1½ pounds (680 g) turkey breasts, cubed
2 cloves garlic, minced
½ leek, chopped
1 cup thinly sliced white mushrooms
½ cup broth
½ teaspoon basil
½ teaspoon dried parsley flakes
¼ teaspoon ground allspice
Salt and black pepper, to taste
½ cup heavy cream

1. Set your Instant Pot to Sauté and melt the butter.
2. Add the turkey and sear for about 4 minutes, stirring constantly.
3. Remove the turkey and set aside on a plate.
4. Add the garlic, leek, and mushrooms to the Instant Pot and cook for 3 minutes, or until the garlic is fragrant.
5. Stir in the cooked turkey, broth, basil, parsley flakes, allspice, salt, and pepper.
6. Lock the lid. Select the Manual mode and set the cooking time for 8 minutes at High Pressure.
7. When the timer beeps, perform a quick pressure release. Carefully remove the lid.
8. Stir in the heavy cream until heated through. Ladle the turkey mixture into six bowls and serve warm.

Per Serving
calories: 251 | fat: 14.3g | protein: 26.8g
carbs: 3.0g | net carbs: 2.5g | fiber: 0.5g

Chapter 15 Appetizers and Snacks

Crispy Pepperoni

Prep time: 5 minutes | Cook time: 8 minutes | Serves 2

14 slices pepperoni

1. Place pepperoni slices into ungreased air fryer basket. Adjust the temperature to 350°F (180°C) and set the timer for 8 minutes. Pepperoni will be browned and crispy when done. Let cool 5 minutes before serving. Store in airtight container at room temperature up to 3 days.

Per Serving
calories: 69 | fat: 5g | protein: 3g
carbs: 0g | net carbs: 0g | fiber: 0g

Parmesan Chicken Nuggets with Mayo

Prep time: 20 minutes | Cook time: 12 minutes | Serves 6

1 pound (454 g) chicken breasts, slice into tenders	¼ cup almond meal
	1 egg, whisked
½ teaspoon cayenne pepper	½ cup Parmesan cheese, freshly grated
Salt and black pepper, to taste	¼ cup mayo
	¼ cup no-sugar-added barbecue sauce

1. Pat the chicken tenders dry with a kitchen towel. Season with the cayenne pepper, salt, and black pepper.
2. Dip the chicken tenders into the almond meal, followed by the egg. Press the chicken tenders into the Parmesan cheese, coating evenly.
3. Place the chicken tenders in the lightly greased Air Fryer basket. Cook at 360°F (182°C) for 9 to 12 minutes, turning them over to cook evenly.
4. In a mixing bowl, thoroughly combine the mayonnaise with the barbecue sauce. Serve the chicken nuggets with the sauce for dipping. Bon appétit!

Per Serving
calories: 268 | fat: 18g | protein: 2g
carbs: 4g | net carbs: 3g | fiber: 1g

Air Fried Cheese Crisps

Prep time: 10 minutes | Cook time: 12 minutes | Serves 2

½ cup shredded Cheddar cheese
1 egg white

1. Preheat the air fryer to 400°F (205°C). Place a piece of parchment paper in the bottom of the air fryer basket.
2. In a medium bowl, combine the cheese and egg white, stirring with a fork until thoroughly combined.
3. Place small scoops of the cheese mixture in a single layer in the basket of the air fryer (about 1-inch apart). Use the fork to spread the mixture as thin as possible. Air fry for 10 to 12 minutes until the crisps are golden brown. Let cool for a few minutes before transferring them to a plate. Store at room temperature in an airtight container for up to 3 days.

Per Serving
calories: 120 | fat: 10g | protein: 9g
carbs: 1g | net carbs: 1g | fiber: 0g

Green Beans with Coconut Cream

Prep time: 5 minutes | Cook time: 2 minutes | Serves 4

11 ounces (312 g) green beans	1 cup coconut cream
	2 teaspoons butter

1. Combine all the ingredients in the Instant Pot.
2. Secure the lid. Select the Manual mode and set the cooking time for 2 minutes at High Pressure.
3. Once cooking is complete, do a quick pressure release. Carefully open the lid.
4. Serve warm.

Per Serving
calories: 184 | fat: 16.6g | protein: 2.9g
carbs: 8.4g | net carbs: 4.4g | fiber: 4.0g

Sesame Broccoli with Colby Cheese

Prep time: 20 minutes | Cook time: 20 minutes | Serves 6

2 eggs, well whisked
2 cups Colby cheese, shredded
½ cup almond meal
2 tablespoons sesame seeds
Seasoned salt, to taste
¼ teaspoon ground black pepper, or more to taste
1 head broccoli, grated
1 cup Parmesan cheese, grated

1. Thoroughly combine the eggs, Colby cheese, almond meal, sesame seeds, salt, black pepper, and broccoli to make the consistency of dough.
2. Chill for 1 hour and shape into small balls; roll the patties over Parmesan cheese. Spritz them with cooking oil on all sides.
3. Cook at 360ºF (182ºC) for 10 minutes. Check for doneness and return to the Air Fryer for 8 to 10 more minutes. Serve with a sauce for dipping. Bon appétit!

Per Serving
calories: 322 | fat: 23g | protein: 19g
carbs: 9g | net carbs: 6g | fiber: 3g

Pork and Scallion Meatball

Prep time: 20 minutes | Cook time: 18 minutes | Serves 8

½ teaspoon fine sea salt
1 cup Romano cheese, grated
3 cloves garlic, minced
1½ pounds (680g) ground pork
½ cup scallions, finely
chopped
2 eggs, well whisked
¹/₃ teaspoon cumin powder
²/₃ teaspoon ground black pepper, or more to taste
2 teaspoons basil

1. Simply combine all the ingredients in a large-sized mixing bowl.
2. Shape into bite-sized balls; cook the meatballs in the air fryer for 18 minutes at 345ºF (174ºC). Serve with some tangy sauce such as marinara sauce if desired. Bon appétit!

Per Serving
calories: 350 | fat: 25g | protein: 28g
carbs: 2g | net carbs: 1g | fiber: 1g

Chili Shrimp and Bacon

Prep time: 45 minutes | Cook time: 8 minutes | Serves 10

1¼ pounds (567g) shrimp, peeled and deveined
1 teaspoon paprika
½ teaspoon ground black pepper
½ teaspoon red pepper flakes, crushed
1 tablespoon salt
1 teaspoon chili powder
1 tablespoon shallot powder
¼ teaspoon cumin powder
1¼ pounds (567g) thin bacon slices

1. Toss the shrimps with all the seasoning until they are coated well.
2. Next, wrap a slice of bacon around the shrimps, securing with a toothpick; repeat with the remaining ingredients; chill for 30 minutes.
3. Air-fry them at 360ºF (182ºC) for 7 to 8 minutes, working in batches. Serve with cocktail sticks if desired. Enjoy!

Per Serving
calories: 282 | fat: 22g | protein: 19g
carbs: 2g | net carbs: 1g | fiber: 1g

Mustard-Cayenne Pork Meatballs

Prep time: 25 minutes | Cook time: 17 minutes | Serves 8

1 teaspoon cayenne pepper
2 teaspoons mustard
2 tablespoons Brie cheese, grated
5 garlic cloves, minced
2 small-sized yellow
onions, peeled and chopped
1½ pounds (680g) ground pork
Sea salt and freshly ground black pepper, to taste

1. Mix all of the above ingredients until everything is well incorporated.
2. Now, form the mixture into balls (the size of golf a ball).
3. Cook for 17 minutes at 375ºF (190ºC). Serve with your favorite sauce.

Per Serving
calories: 275 | fat: 18g | protein: 3g
carbs: 3g | net carbs: 2g | fiber: 1g

Brussels Sprouts with Fennel Seeds

Prep time: 20 minutes | Cook time: 15 minutes | Serves 4

1 pound (454 g) Brussels sprouts, ends and yellow leaves removed and halved lengthwise
Salt and black pepper, to taste
1 tablespoon toasted sesame oil
1 teaspoon fennel seeds
Chopped fresh parsley, for garnish

1. Place the Brussels sprouts, salt, pepper, sesame oil, and fennel seeds in a resealable plastic bag. Seal the bag and shake to coat.
2. Air-fry at 380ºF (193ºC) for 15 minutes or until tender. Make sure to flip them over halfway through the cooking time.
3. Serve sprinkled with fresh parsley. Bon appétit!

Per Serving
calories: 174 | fat: 3g | protein: 3g
carbs: 9g | net carbs: 5g | fiber: 4g

Dijon Beef Meatball and Cheese Kebabs

Prep time: 20 minutes | Cook time: 15 minutes | Serves 4

1 tablespoon Dijon mustard
2 tablespoons minced scallions
1 pound (454 g) ground beef
1½ teaspoons minced
green garlic
½ teaspoon cumin
Salt and ground black pepper, to taste
12 cherry tomatoes
12 cubes Cheddar cheese

1. In a large-sized mixing dish, place the mustard, ground beef, cumin, scallions, garlic, salt, and pepper; mix with your hands or a spatula so that everything is evenly coated.
2. Form into 12 meatballs and cook them in the preheated Air Fryer for 15 minutes at 375ºF (190ºC). Air-fry until they are cooked in the middle.
3. Thread cherry tomatoes, mini burgers and cheese on cocktail sticks. Bon appétit!

Per Serving
calories: 469 | fat: 30g | protein: 3g
carbs: 4g | net carbs: 3g | fiber: 1g

Chili Broccoli Sprouts with Garlic

Prep time: 5 minutes | Cook time: 10 minutes | Serves 4

1 cup water
1 pound (454 g) broccoli sprouts
1 teaspoon sesame oil
1 teaspoon coconut aminos
1 teaspoon minced garlic
½ teaspoon chopped chili pepper
½ teaspoon salt

1. Pour the water into the Instant Pot. Lock the lid and bring the water to a boil on Sauté mode for about 10 minutes.
2. Open the lid and add the broccoli sprouts to the Instant Pot. Let sit in the hot water for 1 minute, then transfer to a bowl.
3. Whisk together the remaining ingredients in a separate bowl until combined. Pour the mixture over the broccoli sprouts and gently toss to combine. Serve immediately.

Per Serving
calories: 55 | fat: 1.3g | protein: 4.3g
carbs: 4.5g | net carbs: 0.5g | fiber: 4.0g

Almond Eggplant with Dill Weed

Prep time: 45 minutes | Cook time: 13 minutes | Serves 4

1 eggplant, peeled and thinly sliced
Salt, to taste
½ cup almond meal
¼ cup olive oil
½ cup water
1 teaspoon garlic powder
½ teaspoon dried dill weed
½ teaspoon ground black pepper, to taste

1. Salt the eggplant slices and let them stay for about 30 minutes. Squeeze the eggplant slices and rinse them under cold running water.
2. Toss the eggplant slices with the other ingredients. Cook at 390ºF (199ºC) for 13 minutes, working in batches.
3. Serve with a sauce for dipping. Bon appétit!

Per Serving
calories: 241 | fat: 21g | protein: 4g
carbs: 9g | net carbs: 4g | fiber: 5g

Spinach Melts with Parsley Yogurt Dip

Prep time: 20 minutes | Cook time: 14 minutes | Serves 4

Spinach Melts:

2 cups spinach, torn into pieces	1 teaspoon baking powder
1 ½ cups cauliflower	½ teaspoon sea salt
1 tablespoon sesame oil	½ teaspoon ground black pepper
½ cup scallions, chopped	¼ teaspoon dried dill
2 garlic cloves, minced	½ teaspoon dried basil
½ cup almond flour	1 cup Cheddar cheese, shredded
¼ cup coconut flour	

Parsley Yogurt Dip:

½ cup Greek-Style yoghurt	parsley, chopped
2 tablespoons mayonnaise	1 tablespoon fresh lemon juice
2 tablespoons fresh	½ teaspoon garlic, smashed

1. Place spinach in a mixing dish; pour in hot water. Drain and rinse well.
2. Add cauliflower to the steamer basket; steam until the cauliflower is tender about 5 minutes.
3. Mash the cauliflower; add the remaining ingredients for Spinach Melts and mix to combine well. Shape the mixture into patties and transfer them to the lightly greased cooking basket.
4. Bake at 330°F (166°C) for 14 minutes or until thoroughly heated.
5. Meanwhile, make your dipping sauce by whisking the remaining ingredients. Place in your refrigerator until ready to serve.
6. Serve the Spinach Melts with the chilled sauce on the side. Enjoy!

Per Serving
calories: 301 | fat: 25g | protein: 11g
carbs: 9g | net carbs: 5g | fiber: 4g

Dill Pickle Spears with Ranch Dressing

Prep time: 40 minutes | Cook time: 10 minutes | Serves 4

4 dill pickle spears, halved lengthwise	½ cup grated Parmesan cheese
¼ cup ranch dressing	2 tablespoons dry ranch seasoning
½ cup blanched finely ground almond flour	

1. Wrap spears in a kitchen towel 30 minutes to soak up excess pickle juice.
2. Pour ranch dressing into a medium bowl and add pickle spears. In a separate medium bowl, mix flour, Parmesan, and ranch seasoning.
3. Remove each spear from ranch dressing and shake off excess. Press gently into dry mixture to coat all sides. Place spears into ungreased air fryer basket. Adjust the temperature to 400°F (205°C) and set the timer for 10 minutes, turning spears three times during cooking. Serve warm.

Per Serving
calories: 160 | fat: 11g | protein: 7g
carbs: 8g | net carbs: 6g | fiber: 2g

Teriyaki Chicken Drumettes

Prep time: 40 minutes | Cook time: 26 minutes | Serves 6

1½ pounds (680 g) chicken drumettes	2 tablespoons fresh chives, roughly chopped
Sea salt and cracked black pepper, to taste	

Teriyaki Sauce:

1 tablespoon sesame oil	2 tablespoons rice wine vinegar
¼ cup coconut aminos	½ teaspoon fresh ginger, grated
½ cup water	2 cloves garlic, crushed
½ teaspoon Five-spice powder	

1. Start by preheating your Air Fryer to 380°F (193°C). Rub the chicken drumettes with salt and cracked black pepper.
2. Cook in the preheated Air Fryer approximately 15 minutes. Turn them over and cook an additional 7 minutes.
3. While the chicken drumettes are roasting, combine the sesame oil, coconut aminos, water, Five-spice powder, vinegar, ginger, and garlic in a pan over medium heat. Cook for 5 minutes, stirring occasionally.
4. Now, reduce the heat and let it simmer until the glaze thickens.
5. After that, brush the glaze all over the chicken drumettes. Air-fry for a further 6 minutes or until the surface is crispy. Serve topped with the remaining glaze and garnished with fresh chives. Bon appétit!

Per Serving
calories: 301 | fat: 21g | protein: 22g
carbs: 4g | net carbs: 3g | fiber: 1g

Kale Chips with Dill Weed

Prep time: 5 minutes | Cook time: 10 minutes | Makes 8 cups

½ teaspoon dried chives
½ teaspoon dried dill weed
½ teaspoon dried parsley
¼ teaspoon garlic powder

¼ teaspoon onion powder
⅛ teaspoon fine sea salt
⅛ teaspoon ground black pepper
2 large bunches kale

1. Spray the air fryer basket with avocado oil. Preheat the air fryer to 360°F (182°C).
2. Place the seasonings, salt, and pepper in a small bowl and mix well.
3. Wash the kale and pat completely dry. Use a sharp knife to carve out the thick inner stems, then spray the leaves with avocado oil and sprinkle them with the seasoning mix.
4. Place the kale leaves in the air fryer in a single layer and cook for 10 minutes, shaking and rotating the chips halfway through. Transfer the baked chips to a baking sheet to cool completely and crisp up. Repeat with the remaining kale. Sprinkle the cooled chips with salt before serving, if desired.
5. Kale chips can be stored in an airtight container at room temperature for up to 1 week, but they are best eaten within 3 days.

Per Serving
calories: 11 | fat: 1g | protein: 1g
carbs: 2g | net carbs: 1g | fiber: 1g

Paprika Cauliflower with Sage

Prep time: 20 minutes | Cook time: 12 minutes | Serves 2

3 cups cauliflower florets
2 tablespoons sesame oil
1 teaspoon onion powder
1 teaspoon garlic

powder
1 teaspoon thyme
1 teaspoon sage
1 teaspoon rosemary
Sea salt and cracked black pepper, to taste
1 teaspoon paprika

1. Start by preheating your Air Fryer to 400°F (205°C).

2. Toss the cauliflower with the remaining ingredients; toss to coat well.
3. Cook for 12 minutes, shaking the cooking basket halfway through the cooking time. They will crisp up as they cool. Bon appétit!

Per Serving
calories: 160 | fat: 14g | protein: 3g
carbs: 8g | net carbs: 5g | fiber: 3g

Bacon-Coated Egg Bites

Prep time: 20 minutes | Cook time: 13 minutes | Serves 4

6 ounces (170 g) (about 9 slices) reduced-sodium bacon
2 hard-boiled eggs, chopped
Flesh of ½ avocado, chopped
2 tablespoons unsalted butter, softened
2 tablespoons

mayonnaise
1 jalapeño pepper, seeded and finely chopped
2 tablespoons chopped fresh cilantro
Juice of ½ lime
Salt and freshly ground black pepper

1. Arrange the bacon in a single layer in the air fryer basket (it's OK if the bacon sits a bit on the sides). Set the air fryer to 350°F (180°C) and cook for 10 minutes. Check for crispiness and cook for 2 to 3 minutes longer if needed. Transfer the bacon to a paper towel–lined plate and let cool completely. Reserve 2 tablespoons of bacon grease from the bottom of the air fryer basket. Finely chop the bacon and set aside in a small, shallow bowl.
2. In a large bowl, combine the eggs, avocado, butter, mayonnaise, jalapeño, cilantro, and lime juice. Mash into a smooth paste with a fork or potato smasher. Season to taste with salt and pepper.
3. Add the reserved bacon grease to the egg mixture and stir gently until thoroughly combined. Cover and refrigerate for 30 minutes, or until the mixture is firm.
4. Divide the mixture into 12 equal portions and shape into balls. Roll the balls in the chopped bacon bits until completely coated.

Per Serving
calories: 330 | fat: 31g | protein: 10g
carbs: 2g | net carbs: 2g | fiber: 0g

Cider-Marinated Pork Belly Chips

Prep time: 5 minutes | Cook time: 12 minutes | Serves 4

1 pound (454 g) slab pork belly	vinegar
½ cup apple cider	Fine sea salt

For Serving (Optional):

Guacamole	Pico de gallo

1. Slice the pork belly into ⅛-inch-thick strips and place them in a shallow dish. Pour in the vinegar and stir to coat the pork belly. Place in the fridge to marinate for 30 minutes.
2. Spray the air fryer basket with avocado oil. Preheat the air fryer to 400°F (205ºC) .
3. Remove the pork belly from the vinegar and place the strips in the air fryer basket in a single layer, leaving space between them. Cook in the air fryer for 10 to 12 minutes, until crispy, flipping after 5 minutes. Remove from the air fryer and sprinkle with salt. Serve with guacamole and pico de gallo, if desired.
4. Best served fresh. Store leftovers in an airtight container in the fridge for up to 5 days. Reheat in a preheated 400°F (205ºC) air fryer for 5 minutes, or until heated through, flipping halfway through.

Per Serving
calories: 240 | fat: 21g | protein: 13g
carbs: 0g | net carbs: 0g | fiber: 0g

Asparagus, Eggplant and Pepper Mix

Prep time: 5 minutes | Cook time: 30 minutes | Serves 2

3 ounces (85 g) asparagus, chopped	1 cup chicken broth
8 ounces (227 g) eggplant, chopped	1 teaspoon salt
1 bell pepper, chopped	1 teaspoon ground cumin

1. Set your Instant Pot to Sauté. Combine all the ingredients in the Instant Pot. Secure the lid and cook for 30 minutes.
2. When done, stir the mixture and serve.

Per Serving
calories: 189 | fat: 12.4g | protein: 10.9g
carbs: 11.1g | net carbs: 6.1g | fiber: 5.0g

Scallops, Bacon and Shallot Kebabs

Prep time: 40 minutes | Cook time: 6 minutes | Serves 6

1 pound (454 g) sea scallops	½ pound (227g) bacon, diced
½ cup coconut milk	1 shallot, diced
1 tablespoon vermouth	1 teaspoon garlic powder
Sea salt and ground black pepper, to taste	1 teaspoon paprika

1. In a ceramic bowl, place the sea scallops, coconut milk, vermouth, salt, and black pepper; let it marinate for 30 minutes.
2. Assemble the skewers alternating the scallops, bacon, and shallots. Sprinkle garlic powder and paprika all over the skewers.
3. Bake in the preheated air Fryer at 400ºF (205ºC) for 6 minutes. Serve warm and enjoy!

Per Serving
calories: 228 | fat: 15g | protein: 15g
carbs: 5g | net carbs: 5g | fiber: 0g

Italian Seasoned Kale

Prep time: 5 minutes | Cook time: 3 minutes | Serves 3

10 ounces (283 g) Italian dark-leaf kale, chopped roughly	1 tablespoon Italian seasonings
	1 cup water

1. Place the kale in a steamer basket and sprinkle with the Italian seasonings. Stir well.
2. Pour the water into the Instant Pot and insert the steamer basket.
3. Secure the lid. Select the Steam mode and set the cooking time for 3 minutes at High Pressure.
4. Once cooking is complete, do a quick pressure release. Carefully open the lid.
5. Serve warm.

Per Serving
calories: 64 | fat: 1.6g | protein: 2.9g
carbs: 10.4g | net carbs: 9.0g | fiber: 1.4g

Zucchini-Bacon Cake with Cotija Cheese

Prep time: 22 minutes | Cook time: 13 minutes | Serves 4

⅓ cup Swiss cheese, grated
⅓ teaspoon fine sea salt
⅓ teaspoon baking powder
⅓ cup scallions, finely chopped
½ tablespoon fresh basil, finely chopped
1 zucchini, trimmed and grated

½ teaspoon freshly cracked black pepper
1 teaspoon Mexican oregano
1 cup bacon, chopped
¼ cup almond meal
¼ cup coconut flour
2 small eggs, lightly beaten
1 cup Cotija cheese, grated

1. Mix all ingredients, except for Cotija cheese, until everything is well combined.
2. Then, gently flatten each ball. Spritz the cakes with a nonstick cooking oil.
3. Bake your cakes for 13 minutes at 305ºF (152ºC); work with batches. Serve warm with tomato ketchup and mayonnaise.

Per Serving
calories: 311 | fat: 25g | protein: 18g
carbs: 5g | net carbs: 3g | fiber: 2g

Lemon Zucchini with Sage

Prep time: 20 minutes | Cook time: 18 minutes | Serves 6

1½ pounds (680g) zucchini, peeled and cut into ½-inch chunks
2 tablespoons melted coconut oil
A pinch of coarse salt
A pinch of pepper

2 tablespoons sage, finely chopped
Zest of 1 small-sized lemon
⅛ teaspoon ground allspice

1. Toss the squash chunks with the other items.
2. Roast in the Air Fryer cooking basket at 350ºF (180ºC) for 10 minutes.
3. Pause the machine, and turn the temperature to 400ºF (205ºC); stir and roast for additional 8 minutes. Bon appétit!

Per Serving
calories: 270 | fat: 15g | protein: 3g
carbs: 5g | net carbs: 4g | fiber: 1g

Italian Tomato Chips with Parmesan

Prep time: 15 minutes | Cook time: 10 minutes | Serves 4

4 Roma tomatoes, sliced
2 tablespoons olive oil
Sea salt and white pepper, to taste

1 teaspoon Italian seasoning mix
½ cup Parmesan cheese, grated

1. Start by preheating your Air Fryer to 350ºF (180ºC). Generously grease the Air Fryer basket with nonstick cooking oil.
2. Toss the sliced tomatoes with the remaining ingredients. Transfer them to the cooking basket without overlapping.
3. Cook in the preheated Air Fryer for 5 minutes. Shake the cooking basket and cook an additional 5 minutes. Work in batches.
4. Serve with Mediterranean aioli for dipping, if desired. Bon appétit!

Per Serving
calories: 130 | fat: 10g | protein: 5g
carbs: 6g | net carbs: 5g | fiber: 1g

Fennel Slices with Parsley

Prep time: 10 minutes | Cook time: 5 minutes | Serves 2

1 cup water
1 fennel bulb, sliced
¾ cup chopped fresh parsley
1 tablespoon olive oil

1 tablespoon coconut aminos
1 teaspoon apple cider vinegar

1. Pour the water into the Instant Pot and insert a steamer basket. Place the sliced fennel in the basket.
2. Secure the lid. Select the Steam mode and set the cooking time for 5 minutes at High Pressure.
3. Once cooking is complete, do a quick pressure release. Carefully open the lid.
4. Remove the fennel from the Instant Pot to a bowl. Add the remaining ingredients to the bowl and gently toss until combined. Serve immediately.

Per Serving
calories: 115 | fat: 7.6g | protein: 2.4g
carbs: 11.4g | net carbs: 7.0g | fiber: 4.4g

Parmesan Bell Pepper

Prep time: 20 minutes | Cook time: 7 minutes | Serves 4

1 egg, beaten
½ cup Parmesan, grated
1 teaspoon sea salt
½ teaspoon red pepper flakes, crushed
¾ pound (340 g) bell peppers, seeded and cut to ¼-inch strips
2 tablespoons olive oil

1. In a mixing bowl, combine together the egg, Parmesan, salt, and red pepper flakes; mix to combine well.
2. Dip bell peppers into the batter and transfer them to the cooking basket. Brush with the olive oil.
3. Cook in the preheated Air Fryer at 390°F (199°C) for 4 minutes. Shake the basket and cook for a further 3 minutes. Work in batches.
4. Taste, adjust the seasonings and serve. Bon appétit!

Per Serving
calories: 163 | fat: 11g | protein: 6g
carbs: 10g | net carbs: 9g | fiber: 1g

Spinach Chips with Chili Yogurt Dip

Prep time: 20 minutes | Cook time: 10 minutes | Serves 3

3 cups fresh spinach leaves
1 tablespoon extra-virgin olive oil
1 teaspoon sea salt
Chili Yogurt Dip:
¼ cup yogurt
2 tablespoons mayonnaise
½ teaspoon cayenne pepper
1 teaspoon garlic powder

½ teaspoon chili powder

1. Toss the spinach leaves with the olive oil and seasonings.
2. Bake in the preheated Air Fryer at 350°F (180°C) for 10 minutes, shaking the cooking basket occasionally.
3. Bake until the edges brown, working in batches.
4. In the meantime, make the sauce by whisking all ingredients in a mixing dish. Serve immediately.

Per Serving
calories: 128 | fat: 12g | protein: 2g
carbs: 3g | net carbs: 2g | fiber: 1g

Cheese Almond Spinach

Prep time: 5 minutes | Cook time: 4 minutes | Serves 4

2 cups chopped spinach
2 ounces (57 g) Monterey Jack cheese, shredded
1 cup almond milk
1 tablespoon butter
1 teaspoon minced garlic
½ teaspoon salt

1. Combine all the ingredients in the Instant Pot.
2. Secure the lid. Select the Manual mode and set the cooking time for 4 minutes at High Pressure.
3. Once cooking is complete, do a quick pressure release. Carefully open the lid.
4. Give the mixture a good stir and serve warm.

Per Serving
calories: 101 | fat: 8.1g | protein: 4.2g
carbs: 2.6g | net carbs: 2.3g | fiber: 0.3g

Paprika Brussels Sprouts with Lemon

Prep time: 5 minutes | Cook time: 5 minutes | Serves 4

2 tablespoons extra-virgin olive oil
1 pound (454 g) Brussels sprouts, outer leaves removed, and washed
1 lemon, juiced
½ teaspoon fresh paprika
½ teaspoon kosher salt
½ teaspoon black ground pepper
1 cup bone broth

1. Set your Instant Pot to Sauté and heat the olive oil.
2. Add the remaining ingredients except the bone broth to the Instant Pot and cook for 1 minute. Pour in the broth.
3. Secure the lid. Select the Manual mode and set the cooking time for 3 minutes at Low Pressure.
4. Once cooking is complete, do a quick pressure release. Carefully open the lid.
5. Remove the Brussels sprouts from the Instant Pot to a plate and serve.

Per Serving
calories: 124 | fat: 7.7g | protein: 5.6g
carbs: 12.2g | net carbs: 7.4g | fiber: 4.8g

Parmesan Broccoli Fries

Prep time: 15 minutes | Cook time: 6 minutes | Serves 4

¾ pound (340g) broccoli florets
½ teaspoon onion powder
1 teaspoon granulated garlic
½ teaspoon cayenne pepper
Spicy Dip:
¼ cup mayonnaise
¼ cup Greek yogurt
¼ teaspoon Dijon

Sea salt and ground black pepper, to taste
2 tablespoons sesame oil
4 tablespoons Parmesan cheese, preferably freshly grated

mustard
1 teaspoon keto hot sauce

1. Start by preheating the Air Fryer to 400ºF (205ºC).
2. Blanch the broccoli in salted boiling water until al dente, about 3 to 4 minutes. Drain well and transfer to the lightly greased Air Fryer basket.
3. Add the onion powder, garlic, cayenne pepper, salt, black pepper, sesame oil, and Parmesan cheese.
4. Cook for 6 minutes, tossing halfway through the cooking time.
5. Meanwhile, mix all of the spicy dip ingredients. Serve broccoli fries with chilled dipping sauce. Bon appétit!

Per Serving
calories: 219 | fat: 19g | protein: 5g
carbs: 9g | net carbs: 6g | fiber: 3g

Turmeric Mushrooms Stew

Prep time: 8 minutes | Cook time: 25 minutes | Serves 2

2 teaspoons butter
½ cup heavy cream
1 cup sliced cremini mushrooms

½ teaspoon white pepper
¼ teaspoon turmeric

1. Set your Instant Pot to Sauté and melt the butter.
2. Add the remaining ingredients to the Instant Pot and stir to combine.
3. Secure the lid and cook for 20 minutes, or until the mushrooms are tender.
4. Serve warm.

Per Serving
calories: 153 | fat: 15.6g | protein: 1.7g
carbs: 2.6g | net carbs: 2.2g | fiber: 0.4g

Simple Purple Cabbage

Prep time: 10 minutes | Cook time: 5 minutes | Serves 2

7 ounces (198 g) purple cabbage, cut into petals

¼ teaspoon salt
½ cup chicken broth
1 teaspoon butter

1. Season the cabbage with salt, then place in the Instant Pot.
2. Stir in the broth and butter.
3. Secure the lid. Select the Steam mode and set the cooking time for 5 minutes at High Pressure.
4. Once cooking is complete, do a quick pressure release. Carefully open the lid.
5. Serve warm.

Per Serving
calories: 54 | fat: 2.5g | protein: 2.6g
carbs: 5.8g | net carbs: 3.3g | fiber: 2.5g

Salmon and Lettuce Salad

Prep time: 10 minutes | Cook time: 4 minutes | Serves 2

6 ounces (170 g) salmon
½ teaspoon salt
1 cup water

1 cup chopped lettuce
1 teaspoon olive oil
2 ounces (57 g) feta cheese, crumbled

1. Season the salmon with salt and wrap in foil.
2. Pour the water into the Instant Pot and insert the trivet. Place the salmon on the trivet.
3. Secure the lid. Select the Manual mode and set the cooking time for 4 minutes at High Pressure.
4. Meanwhile, toss the lettuce with the olive oil in a salad bowl.
5. When the timer beeps, perform a quick pressure release. Carefully remove the lid.
6. Remove the salmon and chop it roughly, then transfer to the salad bowl. Sprinkle with the feta cheese and gently toss to combine. Serve immediately.

Per Serving
calories: 213 | fat: 13.9g | protein: 20.9g
carbs: 1.9g | net carbs: 1.7g | fiber: 0.2g

Zucchini Rings with Cheddar Cheese

Prep time: 15 minutes | Cook time: 3 minutes | Serves 2

1 zucchini	1 cup shredded
2 teaspoon butter,	Cheddar cheese
softened	2 cup water

1. Slice the zucchini into rings and remove the center of every ring.
2. Coat a baking pan with the softened butter and place the zucchini rings in a single layer. Fill each ring with the shredded cheese.
3. Pour the water into the Instant Pot and insert the trivet. Place the baking pan with zucchini rings on the trivet.
4. Secure the lid. Select the Manual mode and set the cooking time for 3 minutes at High Pressure.
5. Once cooking is complete, do a quick pressure release. Carefully open the lid.
6. Let the zucchini rings cool for 5 minutes and serve.

Per Serving
calories: 279 | fat: 22.9g | protein: 15.5g
carbs: 3.9g | net carbs: 2.7g | fiber: 1.2g

Scrambled Egg and Bell Pepper Salad

Prep time: 10 minutes | Cook time: 5 minutes | Serves 2

1 teaspoon butter	milk
2 eggs	1 bell pepper, chopped
2 tablespoons coconut	1 tomato, chopped

1. Set your Instant Pot to Sauté and melt the butter.
2. Crack the eggs in the butter. Pour in the coconut milk and stir the egg mixture until smooth. Sauté for 2 minutes and then scramble again. Cook the eggs for an additional 2 minutes.
3. Transfer the eggs to a salad bowl. Add the chopped bell pepper and tomato and stir well. Serve immediately.

Per Serving
calories: 142 | fat: 10.3g | protein: 7.0g
carbs: 7.2g | net carbs:5.7g | fiber: 1.5g

Paprika Brussels Sprouts with Lemon

Prep time: 5 minutes | Cook time: 5 minutes | Serves 4

2 tablespoons extra-virgin olive oil	½ teaspoon fresh paprika
1 pound (454 g) Brussels sprouts, outer leaves removed, and washed	½ teaspoon kosher salt
	½ teaspoon black ground pepper
1 lemon, juiced	1 cup bone broth

1. Set your Instant Pot to Sauté and heat the olive oil.
2. Add the remaining ingredients except the bone broth to the Instant Pot and cook for 1 minute. Pour in the broth.
3. Secure the lid. Select the Manual mode and set the cooking time for 3 minutes at Low Pressure.
4. Once cooking is complete, do a quick pressure release. Carefully open the lid.
5. Remove the Brussels sprouts from the Instant Pot to a plate and serve.

Per Serving
calories: 124 | fat: 7.7g | protein: 5.6g
carbs: 12.2g | net carbs: 7.4g | fiber: 4.8g

Nutmeg Kale with Flax Seeds

Prep time: 5 minutes | Cook time: 5 minutes | Serves 2

1 teaspoon butter	nutmeg
1 cup chopped kale, Italian dark-leaf	¼ cup water
Salt, to taste	1 teaspoon olive oil
¾ teaspoon ground	1 tablespoon flax seeds

1. Set your Instant Pot to Sauté and melt the butter.
2. Add the kale and sprinkle with the salt and nutmeg. Pour in the water and stir well. Cook for 4 minutes, stirring occasionally.
3. Transfer the kale onto a plate and scatter the olive oil and flax seeds on top. Serve immediately.

Per Serving
calories: 79 | fat: 5.6g | protein: 1.9g
carbs: 4.7g | net carbs:3.1 g | fiber: 1.6g

Creamy Broccoli Purée

Prep time: 10 minutes | Cook time: 6 minutes | Serves 2

7 ounces (198 g) broccoli, chopped
½ cup heavy cream

1. Combine the broccoli and heavy cream in the Instant Pot.
2. Secure the lid. Select the Manual mode and set the cooking time for 6 minutes at High Pressure.
3. Once cooking is complete, do a quick pressure release. Carefully open the lid.
4. Transfer the broccoli and ¼ of the cooking liquid to a blender and blend until a smooth purée is achieved. Serve immediately.

Per Serving
calories: 139 | fat: 11.6g | protein: 3.6g
carbs: 7.2g | net carbs: 4.5g | fiber: 2.7g

Baocn and Onion Guacamole

Prep time: 5 minutes | Cook time: 10 minutes | Serves 8

2 tablespoons avocado oil
½ pound (227 g) no-sugar-added bacon, sliced into small pieces
¼ (4-ounce / 113-g) small onion, thinly sliced
1 avocado, mashed
¼ teaspoon dried cilantro
½ teaspoon kosher salt
1 tablespoon lime juice

1. Set your Instant Pot to Sauté and melt the avocado oil.
2. Add the bacon and cook for about 5 minutes, stirring occasionally, or until crisp.
3. Remove the bacon and place on a paper towel-lined plate. Set aside to cool.
4. Add the onion to the Instant Pot and cook for 1 minute.
5. Spoon the onion into a large mixing bowl, along with the avocado, salt, and cilantro. Crumble the cooked bacon into the bowl and drizzle with the lime juice, stirring, or until your desired consistency is reached.
6. Serve chilled.

Per Serving
calories: 240 | fat: 20.2g | protein: 11.3g
carbs: 3.5g | net carbs: 1.7g | fiber: 1.8g

Cheddar Cauliflower Mash

Prep time: 5 minutes | Cook time: 4 minutes | Serves 4

1 cup water
1 head cauliflower, broken into florets
¼ cup heavy whipping cream
2 tablespoons grass-
fed butter
Pinch of kosher salt
Pinch of freshly ground black pepper
¼ cup shredded full-fat Cheddar cheese

1. Add the water and cauliflower to the Instant Pot.
2. Secure the lid. Select the Manual mode and set the cooking time for 4 minutes at High Pressure.
3. Once cooking is complete, do a quick pressure release. Carefully open the lid.
4. Mash the cauliflower with a potato masher. If necessary, strain out the excess liquid.
5. Stir in the whipping cream and butter. Sprinkle with the salt and pepper.
6. Transfer the cauliflower mixture to a bowl and serve sprinkled with the cheese.

Per Serving
calories: 128 | fat: 11.5g | protein: 3.4g
carbs: 3.7g | net carbs: 2.0g | fiber: 1.7g

Lemon Mushrooms with Thyme

Prep time: 10 minutes | Cook time: 4 minutes | Serves 2

1 cup cremini mushrooms, sliced
½ cup water
1 tablespoon lemon juice
1 teaspoon almond
butter
1 teaspoon grated lemon zest
½ teaspoon salt
½ teaspoon dried thyme

1. Combine all the ingredients in the Instant Pot.
2. Secure the lid. Select the Manual mode and set the cooking time for 4 minutes at High Pressure.
3. Once cooking is complete, do a natural pressure release for 5 minutes, then release any remaining pressure. Carefully open the lid.
4. Serve warm.

Per Serving
calories: 63 | fat: 4.8g | protein: 2.9g
carbs: 3.3g | net carbs: 2.1g | fiber: 1.2g

Cheddar Prosciutto Pierogi

Prep time: 15 minutes | Cook time: 20 minutes | Makes 4 pierogi

1 cup chopped cauliflower
2 tablespoons diced onions
1 tablespoon unsalted butter, melted
Pinch of fine sea salt

½ cup shredded sharp Cheddar cheese (about 2 ounces / 57 g)
8 slices prosciutto
Fresh oregano leaves, for garnish (optional)

1. Preheat the air fryer to 350°F (180ºC). Lightly grease a 7-inch pie pan or a casserole dish that will fit in your air fryer.
2. Make the filling: Place the cauliflower and onion in the pan. Drizzle with the melted butter and sprinkle with the salt. Using your hands, mix everything together, making sure the cauliflower is coated in the butter.
3. Place the cauliflower mixture in the air fryer and cook for 10 minutes, until fork-tender, stirring halfway through.
4. Transfer the cauliflower mixture to a food processor or high-powered blender. Spray the air fryer basket with avocado oil and increase the air fryer temperature to 400°F (205ºC).
5. Pulse the cauliflower mixture in the food processor until smooth. Stir in the cheese.
6. Assemble the pierogi: Lay 1 slice of prosciutto on a sheet of parchment paper with a short end toward you. Lay another slice of prosciutto on top of it at a right angle, forming a cross. Spoon about 2 heaping tablespoons of the filling into the center of the cross.
7. Fold each arm of the prosciutto cross over the filling to form a square, making sure that the filling is well covered. Using your fingers, press down around the filling to even out the square shape. Repeat with the rest of the prosciutto and filling.
8. Spray the pierogi with avocado oil and place them in the air fryer basket. Cook for 10 minutes, or until crispy.
9. Garnish with oregano before serving, if desired. Store leftovers in an airtight container in the fridge for up to 4 days. Reheat in a preheated 400°F (205ºC) air fryer for 3 minutes, or until heated through.

Per Serving
calories: 150 | fat: 11g | protein: 11g
carbs: 2g | net carbs: 1g | fiber: 1g

Artichoke with Garlic Butter

Prep time: 5 minutes | Cook time: 5 minutes | Serves 2

½ cup water
1 artichoke, stem, top, and thorns removed
5 tablespoons salted grass-fed butter
1 teaspoon minced garlic

¼ teaspoon dried oregano
¼ teaspoon dried cilantro
¼ teaspoon fresh lime juice

1. Pour the water into the Instant Pot and insert the trivet. Place the artichoke on the trivet.
2. Secure the lid. Select the Manual mode and set the cooking time for 5 minutes at High Pressure.
3. Once cooking is complete, do a quick pressure release. Carefully open the lid.
4. Remove the artichoke and set aside.
5. Whisk together the remaining ingredients in a small bowl and microwave for about 30 to 40 seconds until melted.
Serve the artichoke with the sauce on the side.

Per Serving
calories: 291 | fat: 29.2g | protein: 2.7g
carbs: 7.6g | net carbs: 4.0g | fiber: 3.6g

Cauliflower with Turmeric

Prep time: 5 minutes | Cook time: 5 minutes | Serves 2

1 teaspoon butter
8 ounces (227 g) cauliflower, shredded
Salt, to taste

½ cup chicken broth
1 teaspoon ground turmeric

1. Set your Instant Pot to Sauté and melt the butter.
2. Stir in the shredded cauliflower and salt and sauté for 1 minute.
3. Pour in the chicken broth and sprinkle with the turmeric.
4. Secure the lid. Select the Manual mode and set the cooking time for 1 minute at High Pressure.
5. Once cooking is complete, do a quick pressure release. Carefully open the lid.
6. Allow to cool for 5 minutes before serving.

Per Serving
calories: 62 | fat: 2.8g | protein: 3.7g
carbs: 6.8g | net carbs: 3.7g | fiber: 3.1g

Cheese Spinach with Dill Weed

Prep time: 5 minutes | Cook time: 5 minutes | Serves 4

2 tablespoons butter, melted
2 cloves garlic, smashed
½ cup chopped scallions
1½ pounds (680 g) fresh spinach
1 cup cubed cream cheese
1 cup vegetable broth
½ teaspoon dried dill weed
Sea salt and ground black pepper, to taste

1. Set your Instant Pot to Sauté and warm the butter.
2. Add the garlic and scallions and cook for 2 minutes until fragrant.
3. Add the remaining ingredients to the Instant Pot and stir until combined.
4. Lock the lid. Select the Manual mode and set the cooking time for 2 minutes at High Pressure.
5. When the timer beeps, perform a quick pressure release. Carefully remove the lid.
6. Serve warm.

Per Serving
calories: 287 | fat: 24.1g | protein: 10.9g
carbs: 9.1g | net carbs: 4.8g | fiber: 4.3g

Vinegary Bok Choy with Sesame Seeds

Prep time: 5 minutes | Cook time: 3 minutes | Serves 2

1 cup water
2 cups bok choy, sliced
1 tablespoon apple cider vinegar
1 teaspoon sesame oil
1 teaspoon sesame seeds
¾ teaspoon salt

1. Pour the water into the Instant Pot and insert a steamer basket. Place the bok choy in the basket.
2. Secure the lid. Select the Steam mode and set the cooking time for 3 minutes at High Pressure.
3. Once cooking is complete, do a quick pressure release. Carefully open the lid.
4. Transfer the bok choy to a plate. Sprinkle with the vinegar, oil, sesame seeds, and salt and gently toss to combine. Serve immediately.

Per Serving
calories: 37 | fat: 3.1g | protein: 1.5g
carbs: 2.1g | net carbs: 1.4g | fiber: 0.7g

Chicken, Egg and Spinach Salad

Prep time: 5 minutes | Cook time: 5 minutes | Serves 1

2 tablespoons avocado oil
3 slices no-sugar-added bacon
¼ pound (113 g) boneless, skinless chicken breasts, cubed
2 eggs, hard-boiled
1 cup chopped spinach
½ avocado, mashed
1 teaspoon ground turmeric
½ teaspoon kosher salt
½ teaspoon freshly ground black pepper

1. Set your Instant Pot to Sauté and warm the avocado oil.
2. Add the bacon and chicken, stirring thoroughly and continuously.
3. Once the bacon is crisp and chicken is cooked through, remove them from the Instant Pot and set aside to cool.
4. Stir together the eggs, spinach, avocado, turmeric, salt, and pepper in a large salad bowl until combined.
5. Crumble the bacon, and then add to the salad along with the cooked chicken. Gently toss and serve immediately.

Per Serving
calories: 555 | fat: 44.3g | protein: 34.3g
carbs: 6.9g | net carbs: 2.8g | fiber: 4.1g

Chicken and Celery Salad

Prep time: 10 minutes | Cook time: 15 minutes | Serves 2

4 ounces (113 g) chicken fillet
1 cup water
1 teaspoon ground
black pepper
7 ounces (198 g) celery stalks, chopped
½ teaspoon salt

1. Place the chicken, water, and pepper in the Instant Pot.
2. Secure the lid. Select the Manual mode and set the cooking time for 15 minutes at High Pressure.
3. Once cooking is complete, do a natural pressure release for 5 minutes, then release any remaining pressure. Carefully open the lid.
4. Remove the chicken and shred with forks, then transfer to a bowl. Add the celery stalks and salt and toss well, then serve.

Per Serving
calories: 146 | fat: 6.4g | protein: 17.9g
carbs: 3.7g | net carbs: 1.8g | fiber: 1.9g

Cayenne Cabbage with Bacon

Prep time: 5 minutes | Cook time: 10 minutes | Serves 4

2 teaspoons olive oil
4 slices bacon, chopped
1 cup vegetable stock
1 head green cabbage, cored and cut into wedges
1 teaspoon cayenne pepper
1 bay leaf
½ teaspoon whole black peppercorns
Sea salt, to taste

1. Set your Instant Pot to Sauté and heat the olive oil.
2. Add the bacon and cook for about 5 minutes, stirring occasionally, or until nicely browned.
3. Add the remaining ingredients to the Instant Pot and stir to incorporate.
4. Lock the lid. Select the Manual mode and set the cooking time for 3 minutes at High Pressure.
5. When the timer beeps, perform a quick pressure release. Carefully remove the lid.
6. Cool for 5 minutes before serving.

Per Serving
calories: 169 | fat: 13.7g | protein: 6.9g
carbs: 7.0g | net carbs: 6.1g | fiber: 0.9g

Ginger Bok Choy

Prep time: 5 minutes | Cook time: 10 minutes | Serves 4

2 tablespoons butter, melted
2 cloves garlic, minced
1 (½-inch) slice fresh ginger root, grated
1 cup vegetable stock
1½ pounds (680 g)
Bok choy, trimmed
1 teaspoon five-spice powder
Celery salt and ground black pepper to taste
2 tablespoons coconut aminos, for serving

1. Set your Instant Pot to Sauté and warm the butter.
2. Add the garlic and sauté for 2 minutes until tender.
3. Stir in the grated ginger and cook for 40 seconds more.
4. Add the remaining ingredients except the coconut aminos to the Instant Pot and mix well.
5. Lock the lid. Select the Manual mode and set the cooking time for 6 minutes at High Pressure.

6. When the timer beeps, perform a quick pressure release. Carefully remove the lid.
7. Remove the Bok choy from the Instant Pot to a platter and serve drizzled with the coconut aminos.

Per Serving
calories: 86 | fat: 6.3g | protein: 3.4g
carbs: 6.9g | net carbs: 2.4g | fiber: 4.5g

Paprika Egg Salad with Green Onions

Prep time: 5 minutes | Cook time: 7 minutes | Serves 2

6 eggs
1 cup water
¼ cup mayonnaise
½ teaspoon ground turmeric
½ teaspoon fresh paprika
½ teaspoon kosher salt
½ teaspoon freshly ground black pepper
¼ cup thinly sliced green onions

1. Beat the eggs in a bowl until frothy.
2. Pour the water into the Instant Pot and insert the trivet. Place the bowl with the eggs on the trivet.
3. Secure the lid. Select the Manual mode and set the cooking time for 7 minutes at High Pressure.
4. Meanwhile, stir together the mayo, turmeric, paprika, salt, and pepper in a small bowl until well combined.
5. When the timer beeps, perform a natural pressure release for 10 minutes, then release any remaining pressure. Carefully open the lid.
6. Remove the eggs and allow to cool for a few minutes. Stir in the mayo mixture and serve topped with the green onions.

Per Serving
calories: 400 | fat: 37.6g | protein: 17.5g
carbs: 3.0g | net carbs: 2.2g | fiber: 0.8g

Cheese Pepperoni Pizza Bites

Prep time: 5 minutes | Cook time: 5 minutes | Serves 4 to 5

1 cup water
2 cups shredded full-fat Mozzarella cheese
1 cup grated full-fat Parmesan cheese
1 (14-ounce / 397-g) can sugar-free or low-

sugar diced tomatoes, drained
16 uncured pepperoni slices, cut in half
1 teaspoon dried oregano
1 teaspoon dried basil

1. Pour the water into the Instant Pot and insert the trivet.
2. Combine the remaining ingredients in a large bowl and stir to incorporate.
3. Spoon the mixture into a greased egg bites mold. Work in batches, if needed. I prefer to stack 2 egg bites molds on top of each other, separated by Mason jar lids. Put the molds on the trivet and loosely cover with aluminum foil.
4. Secure the lid. Select the Manual mode and set the cooking time for 5 minutes at High Pressure.
5. Once cooking is complete, do a natural pressure release for 10 minutes, then release any remaining pressure. Carefully open the lid.
6. Remove the molds and cool for 5 minutes, then serve.

Per Serving
calories: 331 | fat: 25.1g | protein: 22.5g | carbs: 6.3g | net carbs: 4.6g | fiber: 1.7g

Chicken, Cauliflower and Broccoli Salad

Prep time: 5 minutes | Cook time: 10 minutes | Serves 4

2 tablespoons coconut oil
2 cups boneless, skinless chicken breasts, cubed
1 cup water
2 eggs, hard-boiled and sliced
1 avocado, mashed
¼ cup green thinly sliced onions

½ teaspoon dried sage
½ teaspoon ground nutmeg
½ teaspoon ground turmeric
½ teaspoon freshly ground black pepper
1 cup chopped cauliflower
1 cup chopped broccoli
2 tablespoons extra-virgin olive oil

1. Set your Instant Pot to Sauté and melt the coconut oil.
2. Add the chicken and water and mix well.
3. Secure the lid. Select the Manual mode and set the cooking time for 10 minutes at High Pressure.
4. Meanwhile, stir together the egg slices, avocado, green onions, sage, nutmeg, turmeric, and black pepper in a large salad bowl well incorporated. Set aside.
5. Once cooking is complete, do a quick pressure release. Carefully open the lid.
6. Add the cauliflower and broccoli to the Instant Pot, cover, and let sit for 2 minutes.
7. Drain out any excess liquid from the chicken and vegetable mixture. Allow them to cool to room temperature. When cooled, transfer them to the salad bowl and drizzle with the olive oil. Toss well and serve immediately.

Per Serving
calories: 411 | fat: 31.5g | protein: 25.7g | carbs: 9.2g | net carbs: 4.0g | fiber: 5.2g

Chapter 16 Desserts

Chocolate Muffins with Coconut

Prep time: 5 minutes | Cook time: 25 minutes | Serves 5

½ cup coconut flour
2 tablespoons cocoa powder
3 tablespoons erythritol
1 teaspoon baking powder
2 tablespoons coconut oil
2 eggs, beaten
½ cup coconut shred

1. In the mixing bowl, mix all ingredients.
2. Then pour the mixture in the molds of the muffin and transfer in the air fryer basket.
3. Cook the muffins at 350ºF (180ºC) for 25 minutes.

Per Serving
calories: 206 | fat: 16g | protein: 4g
carbs: 13g | net carbs: 6g | fiber: 7g

Chocolate Chip and Pecan Brownies

Prep time: 10 minutes | Cook time: 20 minutes | Serves 6

½ cup blanched finely ground almond flour
½ cup powdered erythritol
2 tablespoons unsweetened cocoa powder
½ teaspoon baking powder
¼ cup unsalted butter, softened
1 large egg
¼ cup chopped pecans
¼ cup low-carb, sugar-free chocolate chips

1. In a large bowl, mix almond flour, erythritol, cocoa powder, and baking powder. Stir in butter and egg.
2. Fold in pecans and chocolate chips. Scoop mixture into 6 -inch round baking pan. Place pan into the air fryer basket.
3. Adjust the temperature to 300ºF (150ºC) and set the timer for 20 minutes.
4. When fully cooked a toothpick inserted in center will come out clean. Allow 20 minutes to fully cool and firm up.

Per Serving
calories: 215 | fat: 18g | protein: 4g
carbs: 22g | net carbs: 19g | fiber: 3g

Lime Coconut Bar

Prep time: 10 minutes | Cook time: 35 minutes | Serves 10

3 tablespoons coconut oil, melted
3 tablespoons Splenda
1½ cups coconut flour
3 eggs, beaten
1 teaspoon lime zest, grated
3 tablespoons lime juice

1. Cover the air fryer basket bottom with baking paper.
2. Then in the mixing bowl, mix Splenda with coconut flour, eggs, lime zest, and lime juice.
3. Pour the mixture in the air fryer basket and flatten gently.
4. Cook the meal at 350ºF (180ºC) for 35 minutes.
5. Then cool the cooked meal little and cut into bars.

Per Serving
calories: 144 | fat: 7g | protein: 4g
carbs: 16g | net carbs: 8g | fiber: 7g

Cinnamon Zucchini Bread

Prep time: 10 minutes | Cook time: 40 minutes | Serves 12

2 cups coconut flour
2 teaspoons baking powder
¾ cup erythritol
½ cup coconut oil, melted
1 teaspoon apple cider vinegar
1 teaspoon vanilla extract
3 eggs, beaten
1 zucchini, grated
1 teaspoon ground cinnamon

1. In the mixing bowl, mix coconut flour with baking powder, erythritol, coconut oil, apple cider vinegar, vanilla extract, eggs, zucchini, and ground cinnamon.
2. Transfer the mixture in the air fryer basket and flatten it in the shape of the bread.
3. Cook the bread at 350F (180ºC) for 40 minutes.

Per Serving
calories: 179 | fat: 12g | protein: 4g
carbs: 15g | net carbs: 7g | fiber: 8g

Vanilla Scones

Prep time: 20 minutes | Cook time: 10 minutes | Serves 6

4 ounces (113 g) coconut flour
½ teaspoon baking powder
1 teaspoon apple cider vinegar
2 teaspoons

mascarpone
¼ cup heavy cream
1 teaspoon vanilla extract
1 tablespoon erythritol
Cooking spray

1. In the mixing bowl, mix coconut flour with baking powder, apple cider vinegar, mascarpone, heavy cream, vanilla extract, and erythritol.
2. Knead the dough and cut into scones.
3. Then put them in the air fryer basket and sprinkle with cooking spray.
4. Cook the vanilla scones at 365F (185ºC) for 10 minutes.

Per Serving
calories: 104 | fat: 4g | protein: 3g
carbs: 14g | net carbs: 6g | fiber: 8g

Vanilla Cookie Cake with Chocolate Chips

Prep time: 5 minutes | Cook time: 15 minutes | Serves 8

4 tablespoons salted butter, melted
⅓ cup granular brown erythritol
1 large egg
½ teaspoon vanilla extract

1 cup blanched finely ground almond flour
½ teaspoon baking powder
¼ cup low-carb chocolate chips

1. In a large bowl, whisk together butter, erythritol, egg, and vanilla. Add flour and baking powder, and stir until combined.
2. Fold in chocolate chips, then spoon batter into an ungreased 6-inch round nonstick baking dish.
3. Place dish into air fryer basket. Adjust the temperature to 300°F (150ºC) and set the timer for 15 minutes. When edges are browned, cookie cake will be done.
4. Slice and serve warm.

Per Serving
calories: 170 | fat: 16g | protein: 4g
carbs: 15g | net carbs: 11g | fiber: 4g

Coffee Mint Pie

Prep time: 15 minutes | Cook time: 25 minutes | Serves 2

1 tablespoon instant coffee
2 tablespoons almond butter, softened
2 tablespoons erythritol
1 teaspoon dried mint

3 eggs, beaten
1 teaspoon spearmint, dried
4 teaspoons coconut flour
Cooking spray

1. Spray the air fryer basket with cooking spray.
2. Then mix all ingredients in the mixer bowl.
3. When you get a smooth mixture, transfer it in the air fryer basket. Flatten it gently.
4. Cook the pie at 365F (185ºC) for 25 minutes.

Per Serving
calories: 313 | fat: 19g | protein: 16g
carbs: 20g | net carbs: 8g | fiber: 12g

Vanilla Doughnut Holes

Prep time: 10 minutes | Cook time: 6 minutes | Makes 20 doughnut holes

1 cup blanched finely ground almond flour
½ cup low-carb vanilla protein powder
½ cup granular erythritol
¼ cup unsweetened

cocoa powder
½ teaspoon baking powder
2 large eggs, whisked
½ teaspoon vanilla extract

1. Mix all ingredients in a large bowl until a soft dough forms. Separate and roll dough into twenty balls, about 2 tablespoons each.
2. Cut a piece of parchment to fit your air fryer basket. Working in batches if needed, place doughnut holes into air fryer basket on ungreased parchment. Adjust the temperature to 380°F (193ºC) and set the timer for 6 minutes, flipping doughnut holes halfway through cooking. Doughnut holes will be golden and firm when done. Let cool completely before serving, about 10 minutes.

Per Serving
calories: 103 | fat: 7g | protein: 8g
carbs: 13g | net carbs: 11g | fiber: 2g

Vanilla Coconut Whipping Cream

Prep time: 5 minutes | Cook time: 1 minute | Serves 5 to 6

1 (14-ounce / 397-g) can full-fat coconut milk, refrigerated	cream
	½ teaspoon vanilla extract
½ cup heavy whipping	⅓ cup Swerve

1. With a large spoon, carefully scoop out the cream portion of the coconut milk, discarding the remaining liquid.
2. In a small bowl, mix the coconut milk with the heavy whipping cream, vanilla, and Swerve and stir until combined.
3. Set the Instant Pot to Sauté mode and pour in the mixture. Melt together for 1 minute, stirring thoroughly.
4. Remove cream mixture from the Instant Pot and whip with an electric mixer, until reaching desired consistency. Refrigerate until ready to serve.

Per Serving
calories: 219 | fat: 22.7g | protein: 2.1g
carbs: 4.7g | net carbs: 2.8g | fiber: 1.9g

Coconut Fudge with Avocado

Prep time: 5 minutes | Cook time: 5 minutes | Serves 6

1 teaspoon grass-fed butter	¼ cup full-fat coconut milk
1 teaspoon raw coconut butter	1 cup dark sugar-free chocolate chips
1 teaspoon vanilla extract	1 tablespoon avocado
½ cup Swerve	½ cup pecans, chopped

1. Press the Sauté button on the Instant Pot. Add all ingredients, stirring very frequently, cook for 5 minutes, or until fudge melts together smoothly. Do not overcook.
2. Turn off Instant Pot and remove fudge. Cool briefly, then carefully pour it into a greased, deep glass dish.
3. Place into freezer for 20 minutes. Cut into 12 squares, and serve. Store leftovers in the refrigerator or freezer.

Per Serving
calories: 97 | fat: 7.8 g | protein: 1.5g
carbs: 10.9g | net carbs: 8.0g | fiber: 2.9g

Chocolate-Coated Cashews with Coconut

Prep time: 5 minutes | Cook time: 5 minutes | Serves 6

2 tablespoons grass-fed butter, softened	2 teaspoons shredded coconut
¼ cup sugar-free chocolate chips	¾ cup cashews, chopped

1. Set the Instant Pot to Sauté mode and melt the butter.
2. Add chocolate chips, shredded coconut and cashews to the Instant Pot, and cook for 5 minutes, or until the chocolate is melted.
3. Pour mixture into a large bowl and refrigerate until firm. Break into pieces and serve.

Per Serving
calories: 202 | fat: 17.6g | protein: 3.7g
carbs: 12.0g | net carbs: 9.3g | fiber: 2.7g

Almond Butter Cakes

Prep time: 5 minutes | Cook time: 30 minutes | Serves 6

1 egg	¼ teaspoon baking soda
½ cup almond flour	
¼ cup almond butter	⅓ cup Swerve

1. Mix the egg, flour, almond butter, baking soda, and Swerve in a large bowl. Use an electric mixer, until a smooth consistency is obtained. Pour the mixture evenly into ramekins.
2. Pour 1 cup water into the Instant Pot, then insert the trivet.
3. Cover the ramekins with aluminum foil, and place on top of the trivet.
4. Lock the lid. Select the Manual mode and set the cooking time for 30 minutes on High Pressure. Once the timer goes off, perform a natural pressure release for 10 minutes, then release any remaining pressure. Carefully open the lid.
5. Remove the mini cakes, and let cool. Serve.

Per Serving
calories: 195 | fat: 17.4g | protein: 6.5g
carbs: 7.0g | net carbs: 3.8g | fiber: 3.2g

Creamy Chocolate Mousse

Prep time: 5 minutes | Cook time: 5 minutes | Serves 5 to 6

2 tablespoons grass-fed butter, softened
¼ cup sugar-free chocolate chips
1 cup full-fat cream cheese, softened
1 tablespoon raw cacao nibs
½ teaspoon vanilla extract
½ cup Swerve
1/3 cup unsweetened cocoa powder
½ cup heavy whipping cream

1. Set the Instant Pot to Sauté mode and melt the butter. Add the chocolate chips, cream cheese, cacao nibs, vanilla, Swerve, and cocoa powder to the Instant Pot. Stir continuously for 5 minutes.
2. Remove the inner pot from the Instant Pot, and refrigerate for at least 20 minutes.
3. Whisk to beat the heavy whipping cream, until stiff peaks form.
4. Using a spatula, gently fold the whipped cream into the cooled chocolate mixture. Serve.

Per Serving

calories: 118 | fat: 10.9g | protein: 1.9g
carbs: 8.2g | net carbs: 5.3g | fiber: 2.9g

Coconut Muffins with Poppy Seeds

Prep time: 10 minutes | Cook time: 10 minutes | Serves 5

5 tablespoons coconut oil, softened
1 egg, beaten
1 teaspoon vanilla extract
1 tablespoon poppy seeds
1 teaspoon baking powder
2 tablespoons erythritol
1 cup coconut flour

1. In the mixing bowl, mix coconut oil with egg, vanilla extract, poppy seeds, baking powder, erythritol, and coconut flour.
2. When the mixture is homogenous, pour it in the muffin molds and transfer it in the air fryer basket.
3. Cook the muffins for 10 minutes at 365°F (185°C).

Per Serving

calories: 239 | fat: 17g | protein: 5g
carbs: 17g | net carbs: 7g | fiber: 10g

Coconut Flakes

Prep time: 5 minutes | Cook time: 3 minutes | Serves 4

1 cup unsweetened coconut flakes
2 teaspoons coconut oil
¼ cup granular erythritol
⅛ teaspoon salt

1. Toss coconut flakes and oil in a large bowl until coated. Sprinkle with erythritol and salt.
2. Place coconut flakes into the air fryer basket.
3. Adjust the temperature to 300°F (150°C) and set the timer for 3 minutes.
4. Toss the flakes when 1 minute remains. Add an extra minute if you would like a more golden coconut flake.
5. Store in an airtight container up to 3 days.

Per Serving

calories: 165 | fat: 15g | protein: 1g
carbs: 20g | net carbs: 17g | fiber: 3g

Vanilla Macadamia Bar

Prep time: 15 minutes | Cook time: 30 minutes | Serves 10

3 tablespoons butter, softened
1 teaspoon baking powder
1 teaspoon apple cider vinegar
1½ cups coconut flour
3 tablespoons Swerve
1 teaspoon vanilla extract
2 eggs, beaten
2 ounces (57 g) macadamia nuts, chopped
Cooking spray

1. Spray the air fryer basket with cooking spray.
2. Then mix all remaining ingredients in the mixing bowl and stir until you get a homogenous mixture.
3. Pour the mixture in the air fryer basket and cook at 345F (174°C) for 30 minutes.
4. When the mixture is cooked, cut it into bars and transfer in the serving plates.

Per Serving

calories: 158 | fat: 10g | protein: 4g
carbs: 13g | net carbs: 5g | fiber: 8g

Chocolate Fat Bombs with Nuts

Prep time: 5 minutes | Cook time: 5 minutes | Serves 7 to 8

2 tablespoons coconut oil
1 cup sugar-free chocolate chips
2 teaspoons shredded coconut
1 cup raw coconut butter
½ cup nuts, chopped

1. Set the Instant Pot to Sauté mode and melt the oil.
2. Add the chocolate chips, coconut, coconut butter, and nuts to the Instant Pot. Cook for 5 minutes, or until the chocolate is melted.
3. Pour mixture into a silicone mini-muffin mold.
4. Refrigerate until firm. Serve. Store leftover fudge in the refrigerator.

Per Serving
calories: 341 | fat: 35.7g | protein: 2.6g
carbs: 10.1g | net carbs: 7.2g | fiber: 2.9g

Vanilla Walnut Fudge with Coconut

Prep time: 5 minutes | Cook time: 5 minutes | Serves 4

2 tablespoons coconut oil
1 cup sugar-free chocolate chips
½ cup coconut milk
½ cup chopped walnuts
2 tablespoons unsweetened coconut flakes
2 tablespoons grass-fed butter, softened
1 teaspoon vanilla extract

1. Set the Instant Pot to the Sauté mode and melt the oil.
2. Stir in the chocolate chips, coconut milk, walnuts, coconut flakes, butter, and vanilla. Cook for 5 minutes, or until the chocolate is melted.
3. Remove the inner pot from the Instant Pot and carefully pour the fudge into a greased, deep glass dish. Smooth the surface with a spatula so the fudge is evenly distributed in the dish.
4. Freeze until firm, about 30 minutes. Slice into squares and serve.

Per Serving
calories: 151 | fat: 13.3g | protein: 2.8g
carbs: 11.3g | net carbs: 8.1g | fiber: 3.2g

Chocolate-Coated Pumpkin Seeds

Prep time: 5 minutes | Cook time: 5 minutes | Serves 5 to 6

2 tablespoons coconut oil
½ cup sugar-free chocolate chips
½ cup pumpkin seeds
½ teaspoon salt (optional)

1. Set the Instant Pot to the Sauté mode and melt the oil.
2. Add chocolate chips, pumpkin seeds, and salt to the Instant Pot, and cook for 5 minutes, or until chocolate is melted.
3. Using a spatula, scrape mixture into a large bowl or a cookie sheet in a single layer.
4. Refrigerate until firm. Serve. Store leftovers in the refrigerator or freezer.

Per Serving
calories: 174 | fat: 15.0g | protein: 4.3g
carbs: 12.6g | net carbs: 9.4g | fiber: 3.2g

Vanilla Custard

Prep time: 5 minutes | Cook time: 7 minutes | Serves 4

6 eggs, beaten
1 cup heavy cream
1 teaspoon vanilla extract
¼ teaspoon ground nutmeg
2 tablespoons erythritol
1 tablespoon coconut flour
1 cup water

1. Whisk the eggs and erythritol until smooth.
2. Then add heavy cream, vanilla extract, ground nutmeg, and coconut flour.
3. Whisk the mixture well again.
4. Then pour it in the custard ramekins and cover with foil.
5. Pour water and insert the trivet in the instant pot.
6. Place the ramekins with custard on the trivet.
7. Set the lid in place. Select the Manual mode and set the cooking time for 7 minutes on High Pressure. When the timer goes off, do a quick pressure release. Carefully open the lid.
8. Serve immediately.

Per Serving
calories: 208 | fat: 17.8g | protein: 9.3g
carbs: 10.2g | net carbs: 9.3g | fiber: 0.9g

Coconut Butter Bars with Chocolate Chips

Prep time: 5 minutes | Cook time: 10 minutes | Serves 16

4 tablespoons grass-fed butter, softened
1 cup raw coconut butter
2 tablespoons raw cacao nibs

½ cup sugar-free chocolate chips
½ teaspoon vanilla extract
½ teaspoon salt
½ cup Swerve

1. In a large bowl, mix together the butter, coconut butter, cacao nibs, chocolate chips, vanilla, salt, and Swerve. Whisk or stir until the mixture reaches a smooth consistency.
2. Pour 1 cup water into the inner pot of the Instant Pot, and insert the trivet. Transfer the mixture from the bowl into a well-greased, Instant Pot-friendly dish.
3. Place the dish onto the trivet, and cover loosely with aluminum foil.
4. Lock the lid. Select the Manual mode and set the cooking time for 10 minutes on High Pressure. Once the timer goes off, perform a natural pressure release for 10 minutes, then release any remaining pressure. Carefully open the lid.
5. Remove the dish. Once sufficiently cooled, cut into 16 bars, serve, and enjoy!

Per Serving
calories: 181 | fat: 19.2g | protein: 0.7g
carbs: 4.7g | net carbs: 3.1g | fiber: 1.6g

Chocolate Mousse with Nutmeg

Prep time: 5 minutes | Cook time: 10 minutes | Serves 6

1 cup coconut milk
1 cup heavy cream
4 egg yolks, beaten
1/3 cup Swerve
¼ teaspoon grated

nutmeg
¼ teaspoon ground cinnamon
¼ cup unsweetened cocoa powder

1. In a small pan, bring the milk and cream to a simmer.
2. In a mixing dish, thoroughly combine the remaining ingredients. Add this egg mixture to the warm milk mixture. Pour the mixture into ramekins.
3. Add 1½ cups water and the trivet to the Instant Pot. Now, lower your ramekins onto the trivet.

4. Lock the lid. Select the Manual mode and set the cooking time for 10 minutes on High Pressure. Once the timer goes off, perform a natural pressure release for 10 minutes, then release any remaining pressure. Carefully open the lid.
5. Serve chilled.

Per Serving
calories: 139 | fat: 11.7g | protein: 4.2g
carbs: 6.1g | net carbs: 4.9g | fiber: 1.2g

Vanilla Cheesecake

Prep time: 20 minutes | Cook time: 35 minutes | Serves 6

½ cup blanched finely ground almond flour
1 cup powdered erythritol, divided
2 tablespoons unsweetened cocoa powder
½ teaspoon baking powder
¼ cup unsalted butter, softened

2 large eggs, divided
8 ounces (227 g) full-fat cream cheese, softened
¼ cup heavy whipping cream
1 teaspoon vanilla extract
2 tablespoons no-sugar-added peanut butter

1. In a large bowl, mix almond flour, ½ cup erythritol, cocoa powder, and baking powder. Stir in butter and one egg.
2. Scoop mixture into 6-inch round baking pan. Place pan into the air fryer basket.
3. Adjust the temperature to 300°F (150°C) and set the timer for 20 minutes.
4. When fully cooked a toothpick inserted in center will come out clean. Allow 20 minutes to fully cool and firm up.
5. In a large bowl, beat cream cheese, remaining ½ cup erythritol, heavy cream, vanilla, peanut butter, and remaining egg until fluffy.
6. Pour mixture over cooled brownies. Place pan back into the air fryer basket.
7. Adjust the temperature to 300°F (150°C) and set the timer for 15 minutes.
8. Cheesecake will be slightly browned and mostly firm with a slight jiggle when done. Allow to cool, then refrigerate 2 hours before serving.

Per Serving
calories: 347 | fat: 30g | protein: 8g
carbs: 30g | net carbs: 28g | fiber: 2g

Coconut Balls

Prep time: 5 minutes | Cook time: 8 minutes | Serves 2

2 tablespoon coconut flakes
1 egg, whisked
2 tablespoons coconut flour
¾ teaspoon vanilla extract
1 teaspoon erythritol
1 tablespoon coconut oil
1 cup water

1. Combine together the whisked egg, coconut flour, coconut flakes, and vanilla extract. Add coconut oil.
2. Add baking powder and erythritol.
3. Make the balls from the coconut flour mixture.
4. Pour the water in the instant pot.
5. Insert the trivet inside and place the ramekin on it. Add coconut balls.
6. Set the lid in place. Select the Manual mode and set the cooking time for 8 minutes on High Pressure. When the timer goes off, do a quick pressure release. Carefully open the lid.
7. Chill the dessert for 5 to 10 minutes or until they are warm.

Per Serving
calories: 141 | fat: 11.3g | protein: 4.0g
carbs: 6.7g | net carbs: 3.1g | fiber: 3.6g

Coconut Cupcakes

Prep time: 5 minutes | Cook time: 8 minutes | Serves 4

3 egg yolks, well whisked
¹/₃ cup Swerve
¼ cup water
3 tablespoons unsweetened cacao powder
¾ cup whipping cream
¹/₃ cup coconut milk
¼ cup shredded coconut
1 teaspoon vanilla essence
Pinch of grated nutmeg
Pinch of salt

1. Place the egg in a mixing bowl.
2. In a pan, heat the Swerve, water and cacao powder and whisk well to combine.
3. Now, stir in the whipping cream and milk; cook until heated through. Add shredded coconut, vanilla, nutmeg, and salt.
4. Now, slowly and gradually pour the chocolate mixture into the bowl with egg yolks. Stir to combine well and pour into ramekins.

5. Add 1½ cups water and the trivet to the Instant Pot. Now, lower your ramekins onto the trivet.
6. Lock the lid. Select the Manual mode and set the cooking time for 8 minutes on High Pressure. Once the timer goes off, perform a natural pressure release for 10 minutes, then release any remaining pressure. Carefully open the lid.
7. Place in your refrigerator until ready to serve.

Per Serving
calories: 115 | fat: 8.4g | protein: 3.9g
carbs: 7.4g | net carbs: 5.7g | fiber: 1.7g

Vanilla Chocolate Chips Soufflés

Prep time: 5 minutes | Cook time: 15 minutes | Serves 2

2 large eggs, whites and yolks separated
1 teaspoon vanilla extract
2 ounces (57 g) low-carb chocolate chips
2 teaspoons coconut oil, melted

1. In a medium bowl, beat egg whites until stiff peaks form, about 2 minutes. Set aside. In a separate medium bowl, whisk egg yolks and vanilla together. Set aside.
2. In a separate medium microwave-safe bowl, place chocolate chips and drizzle with coconut oil. Microwave on high 20 seconds, then stir and continue cooking in 10-second increments until melted, being careful not to overheat chocolate. Let cool 1 minute.
3. Slowly pour melted chocolate into egg yolks and whisk until smooth. Then, slowly begin adding egg white mixture to chocolate mixture, about ¼ cup at a time, folding in gently.
4. Pour mixture into two 4-inch ramekins greased with cooking spray. Place ramekins into air fryer basket. Adjust the temperature to 400°F (205ºC) and set the timer for 15 minutes. Soufflés will puff up while cooking and deflate a little once cooled. The center will be set when done. Let cool 10 minutes, then serve warm.

Per Serving
calories: 217 | fat: 18g | protein: 8g
carbs: 19g | net carbs: 11g | fiber: 8g

Vanilla Chocolate Chip Bites

Prep time: 5 minutes | Cook time: 20 minutes | Serves 5 to 6

3 tablespoons sugar-free chocolate chips
2 tablespoons coconut oil
1 egg
½ cup almond flour
½ teaspoon vanilla extract
½ cup Swerve
15 ounces (425 g) cream cheese

1. Pour 1 cup water into the inner pot of the Instant Pot, then insert the trivet. In a large bowl, combine the chocolate chips, coconut oil, egg, almond flour, vanilla, Swerve, and cheese. Mix thoroughly. Once mixed, evenly pour this mixture into 6 well-greased, Instant Pot-friendly ramekins.
2. Place the ramekins on the trivet, and cover each loosely with aluminum foil.
3. Lock the lid. Select the Manual mode and set the cooking time for 20 minutes on High Pressure. Once the timer goes off, perform a natural pressure release for 10 minutes, then release any remaining pressure. Carefully open the lid.
4. Remove the ramekins. Place in the refrigerator for at least 20 minutes. Let cool, serve, and enjoy!

Per Serving
calories: 188 | fat: 13.9g | protein: 10.1g
carbs: 8.1g | net carbs: 6.7g | fiber: 1.4g

Blueberry Curd with Lemon

Prep time: 5 minutes | Cook time: 15 minutes | Serves 4

4 ounces (113 g) coconut oil, softened
¾ cup Swerve
4 egg yolks, beaten
½ cup blueberries
1 teaspoon grated
lemon zest
½ teaspoon vanilla extract
½ teaspoon ground star anise

1. Blend the coconut oil and Swerve in a food processor.
2. Gradually mix in the eggs; continue to blend for 1 minute longer.
3. Now, add blueberries, lemon zest, vanilla, and star anise. Divide the mixture among four Mason jars and cover them with lids.
4. Add 1½ cups water and a trivet to the Instant Pot. Now, lower your jars onto the trivet.

5. Lock the lid. Select the Manual mode and set the cooking time for 15 minutes on High Pressure. Once the timer goes off, perform a natural pressure release for 10 minutes, then release any remaining pressure. Carefully open the lid.
6. Place in your refrigerator until ready to serve.

Per Serving
calories: 327 | fat: 32.9g | protein: 2.9g
carbs: 7.2g | net carbs: 6.7g | fiber: 0.5g

Chocolate Cake with Coconut

Prep time: 10 minutes | Cook time: 40 minutes | Serves 5 to 6

3 tablespoons sugar-free chocolate chips
2 tablespoons grass-fed butter, softened
2 eggs
1⅓ cups almond flour
1 teaspoon baking powder
1 teaspoon pumpkin purée
½ cup Swerve
½ cup unsweetened coconut flakes
½ cup heavy whipping cream
½ teaspoon ground nutmeg
½ teaspoon ground cinnamon
½ teaspoon vanilla extract

1. In a large bowl, thoroughly mix together all ingredients, until a perfectly even mixture is obtained.
2. Next, pour 1 cup filtered water into the Instant Pot and insert the trivet.
3. Transfer the mixture from the bowl into a well-greased, Instant Pot-friendly pan.
4. Using a sling, place the pan onto the trivet, and cover loosely with aluminum foil.
5. Lock the lid. Select the Manual mode and set the cooking time for 40 minutes on High Pressure. Once the timer goes off, perform a natural pressure release for 10 minutes, then release any remaining pressure. Carefully open the lid.
6. Remove the pan. Allow to cool completely before serving. Add any desired toppings on top of the finished dessert, serve, and enjoy!

Per Serving
calories: 226 | fat: 21.0g | protein: 4.3g
carbs: 8.7g | net carbs: 6.1g | fiber: 2.6g

Cinnamon Pretzels

Prep time: 10 minutes | Cook time: 10 minutes | Serves 6

1½ cups shredded Mozzarella cheese
1 cup blanched finely ground almond flour
2 tablespoons salted butter, melted, divided
¼ cup granular erythritol, divided
1 teaspoon ground cinnamon

1. Place Mozzarella, flour, 1 tablespoon butter, and 2 tablespoons erythritol in a large microwave-safe bowl. Microwave on high 45 seconds, then stir with a fork until a smooth dough ball forms.
2. Separate dough into six equal sections. Gently roll each section into a 12 -inch rope, then fold into a pretzel shape.
3. Place pretzels into ungreased air fryer basket. Adjust the temperature to 370°F (188ºC) and set the timer for 8 minutes, turning pretzels halfway through cooking.
4. In a small bowl, combine remaining butter, remaining erythritol, and cinnamon. Brush ½ mixture on both sides of pretzels.
5. Place pretzels back into air fryer and cook an additional 2 minutes at 370°F (188ºC).
6. Transfer pretzels to a large plate. Brush on both sides with remaining butter mixture, then let cool 5 minutes before serving.

Per Serving
calories: 223 | fat: 19g | protein: 11g
carbs: 13g | net carbs: 11g | fiber: 2g

Pecan Pie with Strawberry Cream

Prep time: 15 minutes | Cook time: 10 minutes | Serves 6

1½ cups whole shelled pecans
1 tablespoon unsalted butter, softened
1 cup heavy whipping cream
12 medium fresh strawberries, hulled
2 tablespoons sour cream

1. Place pecans and butter into a food processor and pulse ten times until a dough forms. Press dough into the bottom of an ungreased 6-inch round nonstick baking dish.
2. Place dish into air fryer basket. Adjust the temperature to 320°F (160ºC) and set the timer for 10 minutes. Crust will be firm and golden when done. Let cool 20 minutes.
3. In a large bowl, whisk cream until fluffy and doubled in size, about 2 minutes.
4. In a separate large bowl, mash strawberries until mostly liquid. Fold strawberries and sour cream into whipped cream.
5. Spoon mixture into cooled crust, cover, and place into refrigerator for at least 30 minutes to set. Serve chilled.

Per Serving
calories: 340 | fat: 33g | protein: 3g
carbs: 7g | net carbs: 4g | fiber: 3g

Chocolate Squares with Almonds

Prep time: 10 minutes | Cook time: 40 minutes | Serves 8

1 cup almond flour
6 tablespoons sugar-free chocolate chips
¼ cup unsweetened cocoa powder
2 tablespoons coconut oil
2 eggs
2 tablespoons raw
cacao nibs
1 cup chopped almonds
½ cup Swerve
¼ cup coconut milk
½ teaspoon vanilla extract
½ teaspoon salt

1. In a large bowl, mix together the chocolate chips, cocoa powder, coconut oil, eggs, cacao nibs, almonds, Swerve, coconut milk, vanilla, and salt. Combine them very thoroughly.
2. Pour 1 cup water into the inner pot of the Instant Pot, and insert the trivet. Transfer the chocolate mixture from the bowl into a well-greased, Instant Pot–friendly dish.
3. Place the dish onto the trivet, and cover loosely with aluminum foil.
4. Lock the lid. Select the Manual mode and set the cooking time for 40 minutes on High Pressure. Once the timer goes off, perform a natural pressure release for 10 minutes, then release any remaining pressure. Carefully open the lid.
5. Remove the dish. Refrigerate for at least 20 minutes. Once sufficiently firm, cut into 8 squares and serve.

Per Serving
calories: 212 | fat: 18.0g | protein: 6.1g
carbs: 13.0g | net carbs: 7.4g | fiber: 5.6g

Vanilla Flan with Rum

Prep time: 5 minutes | Cook time: 10 minutes | Serves 6

6 eggs
1 cup Swerve
1½ cups double cream
½ cup water
3 tablespoons dark rum
Pinch of salt

Pinch of freshly grated nutmeg
¼ teaspoon ground cinnamon
1 teaspoon vanilla extract

1. Start by adding the water and the trivet to your Instant Pot.
2. In a mixing bowl, thoroughly combine eggs and Swerve. Add double cream, water, rum, salt, nutmeg, cinnamon, and vanilla extract.
3. Pour mixture into a baking dish. Lower the dish onto the trivet.
4. Lock the lid. Select the Manual mode and set the cooking time for 10 minutes on High Pressure. Once the timer goes off, perform a natural pressure release for 10 minutes, then release any remaining pressure. Carefully open the lid.
5. Serve well chilled.

Per Serving
calories: 214 | fat: 15.9g | protein: 7.2g
carbs: 6.1g | net carbs: 5.9g | fiber: 0.2g

Chocolate Bites

Prep time: 5 minutes | Cook time: 5 minutes | Serves 7

6 tablespoons sugar-free chocolate chips
4 ounces (113 g) full-fat cream cheese, softened
½ cup full-fat coconut

milk
1 cup heavy whipping cream
½ cup Swerve
½ teaspoon vanilla extract

1. Pour 1 cup water into the inner pot of the Instant Pot, then insert the trivet. In a large bowl, combine the chocolate chips, cream cheese, coconut milk, whipping cream, Swerve, and vanilla. Mix thoroughly and transfer into well-greased egg bites molds.
2. Place molds on top of the trivet, stacking on top of each other, if needed. Cover loosely with aluminum foil.

3. Lock the lid. Select the Manual mode and set the cooking time for 5 minutes on High Pressure. Once the timer goes off, perform a natural pressure release for 10 minutes, then release any remaining pressure. Carefully open the lid.
4. Remove the molds. Freeze for at least 1 hour, then serve. Keep uneaten bites stored in freezer.

Per Serving
calories: 169 | fat: 15.9g | protein: 2.2g
carbs: 5.6g | net carbs: 4.8g | fiber: 0.8g

Vanilla Butter Cake

Prep time: 5 minutes | Cook time: 35 minutes | Serves 4

2 cups almond flour
¾ cup granulated erythritol
1½ teaspoons baking powder
4 eggs

1 tablespoon vanilla extract
½ cup butter, melted
Cooking spray
½ cup water

1. In a medium bowl, whisk together the almond flour, erythritol, and baking powder. Whisk well to remove any lumps.
2. Add the eggs and vanilla and whisk until combined.
3. Add the butter and whisk until the batter is mostly smooth and well combined.
4. Grease the pan with cooking spray and pour in the batter. Cover tightly with aluminum foil.
5. Add the water to the pot. Place the Bundt pan on the trivet and carefully lower it into the pot using.
6. Set the lid in place. Select the Manual mode and set the cooking time for 35 minutes on High Pressure. When the timer goes off, do a quick pressure release. Carefully open the lid.
7. Remove the pan from the pot. Let the cake cool in the pan before flipping out onto a plate.

Per Serving
calories: 179 | fat: 15.9g | protein: 2.1g
carbs: 2.0g | net carbs: 2.0g | fiber: 0g

Chocolate Cakes

Prep time: 5 minutes | Cook time: 20 minutes | Serves 4

1 egg
1 cup almond flour
½ cup sugar-free chocolate chips
¼ teaspoon baking soda
¼ cup unsweetened cocoa powder

1. Pour 1 cup water into the inner pot, then insert the trivet. Using an electric hand mixer, combine egg, almond flour, chocolate chips, baking soda, and cocoa powder.
2. Transfer batter evenly into 4 well-greased ramekins. Cover with aluminum foil. Place the ramekins on top of the trivet.
3. Set the lid in place. Select the Manual mode and set the cooking time for 20 minutes on High Pressure. When the timer goes off, do a quick pressure release. Carefully open the lid.
4. Remove the ramekins. Let the cakes cool, then serve, and enjoy!

Per Serving
calories: 157 | fat: 11.4g | protein: 5.2g
carbs: 19.7g | net carbs: 13.6g | fiber: 6.1g

Cinnamon Cream Puffs

Prep time: 15 minutes | Cook time: 6 minutes | Makes 8 puffs

½ cup blanched finely ground almond flour
½ cup low-carb vanilla protein powder
½ cup granular erythritol
½ teaspoon baking powder
1 large egg
5 tablespoons unsalted butter, melted
2 ounces (57 g) full-fat cream cheese
¼ cup powdered erythritol
¼ teaspoon ground cinnamon
2 tablespoons heavy whipping cream
½ teaspoon vanilla extract

1. Mix almond flour, protein powder, granular erythritol, baking powder, egg, and butter in a large bowl until a soft dough forms.
2. Place the dough in the freezer for 20 minutes. Wet your hands with water and roll the dough into eight balls.
3. Cut a piece of parchment to fit your air fryer basket. Working in batches as necessary, place the dough balls into the air fryer basket on top of parchment.

4. Adjust the temperature to 380°F (193°C) and set the timer for 6 minutes.
5. Flip cream puffs halfway through the cooking time.
6. When the timer beeps, remove the puffs and allow to cool.
7. In a medium bowl, beat the cream cheese, powdered erythritol, cinnamon, cream, and vanilla until fluffy.
8. Place the mixture into a pastry bag or a storage bag with the end snipped. Cut a small hole in the bottom of each puff and fill with some of the cream mixture.
9. Store in an airtight container up to 2 days in the refrigerator.

Per Serving
calories: 178 | fat: 12g | protein: 15g
carbs: 22g | net carbs: 21g | fiber: 1g

Coconut Cream Flan with Blueberries

Prep time: 30 minutes | Cook time: 25 minutes | Serves 6

¾ cup extra-fine almond flour
1 cup fresh blueberries
½ cup coconut cream
¾ cup coconut milk
3 eggs, whisked
½ cup Swerve
½ teaspoon baking
soda
½ teaspoon baking powder
1/3 teaspoon ground cinnamon
½ teaspoon ginger
¼ teaspoon grated nutmeg

1. Lightly grease 2 mini pie pans using a nonstick cooking spray. Lay the blueberries on the bottom of the pie pans.
2. In a saucepan that is preheated over a moderate flame, warm the cream along with coconut milk until thoroughly heated.
3. Remove the pan from the heat; mix in the flour along with baking soda and baking powder.
4. In a medium-sized mixing bowl, whip the eggs, Swerve, and spices; whip until the mixture is creamy.
5. Add the creamy milk mixture. Carefully spread this mixture over the fruits.
6. Bake at 320°F (160°C) for about 25 minutes. Serve.

Per Serving
calories: 250 | fat: 22g | protein: 7g
carbs: 9g | net carbs: 6g | fiber: 3g

Pecan Cookie Bars with Cinnamon

Prep time: 5 minutes | Cook time: 40 minutes | Serves 5 to 6

1 cup almond flour
2 tablespoons butter, softened
½ cup Swerve
½ cup chopped pecans
½ teaspoon vanilla extract
½ teaspoon ground cinnamon
½ teaspoon ground nutmeg
¼ teaspoon baking soda

1. In a large bowl, mix together almond flour and butter. Add Swerve, pecans, vanilla, cinnamon, nutmeg, and baking soda, and stir until an evenly textured dough forms.
2. Add one cup filtered water into the Instant Pot, and insert the trivet.
3. Transfer the mixture from the bowl into a well-greased, Instant Pot-friendly dish or pan.
4. Place the dish onto the trivet, and cover loosely with aluminum foil.
5. Lock the lid. Select the Manual mode and set the cooking time for 40 minutes on High Pressure. Once the timer goes off, perform a natural pressure release for 10 minutes, then release any remaining pressure. Carefully open the lid.
6. Remove the dish. Once sufficiently cooled, cut into bars and serve.

Per Serving
calories: 146 | fat: 15.5g | protein: 1.5g
carbs: 1.5g | net carbs: 0.5g | fiber: 1.0g

Almond and Monk Fruit Cookies

Prep time: 50 minutes | Cook time: 13 minutes | Serves 8

½ cup slivered almonds
1 stick butter, room temperature
4 ounces (113 g) monk fruit
²/₃ cup blanched almond flour
¹/₃ cup coconut flour
¹/₃ teaspoon ground cloves
1 tablespoon ginger powder
¾ teaspoon pure vanilla extract

1. In a mixing dish, beat the monk fruit, butter, vanilla extract, ground cloves, and ginger until light and fluffy. Then, throw in the coconut flour, almond flour, and slivered almonds.

2. Continue mixing until it forms a soft dough. Cover and place in the refrigerator for 35 minutes. Meanwhile, preheat the Air Fryer to 315ºF (157ºC).
3. Roll dough into small cookies and place them on the Air Fryer cake pan; gently press each cookie using the back of a spoon.
4. Bake these butter cookies for 13 minutes. Bon appétit!

Per Serving
calories: 199 | fat: 19g | protein: 3g
carbs: 4g | net carbs: 2g | fiber: 2g

Almond Vanilla Crème

Prep time: 5 minutes | Cook time: 7 minutes | Serves 4

2 cups heavy whipping cream
½ cup water
4 eggs
¹/₃ cup Swerve
1 teaspoon almond extract
1 teaspoon vanilla extract
¹/₃ cup ground almonds
2 tablespoons coconut oil, at room temperature
4 tablespoons cacao powder
2 tablespoons gelatin

1. Start by adding 1½ cups of water and the trivet to your Instant Pot.
2. Blend the cream, water, eggs, Swerve, almond extract, vanilla extract and almonds in a food processor.
3. Add the remaining ingredients and process for a minute longer.
4. Divide the mixture between four Mason jars; cover your jars with lids. Lower the jars onto the trivet.
5. Lock the lid. Select the Manual mode and set the cooking time for 7 minutes on High Pressure. Once the timer goes off, perform a natural pressure release for 10 minutes, then release any remaining pressure. Carefully open the lid.
6. Serve immediately.

Per Serving
calories: 399 | fat: 37.4g | protein: 9.3g
carbs: 9.6g | net carbs: 7.1g | fiber: 2.5g

Cream Cheesecake

Prep time: 10 minutes | Cook time: 25 minutes | Serves 6

1 cup blanched finely ground almond flour
¼ cup salted butter, melted
½ cup granular erythritol
1 teaspoon vanilla extract
1 teaspoon baking powder
½ cup full-fat sour cream
1 ounce (28 g) full-fat cream cheese, softened
2 large eggs

1. In a large bowl, mix almond flour, butter, and erythritol.
2. Add in vanilla, baking powder, sour cream, and cream cheese and mix until well combined. Add eggs and mix.
3. Pour batter into a 6-inch round baking pan. Place pan into the air fryer basket.
4. Adjust the temperature to 300°F (150°C) and set the timer for 25 minutes.
5. When the cake is done, a toothpick inserted in center will come out clean. The center should not feel wet. Allow it to cool completely, or the cake will crumble when moved.

Per Serving
calories: 253 | fat: 22g | protein: 7g
carbs: 25g | net carbs: 23g | fiber: 2g

Cinnamon Cheese Balls

Prep time: 15 minutes | Cook time: 4 minutes | Serves 10

2 eggs, beaten
1 teaspoon coconut oil, melted
9 ounces (255 g) coconut flour
5 ounces (142 g) Provolone cheese, shredded
2 tablespoons erythritol
1 teaspoon baking powder
¼ teaspoon ground cinnamon
Cooking spray

1. Mix eggs with coconut oil, coconut flour, Provolone cheese, erythritol, baking powder, and ground cinnamon.
2. Make the balls and put them in the air fryer basket.
3. Sprinkle the balls with cooking spray and cook at 400F (205°C) for 4 minutes.

Per Serving
calories: 176 | fat: 7g | protein: 8g
carbs: 19g | net carbs: 8g | fiber: 11g

Coconut Pecan Bar

Prep time: 5 minutes | Cook time: 40 minutes | Serves 12

2 cups coconut flour
5 tablespoons erythritol
4 tablespoons coconut
oil, softened
½ cup heavy cream
1 egg, beaten
4 pecans, chopped

1. Mix coconut flour, erythritol, coconut oil, heavy cream, and egg.
2. Pour the batter in the air fryer basket and flatten well.
3. Top the mixture with pecans and cook the meal at 350°F (180°C) for 40 minutes.
4. Cut the cooked meal into the bars.

Per Serving
calories: 174 | fat: 12g | protein: 4g
carbs: 14g | net carbs: 5g | fiber: 9g

Blueberry Coconut Muffins

Prep time: 5 minutes | Cook time: 14 minutes | Serves 3

¼ cup blueberries
¼ teaspoon baking powder
1 teaspoon apple cider vinegar
4 teaspoons butter,
melted
2 eggs, beaten
1 cup coconut flour
2 tablespoons erythritol
1 cup water

1. In the mixing bowl, mix up baking powder, apple cider vinegar, butter, eggs, coconut flour, and erythritol.
2. When the batter is smooth, add blueberries. Stir well.
3. Put the muffin batter in the muffin molds.
4. After this, pour water and insert the trivet in the instant pot.
5. Then place the muffins on the trivet.
6. Lock the lid. Select the Manual mode and set the cooking time for 14 minutes on High Pressure. Once the timer goes off, perform a natural pressure release for 6 minutes, then release any remaining pressure. Carefully open the lid.
7. Serve immediately.

Per Serving
calories: 94 | fat: 4.4g | protein: 3.5g
carbs: 14.5g | net carbs: 8.3g | fiber: 6.2g

Vanilla Chocolate Chip Cookies

Prep time: 20 minutes | Cook time: 11 minutes | Serves 8

1 stick butter, at room temperature
1¼ cups Swerve
¼ cup chunky peanut butter
1 teaspoon vanilla paste
1 fine almond flour
⅔ cup coconut flour
⅓ cup cocoa powder, unsweetened
1½ teaspoons baking powder
¼ teaspoon ground cinnamon
¼ teaspoon ginger
½ cup chocolate chips, unsweetened

1. In a mixing dish, beat the butter and Swerve until creamy and uniform. Stir in the peanut butter and vanilla.
2. In another mixing dish, thoroughly combine the flour, cocoa powder, baking powder, cinnamon, and ginger.
3. Add the flour mixture to the peanut butter mixture; mix to combine well. Afterwards, fold in the chocolate chips.
4. Drop by large spoonfuls onto a parchment-lined Air Fryer basket. Bake at 365ºF (185ºC) for 11 minutes or until golden brown on the top. Bon appétit!

Per Serving
calories: 303 | fat: 28g | protein: 6g
carbs: 10g | net carbs: 5g | fiber: 5g

Cinnamon Almond Pie

Prep time: 10 minutes | Cook time: 35 minutes | Serves 12

2 cups almond flour
1½ cups powdered erythritol
1 teaspoon baking powder
Pinch of salt
½ cup sour cream
4 tablespoons butter, melted
1 egg
1 teaspoon vanilla extract
Cooking spray
1½ teaspoons ground cinnamon
1½ teaspoons Swerve
1 cup water

1. In a large bowl, whisk together the almond flour, powdered erythritol, baking powder, and salt.
2. Add the sour cream, butter, egg, and vanilla and whisk until well combined. The batter will be very thick, almost like cookie dough.
3. Grease the baking dish with cooking spray. Line with parchment paper, if desired.
4. Transfer the batter to the dish and level with an offset spatula.
5. In a small bowl, combine the cinnamon and Swerve. Sprinkle over the top of the batter.
6. Cover the dish tightly with aluminum foil. Add the water to the pot. Set the dish on the trivet and carefully lower it into the pot.
7. Set the lid in place. Select the Manual mode and set the cooking time for 35 minutes on High Pressure. When the timer goes off, do a quick pressure release. Carefully open the lid.
8. Remove the trivet and pie from the pot. Remove the foil from the pan. The pie should be set but soft, and the top should be slightly cracked.
9. Cool completely before cutting.

Per Serving
calories: 221 | fat: 19.0g | protein: 5.6g
carbs: 4.8g | net carbs: 2.4g | fiber: 2.4g

Vanilla Flan

Prep time: 10 minutes | Cook time: 10 minutes | Serves 4

4 egg whites
4 egg yolks
½ cup erythritol
7 ounces (198 g) heavy whipping cream
3 tablespoons water
1 tablespoon butter
½ teaspoon vanilla extract
1 cup water

1. In the saucepan, heat up erythritol and butter. When the mixture is smooth, leave it in a warm place.
2. Meanwhile, mix up water, heavy cream, egg whites, and egg yolks. Whisk the mixture.
3. Pour the erythritol mixture in the flan ramekins and then add heavy cream mixture over the sweet mixture.
4. Pour water and insert the trivet in the instant pot.
5. Place the ramekins with flan on the trivet.
6. Lock the lid. Select the Manual mode and set the cooking time for 10 minutes on High Pressure. Once the timer goes off, perform a natural pressure release for 10 minutes, then release any remaining pressure. Carefully open the lid.
7. Cool the cooked flan for 25 minutes. Serve.

Per Serving
calories: 268 | fat: 25.7g | protein: 7.5g
carbs: 2.2g | net carbs: 2.2g | fiber: 0g

Easy Coconut Cupcakes

Prep time: 5 minutes | Cook time: 10 minutes | Serves 6

4 eggs, beaten
4 tablespoons coconut milk
4 tablespoons coconut flour
½ teaspoon vanilla

extract
2 tablespoons erythritol
1 teaspoon baking powder
1 cup water

1.
2. In the mixing bowl, mix up eggs, coconut milk, coconut flour, vanilla extract, erythritol, and baking powder.
3. Then pour the batter in the cupcake molds.
4. Pour the water and insert the trivet in the instant pot.
5. Place the cupcakes on the trivet.
6. Lock the lid. Select the Manual mode and set the cooking time for 10 minutes on High Pressure. Once the timer goes off, perform a natural pressure release for 5 minutes, then release any remaining pressure. Carefully open the lid.
7. Serve immediately.

Per Serving
calories: 85 | fat: 5.7g | protein: 4.7g
carbs: 9.1g | net carbs: 6.8g | fiber: 2.3g

Vanilla-Mint Ice Cream

Prep time: 5 minutes | Cook time: 5 minutes | Serves 5 to 6

6 egg whites
4 teaspoons vanilla extract
1 teaspoon mint extract
½ cup Swerve
¼ cup slivered

almonds
¼ cup shredded coconut
2²/₃ cups heavy whipping cream
½ cup sugar-free chocolate chips

1. In a large bowl, using a handheld mixer or stand mixer, beat egg whites until stiff peaks form. Gently fold in vanilla, mint, Swerve, almond, coconut, and whipping cream. Mix thoroughly. Cover and freeze for 2 to 4 hours.
2. Press the Sauté button on the Instant Pot. Pour in the chocolate chips, stirring very frequently, cook for 5 minutes, or until they melt together smoothly. Do not overcook. Turn off heat, and remove melted chocolate.

3. Scoop the ice cream into a bowl and drizzle the melted chocolate over it. Store leftovers in freezer.

Per Serving
calories: 350 | fat: 31.3g | protein: 8.9g
carbs: 13.6g | net carbs: 10.3g | fiber: 3.3g

Pumpkin Cheese Cookie

Prep time: 10 minutes | Cook time: 7 minutes | Serves 6

½ cup blanched finely ground almond flour
½ cup powdered erythritol, divided
2 tablespoons butter, softened
1 large egg
½ teaspoon unflavored gelatin
½ teaspoon baking powder
½ teaspoon vanilla extract

½ teaspoon pumpkin pie spice
2 tablespoons pure pumpkin purée
½ teaspoon ground cinnamon, divided
¼ cup low-carb, sugar-free chocolate chips
3 ounces (85 g) full-fat cream cheese, softened

1. In a large bowl, mix almond flour and ¼ cup erythritol. Stir in butter, egg, and gelatin until combined.
2. Stir in baking powder, vanilla, pumpkin pie spice, pumpkin purée, and ¼ teaspoon cinnamon, then fold in chocolate chips.
3. Pour batter into 6-inch round baking pan. Place pan into the air fryer basket.
4. Adjust the temperature to 300°F (150°C) and set the timer for 7 minutes.
5. When fully cooked, the top will be golden brown and a toothpick inserted in center will come out clean. Let cool at least 20 minutes.
6. To make the frosting: mix cream cheese, remaining ¼ teaspoon cinnamon, and remaining ¼ cup erythritol in a large bowl. Using an electric mixer, beat until it becomes fluffy. Spread onto the cooled cookie. Garnish with additional cinnamon if desired.

Per Serving
calories: 199 | fat: 16g | protein: 5g
carbs: 22g | net carbs: 20g | fiber: 2g

Cinnamon Pumpkin Cheesecake

Prep time: 15 minutes | Cook time: 45 minutes | Serves 8

Crust:

1½ cups almond flour
4 tablespoons butter, melted
1 tablespoon Swerve
1 tablespoon granulated erythritol
½ teaspoon ground cinnamon
Cooking spray

Filling:

16 ounces (454 g) cream cheese, softened
½ cup granulated erythritol
2 eggs
¼ cup pumpkin purée
3 tablespoons Swerve
1 teaspoon vanilla extract
¼ teaspoon pumpkin pie spice
1½ cups water

1. To make the crust: In a medium bowl, combine the almond flour, butter, Swerve, erythritol, and cinnamon. Use a fork to press it all together.
2. Spray the pan with cooking spray and line the bottom with parchment paper.
3. Press the crust evenly into the pan. Work the crust up the sides of the pan, about halfway from the top, and make sure there are no bare spots on the bottom.
4. Place the crust in the freezer for 20 minutes while you make the filling.
5. To make the filling: In a large bowl using a hand mixer on medium speed, combine the cream cheese and erythritol. Beat until the cream cheese is light and fluffy, 2 to 3 minutes.
6. Add the eggs, pumpkin purée, Swerve, vanilla, and pumpkin pie spice. Beat until well combined.
7. Remove the crust from the freezer and pour in the filling. Cover the pan with aluminum foil and place it on the trivet.
8. Add the water to the pot and carefully lower the trivet into the pot.
9. Set the lid in place. Select the Manual mode and set the cooking time for 45 minutes on High Pressure. When the timer goes off, do a quick pressure release. Carefully open the lid.
10. Remove the trivet and cheesecake from the pot. Remove the foil from the pan. The center of the cheesecake should still be slightly jiggly.
11. Let the cheesecake cool for 30 minutes on the counter before placing it in the refrigerator to set. Leave the cheesecake in the refrigerator for at least 6 hours before removing the sides and serving.

Per Serving
calories: 407 | fat: 35.8g | protein: 10.3g
carbs: 6.8g | net carbs: 4.3g | fiber: 2.5g

Vanilla Monkey Bread

Prep time: 15 minutes | Cook time: 12 minutes | Serves 6

½ cup blanched finely ground almond flour
½ cup low-carb vanilla protein powder
¾ cup granular erythritol, divided
½ teaspoon baking powder
8 tablespoons salted butter, melted and divided
1 ounce (28 g) full-fat cream cheese, softened
1 large egg
¼ cup heavy whipping cream
½ teaspoon vanilla extract

1. In a large bowl, combine almond flour, protein powder, ½ cup erythritol, baking powder, 5 tablespoons butter, cream cheese, and egg. A soft, sticky dough will form.
2. Place the dough in the freezer for 20 minutes. It will be firm enough to roll into balls. Wet your hands with warm water and roll into twelve balls. Place the balls into a 6-inch round baking dish.
3. In a medium skillet over medium heat, melt remaining butter with remaining erythritol. Lower the heat and continue stirring until mixture turns golden, then add cream and vanilla. Remove from heat and allow it to thicken for a few minutes while you continue to stir.
4. While the mixture cools, place baking dish into the air fryer basket.
5. Adjust the temperature to 320°F (160°C) and set the timer for 6 minutes.
6. When the timer beeps, flip the monkey bread over onto a plate and slide it back into the baking pan. Cook an additional 4 minutes until all the tops are brown.
7. Pour the caramel sauce over the monkey bread and cook an additional 2 minutes. Let cool completely before serving.

Per Serving
calories: 322 | fat: 24g | protein: 20g
carbs: 34g | net carbs: 32g | fiber: 2g

Cinnamon Daikon Cake

Prep time: 10 minutes | Cook time: 45 minutes | Serves 12

5 eggs, beaten
½ cup heavy cream
1 cup almond flour
1 daikon, diced
1 teaspoon ground

cinnamon
2 tablespoon erythritol
1 tablespoon butter, melted
1 cup water

1. In the mixing bowl, mix up eggs, heavy cream, almond flour, ground cinnamon, and erythritol.
2. When the mixture is smooth, add daikon and stir it carefully with the help of the spatula.
3. Pour the mixture in the cake pan.
4. Then pour water and insert the trivet in the instant pot.
5. Place the cake in the instant pot.
6. Set the lid in place. Select the Manual mode and set the cooking time for 45 minutes on High Pressure. When the timer goes off, do a quick pressure release. Carefully open the lid.
7. Serve immediately.

Per Serving
calories: 66 | fat: 5.7g | protein: 3.1g
carbs: 3.5g | net carbs: 3.0g | fiber: 0.5g

Coconut Porridge with Sunflower Seeds

Prep time: 5 minutes | Cook time: 5 minutes | Serves 2

½ cup coconut shreds
1 tablespoon sunflower seeds
2 tablespoons flax seeds
1 teaspoon ground

cinnamon
1 teaspoon stevia powdered extract
1 teaspoon rosewater
½ cup water
1 cup coconut milk

1. Add all ingredients to the Instant Pot.
2. Set the lid in place. Select the Manual mode and set the cooking time for 5 minutes on High Pressure. When the timer goes off, do a quick pressure release. Carefully open the lid.
3. Ladle into two serving bowls and serve warm.

Per Serving
calories: 278 | fat: 19.1g | protein: 7.5g
carbs: 12.1g | net carbs: 8.7g | fiber: 3.4g

Coconut Pie

Prep time: 5 minutes | Cook time: 41 minutes | Serves 8

1 cup almond flour
½ cup coconut milk
1 teaspoon vanilla extract
2 tablespoons butter,

softened
1 tablespoon Truvia
¼ cup shredded coconut
1 cup water

1. In the mixing bowl, mix up almond flour, coconut milk, vanilla extract, butter, Truvia, and shredded coconut.
2. When the mixture is smooth, transfer it in the baking pan and flatten.
3. Pour water and insert the trivet in the instant pot.
4. Put the baking pan with cake on the trivet.
5. Lock the lid. Select the Manual mode and set the cooking time for 41 minutes on High Pressure. Once the timer goes off, perform a natural pressure release for 10 minutes, then release any remaining pressure. Carefully open the lid.
6. Serve immediately.

Per Serving
calories: 89 | fat: 9.2g | protein: 1.3g
carbs: 2.5g | net carbs: 1.5g | fiber: 1.0g

Flax and Coconut Porridge with Blueberries

Prep time: 5 minutes | Cook time: 5 minutes | Serves 4

6 tablespoons golden flax meal
6 tablespoons coconut flour
2 cups water
¼ teaspoon freshly grated nutmeg
¼ teaspoon Himalayan salt

3 egg, whisked
½ stick butter, softened
4 tablespoons double cream
4 tablespoons monk fruit powder
1 cup blueberries

1. Add all ingredients to the Instant Pot.
2. Set the lid in place. Select the Manual mode and set the cooking time for 5 minutes on High Pressure. When the timer goes off, do a quick pressure release. Carefully open the lid.
3. Serve immediately.

Per Serving
calories: 323 | fat: 15.1g | protein: 9.1g
carbs:7.5g | net carbs: 5.0g | fiber: 2.5g

Coconut Lava Cake

Prep time: 5 minutes | Cook time: 4 minutes | Serves 4

1 teaspoon baking powder	1 tablespoon almond flour
1 tablespoon cocoa powder	2 teaspoons erythritol
1 cup coconut cream	1 tablespoon butter, melted
⅓ cup coconut flour	1 cup water

1. Whisk together baking powder, cocoa powder, coconut cream, coconut flour, almond flour, erythritol, and butter.
2. Then pour the chocolate mixture in the baking cups.
3. Pour the water in the instant pot. Insert the trivet.
4. Place the cups with cake mixture on the trivet.
5. Lock the lid. Select the Manual mode and set the cooking time for 4 minutes on High Pressure. Once the timer goes off, perform a natural pressure release for 5 minutes, then release any remaining pressure. Carefully open the lid.
6. Serve immediately.

Per Serving
calories: 217 | fat: 19.1g | protein: 3.5g carbs: 14.1g | net carbs: 8.1g | fiber: 6.0g

Vanilla Pecan Cookie

Prep time: 5 minutes | Cook time: 24 minutes | Makes 12 cookies

1 cup chopped pecans	¾ cup erythritol, divided
½ cup salted butter, melted	1 teaspoon vanilla extract
½ cup coconut flour	

1. In a food processor, blend together pecans, butter, flour, ½ cup erythritol, and vanilla 1 minute until a dough forms.
2. Form dough into twelve individual cookie balls, about 1 tablespoon each.
3. Cut three pieces of parchment to fit air fryer basket. Place four cookies on each ungreased parchment and place one piece parchment with cookies into air fryer basket. Adjust air fryer temperature to 325°F (163°C) and set the timer for 8 minutes. Repeat cooking with remaining batches.
4. When the timer goes off, allow cookies to cool 5 minutes on a large serving plate until cool enough to handle. While still warm, dust cookies with remaining erythritol. Allow to cool completely, about 15 minutes, before serving.

Per Serving
calories: 151 | fat: 14g | protein: 2g carbs: 13g | net carbs: 10g | fiber: 3g

Blueberry Cobbler with Rum

Prep time: 5 minutes | Cook time: 15 minutes | Serves 6

1 cup almond flour	¼ cup coconut cream
3 tablespoons sunflower seed flour	¼ cup water
½ cup Swerve	¼ cup coconut oil, softened
½ teaspoon baking soda	2 tablespoons dark rum
1 teaspoon baking powder	½ teaspoon vanilla
	½ cup blueberries

1. Start by adding 1½ cups water and a metal trivet to your Instant Pot.
2. Mix all ingredients, except for the blueberries, until everything is well incorporated. Spoon the mixture into a lightly greased baking pan.
3. Fold in blueberries and gently stir to combine. Lower the baking dish onto the trivet.
4. Lock the lid. Select the Manual mode and set the cooking time for 15 minutes on High Pressure. Once the timer goes off, perform a natural pressure release for 10 minutes, then release any remaining pressure. Carefully open the lid.
5. Allow the cobbler to cool slightly before serving.

Per Serving
calories: 240 | fat: 9.3g | protein: 5.2g carbs: 4.7g | net carbs: 3.4g | fiber: 1.3g

Chapter 17 Side Dishes

Balsamic Brussels Sprouts with Bacon

Prep time: 5 minutes | Cook time: 12 minutes | Serves 4

2 cups trimmed and halved fresh Brussels sprouts
2 tablespoons olive oil
¼ teaspoon salt
¼ teaspoon ground

black pepper
2 tablespoons balsamic vinegar
2 slices cooked sugar-free bacon, crumbled

1. In a large bowl, toss Brussels sprouts in olive oil, then sprinkle with salt and pepper. Place into ungreased air fryer basket. Adjust the temperature to 375°F (190ºC) and set the timer for 12 minutes, shaking the basket halfway through cooking. Brussels sprouts will be tender and browned when done.
2. Place sprouts in a large serving dish and drizzle with balsamic vinegar. Sprinkle bacon over top. Serve warm.

Per Serving
calories: 112 | fat: 9g | protein: 3g
carbs: 5g | net carbs: 3g | fiber: 2g

Golden Green Beans

Prep time: 5 minutes | Cook time: 8 minutes | Serves 4

2 teaspoons olive oil
½ pound (227g) fresh green beans, ends trimmed

¼ teaspoon salt
¼ teaspoon ground black pepper

1. In a large bowl, drizzle olive oil over green beans and sprinkle with salt and pepper.
2. Place green beans into ungreased air fryer basket. Adjust the temperature to 350°F (180ºC) and set the timer for 8 minutes, shaking the basket two times during cooking. Green beans will be dark golden and crispy at the edges when done. Serve warm.

Per Serving
calories: 37 | fat: 2g | protein: 1g
carbs: 4g | net carbs: 2g | fiber: 2g

Garlic Roasted Eggplant

Prep time: 15 minutes | Cook time: 15 minutes | Serves 4

1 large eggplant
2 tablespoons olive oil
¼ teaspoon salt

½ teaspoon garlic powder

1. Remove top and bottom from eggplant. Slice eggplant into ¼-inch-thick round slices.
2. Brush slices with olive oil. Sprinkle with salt and garlic powder. Place eggplant slices into the air fryer basket.
3. Adjust the temperature to 390°F (199ºC) and set the timer for 15 minutes.
4. Serve immediately.

Per Serving
calories: 236 | fat: 13g | protein: 19g
carbs: 5g | net carbs: 5g | fiber: 0g

Tomato and Zucchini Boats with Feta

Prep time: 5 minutes | Cook time: 10 minutes | Serves 4

1 large zucchini, ends removed, halved lengthwise
6 grape tomatoes, quartered

¼ teaspoon salt
¼ cup feta cheese
1 tablespoon balsamic vinegar
1 tablespoon olive oil

1. Use a spoon to scoop out 2 tablespoons from center of each zucchini half, making just enough space to fill with tomatoes and feta.
2. Place tomatoes evenly in centers of zucchini halves and sprinkle with salt. Place into ungreased air fryer basket. Adjust the temperature to 350°F (180ºC) and set the timer for 10 minutes. When done, zucchini will be tender.
3. Transfer boats to a serving tray and sprinkle with feta, then drizzle with vinegar and olive oil. Serve warm.

Per Serving
calories: 74 | fat: 5g | protein: 2g
carbs: 4g | net carbs: 3g | fiber: 1g

Easy Cremini Mushrooms

Prep time: 10 minutes | Cook time: 10 minutes | Serves 4

8 ounces (227 g) cremini mushrooms, halved
2 tablespoons salted butter, melted
¼ teaspoon salt
¼ teaspoon ground black pepper

1. In a medium bowl, toss mushrooms with butter, then sprinkle with salt and pepper. Place into ungreased air fryer basket. Adjust the temperature to 400°F (205°C) and set the timer for 10 minutes, shaking the basket halfway through cooking. Mushrooms will be tender when done. Serve warm.

Per Serving
calories: 63 | fat: 5g | protein: 1g
carbs: 3g | net carbs: 3g | fiber: 0g

Zucchini Salad with Herb Dressing

Prep time: 5 minutes | Cook time: 7 minutes | Serves 4

2 medium zucchinis, thinly sliced
5 tablespoons olive oil, divided
¼ cup chopped fresh parsley
2 tablespoons chopped fresh mint
Zest and juice of ½ lemon
1 clove garlic, minced
¼ cup crumbled feta cheese
Freshly ground black pepper

1. Preheat the air fryer to 400°F (205°C).
2. In a large bowl, toss the zucchini slices with 1 tablespoon of the olive oil.
3. Working in batches if necessary, arrange the zucchini slices in an even layer in the air fryer basket. Pausing halfway through the cooking time to shake the basket, air fry for 5 to 7 minutes until soft and lightly browned on each side.
4. Meanwhile, in a small bowl, combine the remaining 4 tablespoons olive oil, parsley, mint, lemon zest, lemon juice, and garlic.
5. Arrange the zucchini on a plate and drizzle with the dressing. Sprinkle the feta and black pepper on top. Serve warm or at room temperature.

Per Serving
calories: 195 | fat: 19g | protein: 3g
carbs: 5g | net carbs: 4g | fiber: 1g

Bacon-Wrapped Asparagus

Prep time: 5 minutes | Cook time: 10 minutes | Serves 4

8 slices reduced-sodium bacon, cut in half
16 thick (about
1 pound / 454 g) asparagus spears, trimmed of woody ends

1. Preheat the air fryer to 350°F (180°C).
2. Wrap a half piece of bacon around the center of each stalk of asparagus.
3. Working in batches, if necessary, arrange seam-side down in a single layer in the air fryer basket. Cook for 10 minutes until the bacon is crisp and the stalks are tender.

Per Serving
calories: 110 | fat: 7g | protein: 8g
carbs: 5g | net carbs: 3g | fiber: 2g

Cheese Brussels Sprouts with Pecan

Prep time: 10 minutes | Cook time: 30 minutes | Serves 4

½ cup pecans
1½ pounds (680g) fresh Brussels sprouts, trimmed and quartered
2 tablespoons olive oil
Salt and freshly ground black pepper
¼ cup crumbled Gorgonzola cheese

1. Spread the pecans in a single layer of the air fryer and set the heat to 350°F (180°C). Air fry for 3 to 5 minutes until the pecans are lightly browned and fragrant. Transfer the pecans to a plate and continue preheating the air fryer, increasing the heat to 400°F (205°C) .
2. In a large bowl, toss the Brussels sprouts with the olive oil and season with salt and black pepper to taste.
3. Working in batches if necessary, arrange the Brussels sprouts in a single layer in the air fryer basket. Pausing halfway through the baking time to shake the basket, air fry for 20 to 25 minutes until the sprouts are tender and starting to brown on the edges.
4. Transfer the sprouts to a serving bowl and top with the toasted pecans and Gorgonzola. Serve warm or at room temperature.

Per Serving
calories: 250 | fat: 19g | protein: 9g
carbs: 17g | net carbs: 9g | fiber: 8g

Chili Cauliflower with Cilantro

Prep time: 10 minutes | Cook time: 7 minutes | Serves 4

2 cups chopped cauliflower florets
2 tablespoons coconut oil, melted
2 teaspoons chili powder
½ teaspoon garlic powder
1 medium lime
2 tablespoons chopped cilantro

1. In a large bowl, toss cauliflower with coconut oil. Sprinkle with chili powder and garlic powder. Place seasoned cauliflower into the air fryer basket.
2. Adjust the temperature to 350°F (180ºC) and set the timer for 7 minutes.
3. Cauliflower will be tender and begin to turn golden at the edges. Place into serving bowl.
4. Cut the lime into quarters and squeeze juice over cauliflower. Garnish with cilantro.

Per Serving
calories: 73 | fat: 6g | protein: 1g
carbs: 3g | net carbs: 2g | fiber: 1g

Dijon Cabbage with Cider

Prep time: 10 minutes | Cook time: 10 minutes | Serves 4

1 small head cabbage, cored and sliced into 1-inch-thick slices
2 tablespoons olive oil, divided
½ teaspoon salt
1 tablespoon Dijon mustard
1 teaspoon apple cider vinegar
1 teaspoon granular erythritol

1. Drizzle each cabbage slice with 1 tablespoon olive oil, then sprinkle with salt. Place slices into ungreased air fryer basket, working in batches if needed. Adjust the temperature to 350°F (180ºC) and set the timer for 10 minutes. Cabbage will be tender and edges will begin to brown when done.
2. In a small bowl, whisk remaining olive oil with mustard, vinegar, and erythritol. Drizzle over cabbage in a large serving dish. Serve warm.

Per Serving
calories: 111 | fat: 7g | protein: 3g
carbs: 12g | net carbs: 8g | fiber: 4g

Crispy Crusted Onion Rings

Prep time: 10 minutes | Cook time: 5 minutes | Serves 8

1 large egg
¼ cup coconut flour
2 ounces (57 g) plain pork rinds, finely
crushed
1 large white onion, peeled and sliced into 8 (¼-inch) rings

1. Whisk egg in a medium bowl. Place coconut flour and pork rinds in two separate medium bowls. Dip each onion ring into egg, then coat in coconut flour. Dip coated onion ring in egg once more, then press gently into pork rinds to cover all sides.
2. Place rings into ungreased air fryer basket. Adjust the temperature to 400°F (205ºC) and set the timer for 5 minutes, turning the onion rings halfway through cooking. Onion rings will be golden and crispy when done. Serve warm.

Per Serving
calories: 79 | fat: 3g | protein: 6g
carbs: 6g | net carbs: 4g | fiber: 2g

Parmesan Asparagus

Prep time: 10 minutes | Cook time: 18 minutes | Serves 4

½ cup heavy whipping cream
½ cup grated Parmesan cheese
2 ounces (57 g) cream cheese, softened
1 pound (454 g)
asparagus, ends trimmed, chopped into 1-inch pieces
¼ teaspoon salt
¼ teaspoon ground black pepper

1. In a medium bowl, whisk together heavy cream, Parmesan, and cream cheese until combined.
2. Place asparagus into an ungreased 6-inch round nonstick baking dish. Pour cheese mixture over top and sprinkle with salt and pepper.
3. Place dish into air fryer basket. Adjust the temperature to 350°F (180ºC) and set the timer for 18 minutes. Asparagus will be tender when done. Serve warm.

Per Serving
calories: 221 | fat: 18g | protein: 7g
carbs: 7g | net carbs: 5g | fiber: 2g

Air Fried Kohlrabi Fries

Prep time: 10 minutes | Cook time: 30 minutes | Serves 4

2 pounds (907 g) kohlrabi, peeled and cut into ¼- to ½-inch fries

2 tablespoons olive oil
Salt and freshly ground black pepper

1. Preheat the air fryer to 400°F (205°C).
2. In a large bowl, combine the kohlrabi and olive oil. Season to taste with salt and black pepper. Toss gently until thoroughly coated.
3. Working in batches if necessary, spread the kohlrabi in a single layer in the air fryer basket. Pausing halfway through the cooking time to shake the basket, air fry for 20 to 30 minutes until the fries are lightly browned and crunchy.

Per Serving
calories: 120 | fat: 7g | protein: 4g
carbs: 14g | net carbs: 12g | fiber: 2g

Mashed Cauliflower with Cheddar Cheese

Prep time: 10 minutes | Cook time: 15 minutes | Serves 6

1 (12-ounce / 340-g) steamer bag cauliflower florets, cooked according to package instructions
2 tablespoons salted butter, softened
2 ounces (57 g) cream

cheese, softened
½ cup shredded sharp Cheddar cheese
¼ cup pickled jalapeños
½ teaspoon salt
¼ teaspoon ground black pepper

1. Place cooked cauliflower into a food processor with remaining ingredients. Pulse twenty times until cauliflower is smooth and all ingredients are combined.
2. Spoon mash into an ungreased 6-inch round nonstick baking dish. Place dish into air fryer basket. Adjust the temperature to 380°F (193°C) and set the timer for 15 minutes. The top will be golden brown when done. Serve warm.

Per Serving
calories: 117 | fat: 9g | protein: 4g
carbs: 3g | net carbs: 2g | fiber: 1g

Spinach-Stuffed Poppers

Prep time: 10 minutes | Cook time: 8 minutes | Makes 16 poppers

4 ounces (113 g) cream cheese, softened
1 cup chopped fresh spinach leaves
½ teaspoon garlic

powder
8 mini sweet bell peppers, tops removed, seeded, and halved lengthwise

1. In a medium bowl, mix cream cheese, spinach, and garlic powder. Place 1 tablespoon mixture into each sweet pepper half and press down to smooth.
2. Place poppers into ungreased air fryer basket. Adjust the temperature to 400°F (205°C) and set the timer for 8 minutes. Poppers will be done when cheese is browned on top and peppers are tender-crisp. Serve warm.

Per Serving
calories: 116 | fat: 8g | protein: 3g
carbs: 5g | net carbs: 4g | fiber: 1g

Curried Cauliflower

Prep time: 15 minutes | Cook time: 20 minutes | Serves 4

¼ cup olive oil
2 teaspoons curry powder
½ teaspoon salt
¼ teaspoon freshly ground black pepper

1 head cauliflower, cut into bite-size florets
½ red onion, sliced
2 tablespoons freshly chopped parsley, for garnish (optional)

1. Preheat the air fryer to 400°F (205°C).
2. In a large bowl, combine the olive oil, curry powder, salt, and pepper. Add the cauliflower and onion. Toss gently until the vegetables are completely coated with the oil mixture. Transfer the vegetables to the basket of the air fryer.
3. Pausing about halfway through the cooking time to shake the basket, air fry for 20 minutes until the cauliflower is tender and beginning to brown. Top with the parsley, if desired, before serving.

Per Serving
calories: 165 | fat: 14g | protein: 3g
carbs: 10g | net carbs: 6g | fiber: 4g

Sesame Broccoli with Vinegary Dressing

Prep time: 5 minutes | Cook time: 10 minutes | Serves 4

6 cups broccoli florets, cut into bite-size pieces
1 tablespoon olive oil
¼ teaspoon salt
2 tablespoons sesame seeds
2 tablespoons rice vinegar
2 tablespoons coconut aminos
2 tablespoons sesame oil
½ teaspoon Swerve
¼ teaspoon red pepper flakes (optional)

1. Preheat the air fryer to 400°F (205°C).
2. In a large bowl, toss the broccoli with the olive oil and salt until thoroughly coated.
3. Transfer the broccoli to the air fryer basket. Pausing halfway through the cooking time to shake the basket, air fry for 10 minutes until the stems are tender and the edges are beginning to crisp.
4. Meanwhile, in the same large bowl, whisk together the sesame seeds, vinegar, coconut aminos, sesame oil, Swerve, and red pepper flakes (if using).
5. Transfer the broccoli to the bowl and toss until thoroughly coated with the seasonings. Serve warm or at room temperature.

Per Serving
calories: 180 | fat: 13g | protein: 5g
carbs: 14g | net carbs: 10g | fiber: 4g

Cheddar Broccoli with Bacon

Prep time: 10 minutes | Cook time: 10 minutes | Serves 2

3 cups fresh broccoli florets
1 tablespoon coconut oil
½ cup shredded sharp Cheddar cheese
¼ cup full-fat sour
cream
4 slices sugar-free bacon, cooked and crumbled
1 scallion, sliced on the bias

1. Place broccoli into the air fryer basket and drizzle it with coconut oil.
2. Adjust the temperature to 350°F (180°C) and set the timer for 10 minutes.
3. Toss the basket two or three times during cooking to avoid burned spots.

4. When broccoli begins to crisp at ends, remove from fryer. Top with shredded cheese, sour cream, and crumbled bacon and garnish with scallion slices.

Per Serving
calories: 361 | fat: 25g | protein: 18g
carbs: 11g | net carbs: 7g | fiber: 4g

Green Bean Casserole with Mushrooms

Prep time: 10 minutes | Cook time: 12 minutes | Serves 4

1 pound (454 g) fresh green beans, ends trimmed, strings removed, and chopped into 2-inch pieces
1 (8-ounce / 227-g) package sliced brown mushrooms
½ onion, sliced
1 clove garlic, minced
1 tablespoon olive oil
½ teaspoon salt
¼ teaspoon freshly ground black pepper
4 ounces (113 g) cream cheese
½ cup chicken stock
¼ teaspoon ground nutmeg
½ cup grated Cheddar cheese

1. Preheat the air fryer to 400°F (205°C). Coat a 6-cup casserole dish with olive oil and set aside.
2. In a large bowl, combine the green beans, mushrooms, onion, garlic, olive oil, salt, and pepper. Toss until the vegetables are thoroughly coated with the oil and seasonings.
3. Transfer the mixture to the air fryer basket. Pausing halfway through the cooking time to shake the basket, air fry for 10 minutes until tender.
4. While the vegetables are cooking, in a 2-cup glass measuring cup, warm the cream cheese and chicken stock in the microwave on high for 1 to 2 minutes until the cream cheese is melted. Add the nutmeg and whisk until smooth.
5. Transfer the vegetables to the prepared casserole dish and pour the cream cheese mixture over the top. Top with the Cheddar cheese. Air fry for another 10 minutes until the cheese is melted and beginning to brown.

Per Serving
calories: 250 | fat: 19g | protein: 10g
carbs: 14g | net carbs: 10g | fiber: 4g

Parmesan Zucchini Fritters

Prep time: 15 minutes | Cook time: 10 minutes | Serves 4

2 zucchinis, grated (about 1 pound / 454 g)
1 teaspoon salt
¼ cup almond flour
¼ cup grated Parmesan cheese
1 large egg
¼ teaspoon dried thyme
¼ teaspoon ground turmeric
¼ teaspoon freshly ground black pepper
1 tablespoon olive oil
½ lemon, sliced into wedges

1. Preheat the air fryer to 400°F (205°C). Cut a piece of parchment paper to fit slightly smaller than the bottom of the air fryer.
2. Place the zucchini in a large colander and sprinkle with the salt. Let sit for 5 to 10 minutes. Squeeze as much liquid as you can from the zucchini and place in a large mixing bowl. Add the almond flour, Parmesan, egg, thyme, turmeric, and black pepper. Stir gently until thoroughly combined.
3. Shape the mixture into 8 patties and arrange on the parchment paper. Brush lightly with the olive oil. Pausing halfway through the cooking time to turn the patties, air fry for 10 minutes until golden brown. Serve warm with the lemon wedges.

Per Serving
calories: 190 | fat: 16g | protein: 6g
carbs: 8g | net carbs: 6g | fiber: 2g

Mozzarella Cauliflower Rice Balls

Prep time: 10 minutes | Cook time: 8 minutes | Serves 4

1 (10-ounce / 283-g) steamer bag cauliflower rice, cooked according to package instructions
½ cup shredded Mozzarella cheese
1 large egg
2 ounces (57 g) plain pork rinds, finely crushed
¼ teaspoon salt
½ teaspoon Italian seasoning

1. Place cauliflower into a large bowl and mix with Mozzarella.
2. Whisk egg in a separate medium bowl. Place pork rinds into another large bowl with salt and Italian seasoning.
3. Separate cauliflower mixture into four equal sections and form each into a ball. Carefully dip a ball into whisked egg, then roll in pork rinds. Repeat with remaining balls.
4. Place cauliflower balls into ungreased air fryer basket. Adjust the temperature to 400°F (205°C) and set the timer for 8 minutes. Rice balls will be golden when done.
5. Use a spatula to carefully move cauliflower balls to a large dish for serving. Serve warm.

Per Serving
calories: 158 | fat: 9g | protein: 15g
carbs: 4g | net carbs: 2g | fiber: 2g

Roasted Salsa with Lime Juice

Prep time: 5 minutes | Cook time: 30 minutes | Makes 2 cups

2 large San Marzano tomatoes, cored and cut into large chunks
½ medium white onion, peeled and large-diced
½ medium jalapeño, seeded and large-diced
2 cloves garlic, peeled and diced
½ teaspoon salt
1 tablespoon coconut oil
¼ cup fresh lime juice

1. Place tomatoes, onion, and jalapeño into an ungreased 6-inch round nonstick baking dish. Add garlic, then sprinkle with salt and drizzle with coconut oil.
2. Place dish into air fryer basket. Adjust the temperature to 300°F (150°C) and set the timer for 30 minutes. Vegetables will be dark brown around the edges and tender when done.
3. Pour mixture into a food processor or blender. Add lime juice. Process on low speed 30 seconds until only a few chunks remain.
4. Transfer salsa to a sealable container and refrigerate at least 1 hour. Serve chilled.

Per Serving
calories: 28 | fat: 2g | protein: 1g
carbs: 3g | net carbs: 2g | fiber: 1g

Mozzarella Cauliflower Tots

Prep time: 15 minutes | Cook time: 12 minutes | Serves 16 tots

1 large head cauliflower
1 cup shredded Mozzarella cheese
½ cup grated Parmesan cheese
1 large egg
¼ teaspoon garlic powder
¼ teaspoon dried parsley
⅛ teaspoon onion powder

1. On the stovetop, fill a large pot with 2 cups water and place a steamer in the pan. Bring water to a boil. Cut the cauliflower into florets and place on steamer basket. Cover pot with lid.
2. Allow cauliflower to steam 7 minutes until fork tender. Remove from steamer basket and place into cheesecloth or clean kitchen towel and let cool. Squeeze over sink to remove as much excess moisture as possible. The mixture will be too soft to form into tots if not all the moisture is removed. Mash with a fork to a smooth consistency.
3. Put the cauliflower into a large mixing bowl and add Mozzarella, Parmesan, egg, garlic powder, parsley, and onion powder. Stir until fully combined. The mixture should be wet but easy to mold.
4. Take 2 tablespoons of the mixture and roll into tot shape. Repeat with remaining mixture. Place into the air fryer basket.
5. Adjust the temperature to 320°F (160ºC) and set the timer for 12 minutes.
6. Turn tots halfway through the cooking time. Cauliflower tots should be golden when fully cooked. Serve warm.

Per Serving
calories: 181 | fat: 9g | protein: 14g
carbs: 10g | net carbs: 7g | fiber: 3g

Buttery Asparagus

Prep time: 5 minutes | Cook time: 12 minutes | Serves 4

1 tablespoon olive oil
1 pound (454 g) asparagus spears, ends trimmed
¼ teaspoon salt
¼ teaspoon ground black pepper
1 tablespoon salted butter, melted

1. In a large bowl, drizzle olive oil over asparagus spears and sprinkle with salt and pepper.
2. Place spears into ungreased air fryer basket. Adjust the temperature to 375°F (190ºC) and set the timer for 12 minutes, shaking the basket halfway through cooking. Asparagus will be lightly browned and tender when done.
3. Transfer to a large dish and drizzle with butter. Serve warm.

Per Serving
calories: 73 | fat: 6g | protein: 2g
carbs: 4g | net carbs: 2g | fiber: 2g

Sausage and Cheese Stuffed Mushrooms

Prep time: 10 minutes | Cook time: 8 minutes | Serves 2

6 large portobello mushroom caps
½ pound (227g) Italian sausage
¼ cup chopped onion
2 tablespoons blanched finely ground almond flour
¼ cup grated Parmesan cheese
1 teaspoon minced fresh garlic

1. Use a spoon to hollow out each mushroom cap, reserving scrapings.
2. In a medium skillet over medium heat, brown the sausage about 10 minutes or until fully cooked and no pink remains. Drain and then add reserved mushroom scrapings, onion, almond flour, Parmesan, and garlic. Gently fold ingredients together and continue cooking an additional minute, then remove from heat.
3. Evenly spoon the mixture into mushroom caps and place the caps into a 6-inch round pan. Place pan into the air fryer basket.
4. Adjust the temperature to 375°F (190ºC) and set the timer for 8 minutes.
5. When finished cooking, the tops will be browned and bubbling. Serve warm.

Per Serving
calories: 404 | fat: 25g | protein: 24g
carbs: 18g | net carbs: 14g | fiber: 4g

Broccoli Salad with Almonds

Prep time: 5 minutes | Cook time: 7 minutes | Serves 4

2 cups fresh broccoli florets, chopped
1 tablespoon olive oil
¼ teaspoon salt
⅛ teaspoon ground black pepper
¼ cup lemon juice, divided
¼ cup shredded Parmesan cheese
¼ cup sliced roasted almonds

1. In a large bowl, toss broccoli and olive oil together. Sprinkle with salt and pepper, then drizzle with 2 tablespoons lemon juice.
2. Place broccoli into ungreased air fryer basket. Adjust the temperature to 350°F (180°C) and set the timer for 7 minutes, shaking the basket halfway through cooking. Broccoli will be golden on the edges when done.
3. Place broccoli into a large serving bowl and drizzle with remaining lemon juice. Sprinkle with Parmesan and almonds. Serve warm.

Per Serving
calories: 102 | fat: 7g | protein: 4g
carbs: 6g | net carbs: 4g | fiber: 2g

Garlic Radishes

Prep time: 10 minutes | Cook time: 10 minutes | Serves 4

1 pound (454 g) radishes
2 tablespoons unsalted butter, melted
½ teaspoon garlic powder
½ teaspoon dried parsley
¼ teaspoon dried oregano
¼ teaspoon ground black pepper

1. Remove roots from radishes and cut into quarters.
2. In a small bowl, add butter and seasonings. Toss the radishes in the herb butter and place into the air fryer basket.
3. Adjust the temperature to 350°F (180°C) and set the timer for 10 minutes.
4. Halfway through the cooking time, toss the radishes in the air fryer basket. Continue cooking until edges begin to turn brown.
5. Serve warm.

Per Serving
calories: 63 | fat: 5g | protein: 1g
carbs: 3g | net carbs: 2g | fiber: 1g

Tomato and Arugula Salad

Prep time: 10 minutes | Cook time: 10 minutes | Serves 4

4 green tomatoes
½ teaspoon salt
1 large egg, lightly beaten
½ cup peanut flour
1 tablespoon Creole seasoning
1 (5-ounce / 142-g) bag arugula
Buttermilk Dressing
1 cup mayonnaise
½ cup sour cream
2 teaspoons fresh lemon juice
2 tablespoons finely chopped fresh parsley
1 teaspoon dried dill
1 teaspoon dried chives
½ teaspoon salt
½ teaspoon garlic powder
½ teaspoon onion powder

1. Preheat the air fryer to 400°F (205°C).
2. Slice the tomatoes into ½-inch slices and sprinkle with the salt. Let sit for 5 to 10 minutes.
3. Place the egg in a small shallow bowl. In another small shallow bowl, combine the peanut flour and Creole seasoning. Dip each tomato slice into the egg wash, then dip into the peanut flour mixture, turning to coat evenly.
4. Working in batches if necessary, arrange the tomato slices in a single layer in the air fryer basket and spray both sides lightly with olive oil. Air fry until browned and crisp, 8 to 10 minutes.
5. To make the buttermilk dressing: In a small bowl, whisk together the mayonnaise, sour cream, lemon juice, parsley, dill, chives, salt, garlic powder, and onion powder.
6. Serve the tomato slices on top of a bed of the arugula with the dressing on the side.

Per Serving
calories: 560 | fat: 54g | protein: 9g
carbs: 16g | net carbs: 13g | fiber: 3g

Conclusion

The Keto diet is the safest and healthiest diet plan you can opt for if you want to lose weight and shed fat naturally and effectively. In this book, I discussed everything you need to know about the Keto diet, ranging from its benefits to its stages down to the food you can eat and not eat and a 21-day diet plan to help you get started on your keto diet journey and lots more. By reading and following through with all that you've learned in this book, you can be sure to get desired results in no time. Happy dieting!

Appendix 1: Measurement Conversion Chart

VOLUME EQUIVALENTS(DRY)

US STANDARD	METRIC (APPROXIMATE)
1/8 teaspoon	0.5 mL
1/4 teaspoon	1 mL
1/2 teaspoon	2 mL
3/4 teaspoon	4 mL
1 teaspoon	5 mL
1 tablespoon	15 mL
1/4 cup	59 mL
1/2 cup	118 mL
3/4 cup	177 mL
1 cup	235 mL
2 cups	475 mL
3 cups	700 mL
4 cups	1 L

WEIGHT EQUIVALENTS

US STANDARD	METRIC (APPROXIMATE)
1 ounce	28 g
2 ounces	57 g
5 ounces	142 g
10 ounces	284 g
15 ounces	425 g
16 ounces (1 pound)	455 g
1.5 pounds	680 g
2 pounds	907 g

VOLUME EQUIVALENTS(LIQUID)

US STANDARD	US STANDARD (OUNCES)	METRIC (APPROXIMATE)
2 tablespoons	1 fl.oz.	30 mL
1/4 cup	2 fl.oz.	60 mL
1/2 cup	4 fl.oz.	120 mL
1 cup	8 fl.oz.	240 mL
1 1/2 cup	12 fl.oz.	355 mL
2 cups or 1 pint	16 fl.oz.	475 mL
4 cups or 1 quart	32 fl.oz.	1 L
1 gallon	128 fl.oz.	4 L

TEMPERATURES EQUIVALENTS

FAHRENHEIT(F)	CELSIUS(C) (APPROXIMATE)
225 °F	107 °C
250 °F	120 °C
275 °F	135 °C
300 °F	150 °C
325 °F	160 °C
350 °F	180 °C
375 °F	190 °C
400 °F	205 °C
425 °F	220 °C
450 °F	235 °C
475 °F	245 °C
500 °F	260 °C

Appendix 2: Recipes Index

Made in the USA
Monee, IL
23 February 2021